FROM WALMART
TO AL-QAEDA

AN INTERDISCIPLINARY APPROACH
TO GLOBALIZATION

FROM WALMART TO AL-QAEDA

AN INTERDISCIPLINARY APPROACH TO GLOBALIZATION

DAVID MURILLO

Greenleaf
PUBLISHING

© 2015 Greenleaf Publishing Limited
Published by Greenleaf Publishing Limited
Aizlewood's Mill
Nursery Street
Sheffield S3 8GG
UK
www.greenleaf-publishing.com

Translated from the orginal in Catalan by ESADE's Language Services
Cover by Sadie Gornall-Jones

Printed and bound by Printondemand-worldwide.com, UK

British Library Cataloguing in Publication Data:
    A catalogue record for this book is available from the British Library.

        ISBN-13: 978-1-78353-193-6 [paperback]
        ISBN-13: 978-1-78353-501-9 [hardback]
        ISBN-13: 978-1-78353-194-3 [PDF ebook]
        ISBN-13: 978-1-78353-500-2 [ePub ebook]

To my wife and sons, Mili, Sebastià and Gabriel.

Contents

Figures

Tables

Preface

Gazing at the world

Let us look back at the recent past. In Eastern Europe, Russia annexes Crimea. In the West, the US Administration comes up with a Free Trade Agreement whose aim is to link the EU and the United States. Spain debates whether to suspend what has been termed "universal justice". The governments of the G20 nations discuss new strategies in their long-running battle against tax havens. Meanwhile, the European Parliament is looking at the scope for levying a tax on "speculative capital flows" despite fierce resistance from the financial lobby. The UK is buzzing with a murder committed by a British citizen converted to radical Islamism. A bigger picture is provided by a UN "worst case" forecast that the world's population may climb as high as 16 billion from the 7.1 billion today.[1] The only thing that seems clear is that the biggest population growth will occur in Africa—one of the world's poorest regions. This will increase migratory pressures on an old and frightened Europe.

This is the setting for the great debate on the state of the world. Western societies discuss the role that democracy should play in a complex, interdependent world in which the growth priorities are set by big corporations, investment banks and sovereign funds. Changes in exchange rates, currency interest rates and the public debt risk premium mean that a country previously shunned by major international capital funds is back in favour

[1]   US Census Bureau. Last consulted: 24th of March 2014: www.census.gov/popclock/.

or vice versa. Bailouts are doled out here and there in return for the imposition of legal and constitutional reforms. Governments formerly elected by voters give way to ones run by technocrats who are unpopular with citizens but enjoy market support.

In this context, change is the norm. Everything is transformed and subject to analysis: our understanding of what constitutes risk; how to detect and prevent financial, ecological and social disasters; Man's impact on the ecosystem; ways of governing our collective future. All is subject to public scrutiny but the voter is not always given the choice on what should be done. Having reached this cul-de-sac, one should look for the common thread running through the transformations described so far: globalization. For some, globalization is the cause of these changes, for others it is their consequence. In any case, it is the context in which ever-faster change occurs.

What is globalization? Globalization is both a concept and a cliché, a synonym which we use to speak of the economic system or the state of the world. Globalization can be understood as making the world one, a way of referring to the global economy or an umbrella term for speaking about cultural contrasts, differences, cosmopolitanism or homogenization. When we refer to globalization we talk of the rise of investment funds, disputes over scarce resources and the emergence of so-called "global risks". When analysing globalization, some authors refer to a set of interests and power dynamics that one often finds placed within an older conceptual framework that will be more familiar to readers: Capitalism.

The world and our knowledge of it

The following pages set out to explain the fuzzy, complex and seemingly incomprehensible concept of globalization. The approach taken is one of the few which we consider feasible, namely, that of interrelationship. The very complexity and scope of globalization means any discussion requires examination of the various schools of thought, theories and approaches found among all kinds of discipline, scholar and thinker. Modern societies only began to split knowledge up into different fields some 200 years ago, turning each into the happy hunting ground of knowledge experts—academics. This gave rise to academic disciplines, each of which had its own jargon and elevated some of its members to "guru" status. These disciplines set out certain problems and defended their own canons of knowledge.

Yet the complexity of our setting, the sheer volume and scope of scientific advances and the forces driving ever-greater knowledge specialization often make us overlook the fact that there is only one reality. The world, its *raison d'être* and hence knowledge should be one and the same. Yet this does not appear to be the case. The various branches of knowledge (within which we should include the Arts and Literature)[2] are merely practical divisions. Their boundaries do not obey individual or societal demands but rather follow an arbitrary scheme which we call "scientific".

When the various theories and approaches do not dovetail—Anthropology with Economics, Sociology with Management; Political Theory with Cognitive and Behavioural Sciences—we tend to look the other way. Hyper-specialization makes that possible: one does not have to convince academics in other departments but rather only those in one's own field of knowledge—even if it makes it harder to grasp the real world. It all boils down to the very human desire to shun the unknown and avoid complexity—triggered whenever the various schools of thought fail to agree. Put baldly, it is better to have different explanations of the world than to have none.

When it comes to understanding globalization, this implies that the subject's sheer scope means that one can only grasp it through the various disciplines in which it has been covered. This is our humble yet ambitious purpose in the following pages. It is ambitious because it forces us to break down arbitrary language barriers and ignore the *trompe l'oeil* of academic disciplines. It is humble because it allows us to gain a global view of complexity where the various branches of knowledge converge. A multidisciplinary approach means piecing together shards of knowledge to yield a view of the world that is not necessarily incomplete.

Sociology and other social sciences came up with the idea of the structure underpinning our society. The concept carries strong Marxist connotations but may be better grasped if we express "structure" as the factors conditioning (and hence limiting) the scope for individual or agential choice. This is what we shall examine in this text—the structural elements (cultural, technological, economic, political and institutional) shaping globalization.

As we have already mentioned, to make this leap one first needs to overcome the compartmentalization of knowledge we have inherited and which we continue to reproduce. We shall jump from discipline to discipline to

---

2   Vargas Llosa, M. (2002). *La verdad de las mentiras*. Madrid: Alfaguara, p. 20 *et seq.*

trace out a landscape similar to that which a historian of ideas might sculpt. At the end of the day, any intellectual construct—whatever its predictive, analytical or ideological purpose—is merely an idea for gaining a better understanding of the world. We shall therefore leap from the language of Political Theory to that of Economics, from Anthropology to History, Moral Philosophy to Business Management, International Relations to Finance and Sociology. Above all, we are interested in the global view afforded by Sociology.

A problem-posing approach

Sociology takes a sceptical, critical, problem-posing approach to our knowledge of the world. Berger, in his classic text,[3] uses the image of "acrobats engaged in perilous balancing acts, holding up between them the swaying structure of the social world". As Shakespeare had it, "All the world's a stage" but in this case one might liken it to a theatre with its mechanisms, costumes and power relations. When we consider these aspects, one might see the world as a clock that reveals the conventions and ways of doing things at a given place and time. It provides a cocktail of reasons explaining why the world is the way it is but which also helps us see it in another light.

This great collective dream of globalization is the mantra of *development*. A collective illusion, both mirage and real. Speaking of globalization means diagnosing its problems and perils. Such diagnosis requires discussion of technological revolutions, global threats, ideological, social and cultural tensions. While such things are not always the fruits of globalization, as Thomas Friedman puts it, living in an ever-shrinking world means that we are ever closer to one another.

We would like to pay homage to the scientific and academic ideal of "objectivity" in this eclectic, multidisciplinary quest. The Economist, Sociologist and Business Management expert should aspire to knowledge uncontaminated by vested interests and power networks. Unfortunately, if Foucault's thesis is to be believed, this is hard to achieve in the Social Sciences. Even so, the pretence of objectivity manifests itself mainly in the early chapters, where the author's opinion is given on the choice of sources and in some of the footnotes—which some readers may prefer to skip.

3   Berger, P. (1963). *Invitation to Sociology: A Humanistic Perspective.* New York: First Anchor Books.

The general aim is to take a sceptical, neutral view of the world. This specific purpose takes a back seat in the last chapter, which makes direct proposals of a normative and political nature on where we think globalization should go. That chapter gives guidelines to citizens who feel overwhelmed by the "structure" defined earlier. All in all, the aim is to address one of the shortcomings of Berger's sociological perspective, which overstresses system conditioning and underemphasizes the individual's ability to act (even though this is the only source from whence change can come).

Our itinerary

The first chapter opens with a generic introduction to globalization and current attempts to conceptualize and measure it. There are theoretical and ideological debates on: whether globalization is inevitable; its supposedly democratizing or Western nature; and the various alternatives for interpreting how the world works. Right from the outset, these debates reveal two threads—the political and the economic—from which the neoliberal globalization model has been woven. Despite the evident limitations of this model, it continues to provide a key tool for understanding the world in which we live.

The second chapter is longer and covers the social and technological dimensions of globalization and cultural change. On the one hand, one can see how technological changes have: led to a quantum jump in interdependence and relationships; affected job profiles; and altered our notion of risk (in which we have gone from the 19th century notion of technology as mankind's salvation to the idea of global risks stemming from technology itself). On the other hand, there is the issue of identity (both collective and individual). This chapter also considers the clash between market and traditional values and discusses whether this is bound to elicit identity-reaffirming reactions.

The third chapter begins with a digression on the sociological view of the economy and why we would do well to see globalization through the eyes of the Sociologist (that is, through the lens of the formal and informal institutions governing community life). We also look at attempts to split economic globalization into various stages and how successful they have proved. Some of the main changes produced by economic globalization are examined. These include: the growth of worldwide production networks;

the role of states in championing their nation's firms; the discussion of the so-called Washington Consensus and the current debate on inequality. This panorama helps us understand why there is currently talk of globalization losing its way. It seems we neither know whither the world is bound nor have a shared ideal of progress.

If today's world reveals how the wall between the real economy and the financial one is growing ever higher, Chapter 4 tries to explain why. This may well be the most complex part of the book for the lay reader. We discuss a key feature of the global economy, its financialization. This is a new development, historically speaking and is a key, albeit somewhat abstract, concept. Accordingly, we delve into its economic foundations (to wit, global macroeconomic maladjustments) and their causes and consequences. We thus begin to understand speculation, the growing gulf between social and economic interests, changes of culture (now financial)—of individuals and companies who, through their deeds, have breathed life into tax havens, hedge funds, Sovereign Funds and rating agencies.

This marks the end of extended discussion of the structural side. The three remaining chapters cover the agents that determine change. These agents include: multinationals; states; international organizations and of course the citizens who vote for or are voted in by governments and sit on company boards. Such agents work in an antlike fashion to nurture international bodies, which in turn mobilize a set of cultures, modus vivendi, set objectives and create their own *Weltanschauung* or "world-view".

The fifth chapter thus discusses the position of large corporations in the world, their thought patterns and "reproduction" mechanisms. This itinerary begins with the genesis of multinationals' rapid growth and vast accumulation of power. The question that springs to mind is: to what extent are large companies drivers of change and to what extent are they obstacles to the changes wrought by globalization? To answer it, we put management (particularly as an ideology) under the magnifying glass. We look at its main flaw from the social standpoint, which is its instrumentalization, the reduction of a discipline and profession to a procedure based on a questionable premise: the maximization of profits. This chapter also provides ways in which management as a discipline is trying to get out of this rut and to incorporate social expectations into the way firms are run. Here we also weigh up the chances of real change to the model.

The sixth chapter covers the workings of the nation-state as the main actor on the international stage and which currently seems to be doing such a poor job of meeting citizens' expectations. We make use of the precise notion of sovereign states that emerged at the end of the Thirty Years' War in 1648 and compare it with the realities of power in today's world. We then go on to examine the elements that allow one to speak of a crisis in the nation-state and its waning capabilities in a globalizing world. This debate gives rise to another, namely: what hopes can one have that a new model of supra-national global governance will emerge that is both democratic and capable of solving the grave problems facing the whole world?

The seventh and last chapter explains the present geopolitical scene in terms of a reorganization of institutional, cultural and economic-military sources of power from 2008 onward. This yields a range of scenarios for redressing present imbalances. We also put forward the European model as the seed of global federalism—a goal that some still see as beyond reach. This proposal is based on certain values which (despite the knocks of the last few years) remain valid and may be improved on and generalized to deal with the problems we all share. It is a model for shaping an inclusive world that is worth living in. It is a goal that we should all strive for.

Note to the reader

The book's itinerary should help the reader gain a sound grasp of global-ization. Where the reader may find the going tougher—for example, the sections on Economics and Finance—we have provided ample footnotes furnishing explanations and definitions. All the reader needs to gain a good understanding of the theme is a healthy dose of curiosity and a willingness to go beyond stereotyped views of the world. At the end of the day, curiosity is one's best ally for rising to intellectual challenges.

In addition, one should also note the world is changing fast, reshaping disciplines in the process. One hardly need say that the world we live in is very different from that of our grandparents and it is unlikely our grand-children's world will be much like today's. Sociology, as we have presented it so far, largely reproduces the world of the Greek philosopher, Parme-nides of Elea. His vision of the world is fixed and unalterable. By contrast, another Greek philosopher, Heraclitus of Ephesus, stressed the malleable, ever-changing nature of the world. I personally identify more with the latter. Thus, our purpose here has been to understand the structure to better focus on the nature and direction of change. As social psychologists argue, there can be no hope without change and without hope life is not worth living.

Acknowledgements

I should like to end this introduction with a section of acknowledgements. I owe much to Josep Miralles, colleague and Professor of ESADE's Department of Social Sciences, with whom I jointly taught the course on which much of this book is based. Prof. Miralles is the author of the early material on which the first and second chapters were to be based. His work has been a source of inspiration and reflection for many of the readings, themes and issues here. One of his reflections continues to occupy me, namely: what prospect is there of change being brought about by those of us who study this field? I believe I have made some progress in coming up with my own answer to this question, as I hope will be seen from the last chapters of this book.

There are not only atomizing trends in society but also in academe, where each faculty member wages his or her own private war. Here, I must confess that much of the intellectual baggage unpacked in this book is based on the sterling work done by other members of the Department. Thus I have drawn on the knowledge of Àngel Castiñeira on geopolitical matters, and on that of Josep Maria Lozano and Marc Vilanova in the Management section. A debt of gratitude is also owed to other (now retired) honorary professors from the Department both with regard to content and methodology. Among these, I would like to mention Carles Comas, whose notes I was privileged to draw on as a junior lecturer over a decade ago in an ambitious course titled Society, Economics and Culture and which—now that I think of it—was to lead me to the Ignatian notion of *magis*.

I should like to thank the Department's Assistant Professors who have striven (and continue to strive) to improve the text through their comments and critiques. Here special thanks are due to: Carlos Abundis; Joan Carrera; Toni Comín; Federico de Gispert; Jorge de los Ríos; Esther Hennchen; Teodor Mellén; Pol Morillas; Lluís Sáez; Alejandro Santana; and Daniela Toro. Josep Miralles; Àngel Castiñeira; Ferran Macipe; Joan de Déu Prats; and my wife Milagros Paseta, have all made invaluable comments, too. Last but not least, I should like to thank ESADE students (now well over a thousand) who have had to grapple with the content found here and who have given me the chance to pen these lines.

One teacher said that he did not know whether his students had learned much but that he could say that they had forced him to learn more about what he taught them. I hope that readers embarking on this exploration of globalization will understand today's world a little better by the time they finish the book.

Sant Cugat del Vallès (Catalonia), March 2014

1
Introduction to globalization

1.1 Images of a complex world

Is the world of today very different from that which our grandparents or our great-great-grandparents knew? Are we really living in a radically different world from that in which our ancestors lived? How has this world changed and what are the consequences of these changes for international relations, the economy, cultures or the environment? Or for the way business is done? The following pages seek to explain the different ramifications of the word globalization, so widely used yet at the same time so blurred and controversial. To do this we will need to explore its dimensions, its problems and its interpretations. Let's start to answer these and other questions by taking a look around us and exploring some examples of these changes that we have come to attribute to globalization.

Let's first go back to October 1998. A Spanish judge, Baltasar Garzón, issued a court order against former president of Chile and former commander-in-chief of the Chilean armed forces, General Augusto Pinochet, who at the time was on a private visit to the UK. The purpose of the order was to investigate crimes against humanity committed in the period during which he was head of government, after the 1973 coup. The arrest warrant gave rise to a long legal and diplomatic dispute that led to the former dictator being placed under house arrest in London and subsequently extradited months later to Chile, where no trial was held. For a large part of Chilean society, controversy was assured: the warrant and extradition order were perceived not only as an aggression to Chilean national sovereignty but also as an overreaching of the judge's area of jurisdiction, which should have been restricted to Spanish borders.[1] To what extent was the indictment correct? And to what extent was the order a new phenomenon?

Now let's move forward in time to 2010. A curious pseudo-documentary appeared on the Internet: *Xmas without China*.[2] It is the story of a young Chinese immigrant in California who challenges his neighbours to live through the month before Christmas without using or buying goods made in China. Is it possible? Although the outcome is predictable, the documentary is no less interesting for that. Obviously, the answer is no. The sight of a middle-class family having to go without toys, TV sets and a host of other products is a palpable demonstration of how different consumer habits are nowadays. It is also a way of asking ourselves how far it is possible to carry out patriotic consumption initiatives such as the "Buy American" campaign promoted by then President George W. Bush. Is it really possible to go back to consuming "home-made" products? According to the documentary, no. Furthermore, what does this tell us about the degree not only of interrelation but also of interdependence—so far, economic—between countries?

Let's now move on a year, to Libya in 2011. A large part of the international community, led by Western countries with a few Arab allies, decided to intervene in the conflict confronting proponents and opponents of Muammar al-Gaddafi's regime. It was not the first international intervention in the internal affairs of a sovereign country, and it will not be the last. From the juridical and diplomatic perspective, the most interesting aspect is the legal point of departure from which the international community, with the UN and its Security Council at the forefront, decided to give the operation the go-ahead. They used a feature of international law that allows foreign intervention to protect citizens from their own rulers, known as the responsibility to protect.[3] A contested and controversial doctrine with an uncertain future, but one that was nevertheless wielded in 2011 in the operation that toppled Colonel Gaddafi's dictatorial regime. What does this intervention tell us about the notion of sovereignty in the 21st century? And about the capacity to present a joint global proposal on issues of global interest such as human rights?

1   BBC News (2001). Special report: The Pinochet file. Monday 9 July 2001, http://news.bbc.co.uk/2/hi/special_report/1998/10/98/the_pinochet_file/198306.stm.

2   Dwyer A. & T. Xia (2012). Xmas without China. Trailer at: http://caamfest.com/2013/films/xmas-without-china/.

3   Bajoria J. (2011). Libya and the responsibility to protect. *Council on Foreign Relations*. 24 March 2011. www.cfr.org/libya/libya-responsibility-protect/p24480.

Let's move on again, in time and space, to East Asia: the Sea of Japan, the waters of which extend to Korea, China and Russia, in addition to Japan itself. In the summer of 2013 the international media reported on the grave ecological and health impact of the leak from the nuclear plant at Fukushima. The plant was incapable of stemming the emission of radioactive particles released by its core, which had been exposed to the elements since the nuclear disaster in March 2011.[4] Although Fukushima is on the Pacific coast, the first countries to be alerted by the consequences of this leak were its neighbours to the west of the Japanese archipelago. The notion of risk, how it is understood and its geographical limits, have changed for good. Globalization and technological development not only bring us closer to risk but also make us increasingly vulnerable and incapable of protecting ourselves from it. Meanwhile, the number of potential ecological, financial and public health hazards grows steadily. What option do we have in the face of situations such as Fukushima or other similar events that will occur in a world overpopulated with nuclear power plants (not to mention weapons) subject to safety protocols that are not always homogeneous?

This extended list of large and small transformations that alter societies and ways of living and seeing the world, could include the—some would say—global protests against the closure of the computer services company Megaupload at the beginning of 2012.[5] This Hong Kong based company provided the means to store and share electronic files of often dubious origin, and ceased its operations as a result of the application of the SOPA (Stop Online Piracy Act) bill submitted to the US Congress, which broadened the scope for prosecuting and censoring web activities regarded as criminal.

We could mention the many attacks perpetrated in far-flung geographical settings by the terrorist franchise known as Al-Qaeda from the 1990s to the present.[6] Or the proliferation of e-commerce companies, many of them located in countries considered as tax havens, which can supply you more

4   Kubota Y. & Y. Obayashi (2013). Wrecked Fukushima storage tank leaking highly radioactive water. *Reuters*. August 20, 2013. www.reuters.com/article/2013/08/20/us-japan-fukushima-leak-idUSBRE97J02920130820.

5   Wikipedia (2012). Protests against SOPA and PIPA. http://en.wikipedia.org/wiki/Protests_against_SOPA_and_PIPA#Protests_of_January_18.2C_2012 (consulted 7 October 2013).

6   For a partial (up to 2007) but geographically representative map of these attacks, see American Progress: https://maps.google.com/maps/ms?ie=UTF8&om=1&source=embed&oe=UTF8&msa=0&msid=100547042535873345331.0004384ce0e13337be966.

cheaply and often more quickly than before with any item (clothes, books, guns or gardening products). This comes naturally at the cost of the progressive desertification of the commercial foundations of cities and towns and, inevitably, the tax base on which is built the so-called welfare state of what we regard as the developed countries.

For all these reasons, this and other lists of events are a clear demonstration of the magnitude of the transformation of the way we live and understand the world around us. Facts that in our private lives often go unnoticed, but that seen in perspective, with our gaze focused on the social change that is going on under our noses, truly reveal the radical alteration of forms of interrelation of societies and countries, its impact on the planet, and the challenges we have to face. Let's begin, though, by putting names to this mesh of transformations that we call globalization.

1.2 Theoretical framework

1.2.1 Core concepts

Any quick consultation in a library, in the thousands of volumes devoted to studying the limits and characteristics of globalization, brings home to us the difficulty of reaching a single definition satisfying the different academic and ideological emphases and biases of their authors. We can, however, seek to understand it through the concepts with which it is usually associated. Thus we talk of globalization as a set of changes that transform relations between countries and individuals in a society. The core elements of these changes are:[7]

- **Internationalization**: intensification of cross-border interactions and interdependence between countries.

- **Liberalization**: the process of removal of restrictions imposed by governments on movements between countries in order to create an "open" and "integrated" world economy.

- **Universalization**: spreading of products, objects and experiences to all the corners of the Earth.

---

7   Baylis J. & S. Smith, eds. (2001). *The Globalization of World Politics*. Introduction. Oxford University Press.

- **Westernization**: some (especially critics of cultural imperialism) have defined globalization as a progressive process of cultural transformation of the planet towards Western-based cultural patterns.

- **Deterritorialization**: the radical change in geography whereby places, distances and territorial borders lose a large part of their value and influence.

1.2.2 Central debates

In the above sections we have succeeded in giving the concept of globalization an elementary theoretical framework: what we refer to when we talk about globalization and what core elements characterize it. Having said that, we would now do well to explore the marrow of the ideological debate that lies behind it. The Sociology Department of Emory University in the US has compiled a list of the debates inherent in the discussion of the concept of globalization. While not exhaustive, the list will be useful to us to understand the ferocity of the subsequent debate:[8]

Is globalization really *a new phenomenon or does it originate from long ago*? When could we pinpoint the beginning of the globalization process? Was it in the 16th century with the European powers' fever to *conquer* new territories? Or was it in the second half of the 19th century during the process of colonial expansion that brought those same countries to carve up Africa and squabble over the economically juiciest territories of China? And why not place the first globalization in Roman times with the spread of Roman law, when in the 1st century AD Paul of Tarsus (in present-day Turkey) fell off his horse and said to the guards who surrounded him, "I am a Roman citizen"? Then again, did globalization take a leap forward at the end of the Second World War when the Soviet and Western blocs linked their respective economies more intensely? Or did this leap forward happen after the fall of the Berlin Wall? Or was it in 2001, when China finally joined the World Trade Organization to transform world trade laws from top to bottom?

Does globalization *help us or harm us*? Or to be more exact: who does it help and who does it harm? Is there any sense in making statements such as these in general terms? What indicators should we use to answer these questions with a degree of precision? On the one hand, we talk about the global growth of inequality: as we will see presently, our societies, particularly in

8   Lechner F. (2001). The Globalization Website: www.sociology.emory.edu/globalization/debates.html#cultural.

the advanced economies, far from advancing towards the even distribution of wealth, are heading in the opposite direction. Yet on the other hand we observe how the growth of what we still call emerging economies causes the poverty rate to diminish. We talk of the Korean miracle, the Chinese miracle, and the development of Africa, Brazil and Peru. Have these countries not developed thanks to globalization?

Is this phenomenon basically *economic or cultural*? If there were some way of comparing these two dimensions, where should we place the emphasis? If we concentrate on issues such as the distribution of wealth and its impact on the economic—and therefore diplomatic—power of states, we will have to give pre-eminence to the economic side. However, if we focus our attention on aspects such as global terrorism, the spread of the Internet and the patterns of demographic transformation of our cities and towns, would it not be reasonable to stress the cultural side of globalization? And what of the processes of individualization, of segregation of the individual from the social mainstream, which ultimately transform even those societies until now regarded as communitarian, such as Asian societies of Confucian tradition or Muslim societies?

A highly controversial question: is globalization *a process or a project*? Is there somebody behind it, or is it inevitable like an apple falling from a tree? For those who defend understanding globalization as a process, any attempt to stem the tide is to deny the future. Putting the brakes on globalization is tantamount to trying to imitate what are considered to be historic failures such as the autarchic or semi-autarchic Socialist countries (North Korea, Cuba and, to an extent, the former USSR). For those who regard globalization as a project, it is not possible to understand globalization without winners and losers, without the presence of powerful interests and the need for someone to do something in order for this inevitability of economic and financial globalization to appear.

And another one: does globalization spell *the end of nation-states … or just the opposite*? We talk of the incapacity of states to cope with the array of challenges posed by the contemporary world. However, far from observing a decline in the number of states we see the contrary: a rise in this number.[9] A quick look at the United Nations Assembly or the map of Europe today compared with that of 20 years ago allows us to weigh up this increase. Yet at the same time we see the efforts to create supra-national bodies such as the

9   EU (2013). List of countries, territories and currencies. Publications Office. http://publications.europa.eu/code/en/en-5000500.htm.

European Union; the gradual transfer, sometimes voluntary and sometimes forced, of sovereignty to international bodies. Is not all this also the result of globalization? Where, then, does this leave states? More numerous and weaker? Or more numerous in name but with a greater difference between them in terms of effective power depending on their demographic size, economic capacity, natural resources and so on? In short, what does the future hold for nation-states in a globalized world?

1.2.3 Key trends

On the basis of the above, we are now in a position to deal with a quite popular definition of globalization, put forward by one of its main promoters, journalist Thomas Friedman. According to Friedman, globalization is "the inexorable integration of markets, nation-states and technologies to a degree never witnessed before, and in a way that is enabling the world to reach into individuals, corporations and nation-states farther, faster, deeper, cheaper than ever before."[10] Mahajan takes us one level further down and shows us the socioeconomic characteristics[11] of this globalization:

- International trade: increases at a faster rate than the growth of the world economy.
- International capital flow: increases, including foreign direct investment, at a higher rate than that of world trade.
- Growing importance of multinational corporations in the world economy.
- Transfer of sovereignty towards international organizations and agreements.
- Increase in the cross-border data flow using technologies such as the Internet, satellite communication, etc.
- Growing migration; numbers of trips and international tourism also on the rise.
- Growth in international terrorism throughout the world.
- Spread of multiculturality and growing individual exposure to cultural diversity.[12]

10   Friedman T. (1999). *The Lexus and the Olive Tree*. Anchor Books.
11   Mahajan S. (2006). *Globalization and Social Change*. New Delhi: Lotus Press.
12   Accompanied by a reduction in diversity through assimilation, hybridization or westernization (Americanization) or sinicization of cultures.

- Greater international cultural exchange via large global corporations arriving through Hollywood, Bollywood or the Korean wave
  (*Hallyu*).

1.2.4 Can we measure it? Explanatory magnitudes

Several academics and research centres have attempted to delimit and
measure the development of this globalization applied to countries using
variables such as their degree of global connectivity or their integration and
interdependence in the economic, social, technological, cultural, political and ecological spheres. Thus the ranking of the Swiss think-tank KOF
(2010)[13] listed the ten countries as follows: Austria, Netherlands, Switzerland, Sweden, Denmark, Canada, Portugal, Finland and Hungary. All European, except for one North American. The same index for 2013 put Belgium
in first place and Singapore in fifth, while Canada dropped out of the top
ten.

For its part, the list compiled by A.T. Kearney and *Foreign Policy*[14] put in
the first ten places Singapore, Switzerland, USA, Ireland, Denmark, Canada,
Netherlands, Australia, Austria and Sweden. All Western countries with the
exception of Singapore. Obviously, the use of different variables yields different results. In any event, it is interesting to note that countries that we
consider to be at the eye of the hurricane of globalization such as China
or India occupy positions as low as 63 and 51 and 11 and 61 respectively.
South Korea, a dynamic exporting country, stands at only 57 and 29 in the
two indices.

The selection of variables and especially how they are weighted in the
final result obviously focus the debate on the methodology used in indices of this type. Why do these variables appear and not others? Why should
this weight be given to some indicators as opposed to others? The choice
undoubtedly reveals preferences and intentions, quite apart from giving clues to the author's ideological bias: does it defend economic globalization or give priority to the cultural sort? Does it take regulation on
globalization to be a positive phenomenon—a step forward—or a disrup-
tive factor? Nonetheless, these indices serve to show how attempts are

13   Dreher A. (2010). KOF Index of Globalization. See: http://globalization.kof.
     ethz.ch/static/pdf/variables_2010.pdf and http://globalization.kof.ethz.ch/
     static/pdf/definitions_2010.pdf.
14   Foreign Policy (2007). The Globalization Index. www.foreignpolicy.com/
     articles/2007/10/11/the_globalization_index_2007.

being made, especially in one of the leading disciplines in the analysis of globalization, economics, to measure this multifaceted and complex phenomenon.

If we take the example of the methodology used in the KOF Index[15] we will see that this index consists of three main components with similar relative weights. Nevertheless, they are curious components to say the least:

A. Economic globalization [36%]

   i) Actual flows (50%)
   - Trade (percentage of GDP) (21%)
   - Foreign direct investment, stocks (percentage of GDP) (28%)
   - Portfolio investment (percentage of GDP) (24%)
   - Income payments to foreign nationals (percentage of GDP) (27%)

   ii) Restrictions (50%)
   - Hidden import barriers (24%)
   - Mean tariff rate (27%)
   - Taxes on international trade (percentage of current revenue) (26%)
   - Capital account restrictions (23%)

B. Social globalization [37%]

   i) Data on personal contact (34%)
   - Telephone traffic (25%)
   - Transfers (percentage of GDP) (3%)
   - International tourism (26%)
   - Foreign population (percentage of total population) (21%)
   - International letters (per capita) (24%)

   ii) Data on information flows (35%)
   - Internet users (per 1,000 people) (33%)
   - Television sets (per 1,000 peoplc) (36%)
   - Trade in newspapers (percentage of GDP) (31%)

   iii) Data on cultural proximity (31%)
   - Number of McDonald's restaurants (per capita) (45%)
   - Number of Ikea (per capita) (45%)
   - Trade in books (percentage of GDP) (10%)

15   Dreher A., N. Gaston & P. Martens (2008). *Measuring Globalization—Gauging its Consequences*. New York: Springer.

C. Political globalization [26%]

- Embassies in country (25%)
- Membership of international organizations (28%)
- Participation in UN Security Council Missions (22%)
- International treaties (26%)

The arbitrariness of the magnitudes, their Western bias, their temporariness and their numerical contribution to the overall weight of the indicator make this sort of index a historical curiosity and make us wonder about the usefulness of comparing, over time and across cultural differences, well-known variables that are no doubt destined to become irrelevant in a historic perspective. To give some examples: why is one of the key variables of this indicator the number of Ikea stores, and not the American Walmart or the Korean Hyundai? Why is trade in newspapers considered important, yet use of Internet news media not so? And why do the national and international press have the same weight? (After all, aren't we talking about globalization?) Why does the number of TV sets matter, but not the number of smartphones or tablets? Talking today about the volume of postal mail or trade in physical books as explanatory magnitudes already sounds old-fashioned.

So why do we go on trying to measure globalization? Probably because indices such as those above attempt to capture a series of magnitudes that, in a historical perspective, have indeed been important in understanding how we got here.[16] These magnitudes[17] have to do, for example, with:

- The fall in communication and transport prices (phone calls, transport by road, rail, sea or air)

- The growth in international operations (i.e., outside their home country) by transnational corporations (TNCs) in volume of assets, sales, exports

- The rise in international capital transfers (purchase and sale of public debt, equity and foreign direct investment)

- The increase in foreign direct investment by TNCs.

---

[16]   See OECD (2008). Economic Outlook. www.oecd.org/eco/outlook/38628438. pdf and Held D., A. McGrew, D. Goldblatt & J. Perraton (1999). *Global Transformations: Politics, Economics, and Culture*. Stanford University Press.

[17]   World Bank (2013a). Indicators. http://data.worldbank.org/indicator.

1.2.5 Unanswered questions

Aside from the shake-ups caused by the economic fluctuations of the moment, the curve described by globalization is ascending. However, although the best tool for predicting the future is to observe the past, does this mean that globalization (at least on the basis of the variables set out above) presents an inevitable race to infinity? From the perspective of the ecological sustainability of the planet we already know that the answer is no: we have one planet, not two. Furthermore, we know, especially since the Great Crisis of 2008, that the unanswered questions hanging over us, and therefore over globalization, are also numerous.[18]

High oil and raw material prices; turmoil in the Middle East; a financial system that is still far from having recovered; the impact on public deficits of bailouts for financial institutions; the squeeze on credit and consumption; growing inequality, poverty, unemployment and (in the West) hopelessness. Further erosion of the middle classes (indebted, impoverished and with fewer opportunities for the future) and distrust in the Anglo-Saxon model of laissez-faire capitalism and the ability to sustain the welfare state. All this makes us think that a lot of things have to change, and that the attitude to globalization will be increasingly critical and complex, particularly in those countries considered up to now to be the great beneficiaries of globalization: the West. But we should leave crossing those bridges until we come to them. For now, we can outline a series of theories that will help us to understand how we have arrived at this juncture.

1.3 Four theories of globalization

1.3.1 World-systems theory (Wallerstein)[19]

Part of so-called dependence theory, of Marxist inspiration, it is based on the central idea that we stand at a moment of expansion of a set of economic rules governed by the division of global labour, which are imposed by the world market and guided by the liberal philosophy of growing accumulation of capital. These rules can be traced back to the 16th century, with

18   Here I follow Roubini N. (2011). Is Capitalism Doomed? Project Syndicate. September 2011.

19   Wallerstein I. (2004): "The Modern World System as a Capitalist World Economy." In Lechner F. & J. Boli, eds. (2008): *The Globalization Reader*, Third Edition. Malden MA: Blackwell Publishing. Chapter 6; pp. 55-61.

the expansion of international trade as a result of Europe opening up to the world. One key element of this theory is that we are up against a single global economy governed by a hard core of power led by transnational corporations (TNCs), with support from increasingly debilitated states. The actions of these TNCs are aimed at protecting and increasing their market share (and therefore their share of power) by exerting pressure on international organizations (IOs) and states, in order to enable them to generate oligopolistic markets and reduce competition.

The unequal trade exchange that occurs between the countries of the periphery (underdeveloped and emerging countries, suppliers of low value-added products) and the core (the West, sellers of high value-added products) shapes a dual global market in which one side hoards profits, well-paid jobs and opportunities at the expense of the other. On this economic structural foundation, Wallerstein talks about what in Marxist terminology we would call an ideological superstructure (a **geoculture**) which hinges on consumerism, and makes the exploitation of one set of countries by the other sustainable over time.[20]

Along the same line of thought but from a more strictly sociological perspective, Leslie Sklair[21] identifies as the hub of the system the transnational capitalist class: the group comprised of corporate executives, bureaucrats in international organizations and global media that exert their power in the sphere of ideas in order to control the discourse on globalization and weld it to their own interests. This set of ideas is based on a twofold belief: that all human progress is founded on economic development, and that there is only one route to development, which since the 1990s has been known rather vaguely as the Washington Consensus, as we will see presently. According to

20   However, things are changing. If we observe the location of the decision-making centres of the major corporations that appear in the Fortune Global 500 index between 1980 and 2000, only 24 (5%) of the top 500 corporations were located in so-called emerging countries. By 2010 their presence in the ranking stood at 17% and the estimates for 2025 are 46%. This means that the headquarters of 229 of the top 500 companies would be located in emerging countries, most of them in China. See: McKinsey (2013): Urban world: The shifting global business landscape. October 2013: www.mckinsey.com/~/media/McKinsey/dotcom/Insights/Urbanization/Urban%20world%20The%20shifting%20global%20business%20landscape/MGI%20Urban%20world%203_Full%20report_Oct%202013.ashx.

21   Sklair L. (2002): "Sociology of the Global System." In Lechner F. & J. Boli, eds. (2008): *The Globalization Reader*, Third Edition. Malden MA: Blackwell Publishing. Chapter 7; pp. 62-9.

Sklair, examples of this transnational class would include chambers of commerce, the World Economic Forum, the Trilateral Commission and Rotary clubs. Its individuals foster increasingly homogeneous cultural patterns, and are responsible for the bulk of the transnational activities that make up the sorts of interaction among individuals in institutional contexts that cross the borders of states.

1.3.2 Neorealism (Keohane and Nye)

In opposition to Machiavelli or Hobbes' classic view of political realism, the Americans Keohane and Nye[22] hold that we can no longer understand the world, and international relations in particular, as a permanent clash between states pursuing their own interests (mainly security and power). The authors state that globalization is a complex system in which transnational activities, IOs and TNCs have gained influence and plunged us into a world dominated by complex interdependence. The characteristics of this would be:

- **The use of force becomes less practical.** Let's take an example: China could resolve its territorial conflicts with its South China Sea neighbours militarily without much difficulty, yet beyond the complex interplay of current geostrategic and military alliances, this theory highlights the series of impacts of various types—not only economic—that this action would have for, among others, the supply chains of Chinese companies located in, for example, Cambodia or Vietnam; or in the Chinese communities established in the Philippines. The observation of this series of reactions motivated by the interrelation and interdependence of Chinese interests in the region would advise against direct military action. In the same way, there is no sense in thinking that commercial disputes between, say, the US and the EU will be settled by military force.

- **The hierarchy of issues of each actor is less evident:** take the case of Deutsche Bank or Banco Santander. As their names indicate, these were originally German and Spanish concerns respectively. Nowadays, a quick glance at the countries in which they operate, their main source of revenue or the profile of their employees would

---

22   Keohane R. & J. Nye (2000): "Realism and Complex Interdependence." In Lechner F. & J. Boli, eds. (2008): *The Globalization Reader*, Third Edition. Malden MA: Blackwell Publishing. Chapter 8; pp. 70-8.

lead us to question what it means for an enterprise to be German or indeed European. If in the past a German Chancellor could say that whatever was good for Deutsche Bank was good for Germany, does that statement still hold today? Can we identify its interests and the interplay of alliances and collaborations that determine its actions in the global sphere? According to Keohane and Nye, this is an increasingly complex exercise.

- **There are multiple centres of power**: finally, an observation: far from the classical assumption that arose out of the Treaty of West-phalia (1649) to the effect that the only important players on the international stage are states, the authors take note of the transfor-mation affecting international relations, which has led to the pro-liferation in the global sphere of multiple actors, with a wide variety of origins and objectives and, as we have just mentioned, interests that are not always obvious. These include the major IOs such as the European Union, the World Trade Organization and the World Bank; global NGOs such as Oxfam, Greenpeace and Amnesty Inter-national; corporations such as Walmart, PetroChina, Volkswagen and Samsung; they all exercise their own diplomacy, interacting and pressurizing the rest of the actors, each with their own respec-tive strength and resources, in order to achieve their goals.

1.3.3 World polity theory (Boli and Meyer)[23]

Boli and Meyer bring the emphasis back to the cultural side of globalization. We gain insight into it not through states but through the generation of a pro-globalization culture. The central idea is that states compare themselves to each other; they copy each others' organizational and management pat-terns. The outcome is that they behave in an increasingly similar way. The elites are educated in the same schools and universities, they reproduce the same cultural patterns and they use and turn into public policies the same bodies of doctrine (theories, paradigms, tools). The effect of this conversion to a single role model among the ruling classes of each country is the cre-ation of IOs guided by increasingly homogeneous patterns.

---

23   World polity theory is also known as neo-institutional or world society the-ory. Lechner F. (2001). The Globalization Website. www.sociology.emory.edu/globalization/theories02.html.

IOs and states thus take it upon themselves to disseminate a set of common principles and values that will influence and transform their own societies, activating isomorphic mechanisms that cause citizens to assimilate and appropriate the behaviour of the ruling classes. On the most superficial, most easily observable level, we can find this cultural homogenization in patterns of dress, standard labour dynamics, the extension of a uniform pattern of incentives to compensate work. Economic language, patterns of consumption and work organization systems will be homogenized. From Bolivia to Singapore, Belgium, Kazakhstan and India, cultural manifestations are tending to converge, both inside and outside the workplace.

1.3.4 World culture theory (Roland Robertson)

According to Robertson,[24] globalization does not imply homogenization. On the contrary, it is a powerful process of relativization. World society is not governed by a common set of values but by growing confrontation between different ways of organizing the relationships that are generated. The search for **essences** (values and principles) is inherent in globalization and translates as a growing problem of personal identity. This construction of identity thus becomes an issue about how to give meaning to the tension/collision between the local and homogeneous and that which is different.

We are therefore to understand globalization as the process of *compression* of the world and the *intensification* of consciousness of the world as a result of the acceleration of global *interdependence*. The meaning of living on this planet thus becomes a universal question that individuals and societies will answer from very different perspectives. For Robertson, globalization involves permanent interaction and comparison of different ways of life. The search for a limited set of common principles to answer these questions, he will say, is an impossible task, and this goal is not in itself a basis for any world order. For Robertson, the fact that there is global awareness does not imply the existence of a global consensus.

At the end of the 20th century, globalization itself is a problem, as it leads us towards a cultural clash between different formulations and conceptions

---

24 Here we follow Robertson, R. (1991). "The Globalization Paradigm: Thinking Globally." In *Religion and Social Order*. Greenwich: JAI Press, pp. 207-24; Robertson, R. (1992); *Globalization: Social Theory and Global Culture*. London: Sage; and the summary written by Lechner F. (2001) at The Globalization Website. http://sociology.emory.edu/faculty/globalization/theories03.html.

of the world. In this conflict, religious traditions play a special role, as they can be mobilized to provide an ultimate justification for one's way of understanding the world. So we live in a world that is increasingly integrated, but not more harmonious. The problem of globality is therefore the problem of relativization.

For Robertson, globalization should be regarded as occurring in several stages. These are:

- A germinal European stage, starting in the 15th century, which spread a series of ideas about society, the individual and humanity

- A fundamental stage that began in the 1870s, in which contemporary world society truly took shape, characterized by the spread of ideas such as individual rights and identities, and the growing inclusion of non-European societies in this process

- A stage that started in the 1920s, marked by a struggle for hegemony, lasting until after the Second World War

- A period of uncertainty since 1960.

Globalization thus presents the following key elements:

- **Relativization**: each unit in the new world order (societies, international system, individuals and humanity as a whole) is shaped in dialogue with the rest of the players with which it interacts.

- **Emulation**: although globalization does not create a common culture in which everyone shares the same beliefs and values, it does generate a common ground in which the various actors pursue their goals by comparing themselves to the rest.

- **Glocalization**: the universal ideas and processes that form part of globalization are necessarily interpreted and absorbed in different ways. The concept of glocalization captures the way in which the two opposing forces of homogenization and heterogenization intertwine and act at the same time.

- **Interpenetration**: universalism and particularism are two sides of the same coin—we find a universalization of particularism (the particular reaches everywhere and is experienced throughout the globe) and a particularization of universalism (the experience of being part of a whole is lived and interpreted in an individual or particularized way).

- **Contestation**: globalization is a process that is questioned, giving rise to different ideologies that oppose and confront each other. The paradigmatic case of this is Islamic fundamentalism.

1.4 Explaining globalization: ideologies

The above section on Robertson's world culture theory brings us to analyse the present and try to understand the various ideologies that seek not only to explain globalization but also to channel it in one direction or another. This is a particularly important point in that, as we will see, ideologies are guidelines that provide a response to the dynamics, problems or situations described by the theories discussed above.

Steger, in his essay on globalization,[25] gives a definition of ideology that will suit us well to pursue the goal we have just set. According to the author, ideologies are those ideas and beliefs that are widely shared and accepted as *true* by significant groups of people in a society. A large part of the success of ideologies in general thus lies in their functionality: they have the capacity to offer a template for explaining the world; they help to organize the information that we receive; and they convert complexity into easily interpretable patterns. Furthermore, ideologies are proselytical: they seek followers and attempt to gain consensus. They also strive to impregnate society with their standards and values. In the public political sphere it is important to emphasize that ideologies set an agenda of topics for discussion (what *must* be debated and what is *unquestionable*); they problematize some issues; they make assumptions and claims about the reality that surrounds us; they expose *truths*; and they qualify certain actions or facts as *good* or *bad*. However, we stress the essential feature of their proselytical nature: their political dimension, made explicit in the will to turn theoretical assumptions into concrete and specific social action.

In the theorem that bears his name, sociologist William I. Thomas (1863–1947) highlighted the importance that theories have in the sphere of the transformation of reality. According to the Thomas theorem, if men define situations as real, they are real in their consequences.[26] Similar concepts

---

25   Here we will follow Steger M. (2010). *Globalization: A Very Short Introduction.* Oxford. Particularly the section entitled "What is an ideology?" pp. 98 ff.

26   Merton R. (1995). The Thomas Theorem and The Matthew Effect. *Social Forces.* 74(2): 379-424.

such as circularity, performativity and the double hermeneutic in social processes have been studied and formulated by several authors in the 20th and 21st centuries. For our purposes, the most important aspect is the way they transform reality: adhering to an ideology means adjusting our world-view, values, ideas and policy recommendations to the framework established by the ideology in question. Let's take a look at this extreme in the various ideologies (or globalisms) that attempt to explain this complex and multidimensional phenomenon we call globalization.

1.4.1 Neoliberal globalization

Globalization of the neoliberal sort reproduces the set of ideas, principles and values that have done most to help shape the world in which we have lived since the 1980s,[27] and will therefore receive special attention not only in this section but also in the coming chapters. Personalized in the political sphere by Ronald Reagan and Margaret Thatcher, the intellectual facet of its political formulation can be attributed to economists such as Friedrich Hayek, Milton Friedman and Gary Becker. From the institutional perspective we would find as traditional proponents of this ideology IOs such as the IMF, the WTO and the WB, together with the World Economic Forum (WEF) and the major corporations.

The central idea on which such diverse organizations and groups converge can be summarized as follows: the extension of the framework for analysing reality adopted by neoclassical economics (a particular interpretation of economics based on the ideas of Adam Smith) to account for the action of the individual in society as a whole (from public policies to family relationships, the functioning of organizations and, of course, the economy and international relations). Essentially, neoliberalism attempts to use economics as the yardstick for the interaction of individuals, societies and organizations with the world.

The series of guidelines and recommendations for public policies rests on the above-mentioned Washington Consensus, which we will discuss in detail later on. These ideas form part of the regular diet of a large part of today's economic and political elites and are conveyed continuously in the global media, generating a discourse that is strong, ever-present and therefore difficult to withstand. As regards the object of our interest, i.e., the

---

27   Judt T. & T. Snyder (2012). *Thinking the Twentieth Century*. London: Penguin Press.

explanation of the specific dynamics of globalization, this ideology makes five main statements:[28]

- Globalization is defined as the integration and global liberalization of markets.

- Globalization, as a phenomenon, is inevitable.

- No one is in charge of globalization.

- Globalization benefits everyone.

- Globalization promotes the spread of democracy in the world.

Insofar as it is the ideological framework that still today serves to understand most of the action of the economic and political agents that operate in economic globalization, it is hardly surprising that it attracts most of the attention and criticism of the rest of the ideological options. Among these we will mention:

- **Its inevitability**: if it is inevitable, why does it push to achieve a particular set of public policies that furthermore are at odds with the basic premise of neoliberalism, which advocates the reduction of government action on the economy?

- **The depoliticization of globalization**: is there really nothing to discuss when it comes to globalization? Shouldn't the will of the citizens be the ultimate rationale about what direction we want this globalization to take?

- **On the subject of its effective management**: is there really no one in charge? If so, what is the role of the major IOs such as the International Monetary Fund, the World Bank and the World Trade Organization?

- **Does it really benefit everyone?** If so, how can we justify the increase in inequality or, as economists such as Stiglitz and Rodrik hold, the growing public opposition to markets, especially financial markets?

- **Does it really promote democracy?** Can we establish a causal, and therefore one-way, relationship between globalization and democracy? And beyond this, what is the impact of this globalization on the quality of our increasingly weakened democracy? Why does

28   In this and the next two ideologies we follow the analysis made by Steger (2010). op. cit.

support for democracy seem to wane, precisely in countries such as those of Europe, affected by economic turmoil arising out of financial globalization?

The demonstrations of the anti-globalization movement, subsequently known as the alter-globalization movement, throughout the 1990s and the beginning of this century, and the two big crises—that of the Internet bubble at the beginning of the 2000s and especially that of 2008—have cast a profound doubt on the present ideology yet have not managed to replace it. Its continuance can largely be attributed to the precariousness of its ideological alternatives. Let's take a look at this.

1.4.2 The alter-globalization movement

Articulating the result of social and political dynamics such as those of the alter-globalization movement in a series of statements is not a straightforward task. The dynamics developed in South and Central America in opposition to neoliberal economic globalization, and events in the US and Europe from, for example, the 1990s marches in Seattle, Genoa and Barcelona to the rise of the Occupy Wall Street movement and the Indignants in the Spanish State, cover a wide spectrum. Once again following Steger in his attempt to articulate a single ethos for the alter-globalization movement, the statements and proposals he makes can be summed up as follows:

- Globalization leaves a whole series of countries behind: a huge global Marshall Plan should be promoted, financed by the developed countries (from the "Great North" to the "Great South").

- The globalization of financial markets has been to the detriment of the planet's economy and societies. According to Tobin, this requires throwing sand in the cogs of financial globalization by means of a global tax on flows of speculative capital (the so-called Tobin Tax).[29]

- He calls for the abolition of tax havens.

- He urges the signing of global binding environmental agreements to develop and extend the scope of the Kyoto Protocol.[30]

---

29   See *The Economist* dictionary of economics: www.economist.com/economics-a-to-z/t#node-21529373 (accessed 28 January 2015).

30   UN Framework Convention on Climate Change (2013). Kyoto Protocol: http://unfccc.int/kyoto_protocol/items/2830.php (accessed 7 October 2013).

- He calls for more equitable global development.

- He wants the creation of a new institution working for worldwide development, funded by the rich countries and managed by its beneficiaries, the developing countries.

- He demands the reform of the ILO to apply more stringent international labour standards capable of preventing divergence between the labour standards of Northern and Southern countries.

- He wants to introduce greater transparency and accountability into governments and IOs.

- He wants to make globalization sensitive to gender issues, by encouraging values considered to be of prime importance by, among others, feminist ethics (care of the environment, peace, care of those who suffer, co-operation, solidarity and participative and inclusive democracy).

Historically, we find among its main protagonists and promoters the World Social Forum, radical left-wing groups such as the Zapatista Movement and ATTAC, thinkers such as Noam Chomsky and politicians such as the American Ralph Nader. Today, movements such as the Indignants and Occupy Wall Street represent their historical continuity. It is important to note that since the last decade of the 20th century a large part of its political ideology has been incorporated into the programme proposals of left-wing parties worldwide, trade unions, and some of the leading NGOs that work for development (Oxfam, for example). It has also served as an intellectual ferment for leading publications such as the French *Le Monde Diplomatique*.

Although a large part of the programme of the alter-globalization movement—the Tobin Tax, the persecution of tax havens, the not always successful attempt to strengthen global environmental initiatives, concern about equity—has found its way into the political initiatives of a wide variety of parties and institutions, especially since the crisis of 2008, we need to recognize the difficulty of its political articulation in practice. This weakness hinges to a large extent on the gap between the proposals of this group and the interests and power dynamics that dominate the international sphere. Thus, the ambition of many of the proposed reforms and a degree of powerlessness when it comes to articulating concrete policies in order to implement them show how the battle of ideas is often at odds with the everyday management of reality. In other words, identifying a problem and opting for a particular solution does not necessarily imply progress towards sorting it out in the real world.

1.4.3 Jihadist globalism

It is interesting to observe how ideologies such as those above, formulated historically mainly from Western countries, have recently been confronted with other alternative ideologies that have come to compete intellectually with regard to the meaning of globalization and how it should be conducted. Since the 1990s, jihadism has become a loose movement bound together by a restrictive and radical interpretation of the Koran and centred on combating what is identified as Western imperialism,[31] a form of impoverishing cultural imperialism which fosters values that are considered to clash with the tradition of Islam. Among these values we find materialism and secularism.

In recent decades jihadist globalism has become widely known thanks to its armed wing, Al-Qaeda, a brand name and a franchise made up of a number of loosely linked armed groups that operate throughout the entire geography of the planet and, if we are to take notice of the opinion polls conducted on the subject, has little or fairly little popular support among the citizens of these countries.[32] It is also well known for the famous attacks committed in the US, the UK, Spain, Indonesia, Mali, Algeria and elsewhere. The characteristics of the jihadist movement have been summarized by Steger as follows:[33]

- It is a movement that articulates the popular desire in the Arab world to avail themselves of strong leaders prepared to sacrifice their lives as martyrs for a just cause.

- It reflects a will to democratize: to return power to the masses, as it is now usurped by rulers at the service of Western and their own interests.

31   One text that articulates much of the content set out in this section would be *Letter to America* by Bin Laden. See Bin Laden O. (2002): Letter to America. In O'Tuathail G., S. Dalby & P. Routledge, eds. (2003). *The Geopolitics Reader*. New York: Routledge Press. pp. 265-9.

32   See the summary of data by country in Gerges F. (2009). Al-Qaida today: a movement at the crossroads. *Open Democracy*. 14 May 2009, www.opendemocracy. net/article/al-qaida-today-the-fate-of-a-movement. The above analysis should not prevent us from bearing in mind that a large proportion of the citizens of Islamic countries may nevertheless support politico-religious groups considered in the West to be conservative or highly conservative. This list would include the Muslim Brotherhood and Salafist currents in Egypt, Hamas and Hezbollah in Palestine and Lebanon, and the more moderate but equally conservative Justice and Development Party, of Erdoğan, in Turkey. Religious conservatism and jihadism are therefore not equivalent concepts.

33   Steger (2010). op. cit. 121.

- It has no defined centre.[34]

- Its appeal also goes out to the Muslim population living in non-Muslim countries (for example, 3 million people in France and more than 100 million in India).

- It has a global strategy for the world: the articulation of a single human community governed under the precepts of the Koran (or, to be more exact, its interpretation of the Koran).

Two concepts that are central to its mind-set are the *ummah* or community of believers which encompasses all the planet's Muslims; and *jihad*, the strife or supreme effort that, in the Koran, Allah demands from the believers to face a situation of special difficulty.[35] The reactions that this movement has generated worldwide have marked an important part of the events of recent years, especially in the Middle East, quite apart from the long list of human losses. From President George W. Bush's War on Terror to President Obama's operations with unpiloted aircraft (drones) and military interventions in Somalia, Afghanistan, Iraq, Pakistan and Mali, our world today cannot be understood without reference to this religious and political phenomenon that is so closely linked to globalization.

1.4.4 Authoritarian globalism

Jihadist globalism is not the only type of globalism with a non-Western origin. In recent years, especially since the economic rise of China, a new cluster of ideas has come to be considered a separate ideology and treated as a single entity labelled as the authoritarian and antiliberal model. According to this reading, authoritarian globalism is based on the defence of an ideological model consisting in countering the deregulated antistate model of globalism advocated by the West. Its core characteristics are as follows:[36]

---

34 Note on this point that Islam, unlike Catholicism, has no defined hierarchy in the form of an organized church.

35 A detailed analysis of the word jihad—in fact, an onomatopoeia that expresses the notion of effort—would take us a great deal further than the outline we provide here. But for the introductory purpose we propose, an overall idea of the term is sufficient.

36 For an economic reading of the importance of this ideological phenomenon, see *The Economist* (2012). The rise of state capitalism. 21/01/2012. www.economist.com/node/21543160.

- Recovery of state control over the economy and politics after decades of debilitation following the strong influx of globalization.

- Withdrawal from international commitments on the understanding that, far from opting to build a global institutional and regulatory framework, the current priority should be to reinforce the role of the state.

- Strengthening of the internal social stability of each country as the ultimate goal of political action.

- Differentiation between two basic concepts: **rule of law** (the notion of a model of social order that rests on the principle of obedience to the law), a positive and universalizable principle, is contraposed to the concept of **democracy**, a mere model of articulation of the processes of political deliberation that takes many forms. These forms include liberal, communitarian and *single-party* (*sic*) democracy, and although positive, democracy cannot be seen as universalizable because it depends on the cultural and institutional contexts of each country.[37]

- Relativism with regard to values such as human rights, minority rights and political and trade union rights (as there is no single interpretation of these concepts it is pointless to want to universalize them).

- Establishment of a realpolitik focusing on its own interests (recovering a classical view of international relations whereby these relations must be based on the pre-eminence of the defence of the particular interests of each country in the international sphere).

The discussion as to whether or not this is a new type of globalism has been with us for some years now. What does seem to be evident is that certain attitudes in international politics or economic action guidelines in domestic policy have come to break the "Western" or "neoliberal" consensus (depending on one's persuasion) on the management of the various aspects of globalization. In the area of international affairs, countries

---

37   Note the loss of confidence in democracy as an institution, especially in countries recently incorporated into the liberal model: Pew (2011). *Twenty Years Later Confidence in Democracy and Capitalism Wanes in Former Soviet Union* (December 5, 2011), www.pewglobal.org/2011/12/05/confidence-in-democracy-and-capitalism-wanes-in-former-soviet-union/.

such as China and Russia show growing resistance to being carried along by Western countries in the resolution of conflicts such as that in Syria. In the economic sphere, we find the wave of nationalizations of companies in the energy sector in countries such as Argentina and Bolivia. In the domestic social or political sphere, the growing repression and the open use of censorship against the media, political opposition, ethnic or religious minorities or groups with a particular sexual orientation in many of the world's countries show the reassertion of an alternative political model.

The discussion, for example, surrounding the Asian growth model and the existence or otherwise of an oriental or Confucian style of democracy, more authoritarian and illiberal, with distinctively non-Western features, is a long-standing one. At present this model feeds off the growing disrepute and lack of solutions to the many problems that affect us globally and that originate from the West.[38] To what extent this model is on the rise or whether we are simply seeing a series of more or less ephemeral manifestations is quite another matter for discussion.

1.4.5 Anti-globalization groups

The last group consists of a catch-all formed by those movements that are opposed to globalization.[39] This is a group apart, insofar as it makes no attempt to offer a set of global guidelines to respond to or tackle the social, economic, ecological and political dynamics that exist under this umbrella concept we call globalization. They have no package of recipes for the world; they do not want to enter into dialogue or seek to win more supporters than those who belong to the nation-states in which they operate. The characteristics of these groups would be a compendium of the following elements:

- Fear of everything that comes from abroad.

- Reaction against any ceding of state sovereignty.

- Defence of protectionist measures in the areas of trade, identity and migration.

---

38 The paradigmatic case can be found in the proposal made by the former Prime Minister and founding father of Singapore, Lee Kuan Yew, one of the veritable categorizers of the Confucian-authoritarian growth model. See Zakaria, F. (1994): Culture is Destiny—A Conversation with Lee Kuan Yew. *Foreign Affairs*; Mar/Apr 1994; 73, 2.

39 Here we refer once again to Steger (2010). op. cit.

- A general view that is opposed to globalization, resting on the terrain of diplomacy and voluntary isolationism.

- A will to sustain their theses through an emotional populism that seeks to involve the common citizen in their proposal ("we say what the man in the street is thinking").

Here we find European and US conservative or extreme right-wing groups with historic figures such as Le Pen and Pat Buchanan and also, albeit with obvious differences, certain indigenist and religious movements in various parts of the world. The central element of all these groups is their rejection of globalization and their unwillingness to articulate joint proposals aimed at putting it right or redirecting it.

1.5 How should we "read" today's world?

Having conducted this first overview of globalization and the debates, theses, theories and interpretations that surround it, we are now in a position to look at the present from the perspective of various authors. How should we read today's world? In 2008, the French citizen of Bulgarian origin Tzvetan Todorov made an interesting division of countries by blocs in his book *The Fear of Barbarians*:[40]

- **The bloc of hunger**: those who have had the feeling that they have been kept apart for decades or perhaps centuries from the generation of wealth and now want to enjoy their new global status. This is the case of China and India, and also Brazil, Mexico, South Africa and Russia.

- **The bloc of resentment**: those countries that still perceive globalization as a humiliation, real or imaginary, the culprits being the Western countries. This would include many of the Muslim countries, parts of Latin America (Venezuela, Cuba and Bolivia) and some Asian countries.

- **The bloc of fear**: the West. Those countries that are afraid of the first two blocs; either of their economic development or of their capacity, real or imaginary, to generate violence.

40 Todorov T. (2010). *The Fear of Barbarians: Beyond the Clash of Civilizations*. University of Chicago Press.

- **The group of the undecided**. These countries are not aligned with any of the above blocs but could be, depending on circumstances. In the meantime, says Todorov, their natural resources are plundered thanks to corrupt leaders and ethnic conflicts.

Along the same lines as Todorov, and almost at the same time as him, we find the perception of French political scientist Dominique Moïsi.[41] According to him, beyond economics and culture shock, states of mind are of fundamental importance in understanding the world. This state of mind fluctuates historically, and at present provides us with the following divisions:

- **The group of humiliation**: one part of the world that is generically identified with Islam falls into this group. Humiliation leads to hopelessness; it translates as powerlessness, frustration and a feeling of loss of control over one's own future. A sensation that leads these people to put the blame for their own situation on others.

- **The group of hope**: currently located in Asia. Their growth and their upbeat attitude are proof that there is modernity beyond Westernization. China and India are the prime examples. Hope translates as self-esteem, self-confidence and the capacity to interact with others positively and confidently. Their maxim is "I want to do it and I will do it."

- **The group of fear**: this last bloc encompasses the West, essentially Europe and the US. It is a group of countries in the midst of a crisis of identity and confidence that perceive threats everywhere: the threat of external dependence, of being overrun by immigration, of the impact of the never-ending crisis, of the incapacity of democracy to solve their problems, of the lack of leaders, of the malfunctioning of their institutions, and so on.[42]

---

41 Moïsi, D. (2009). *The Geopolitics of Emotion: How Cultures of Fear, Humiliation, and Hope are Reshaping the World*. New York *et al.*: Doubleday.

42 If we take a look at the many and varied studies on confidence conducted in Western countries since the onset of the crisis we cannot help but agree with him, at least on this particular point. In the survey by BVA/Gallup, France comes out top in pessimism. See *Le Parisien* (2011). Les Français champions du monde … du pessimisme! 03.01.2011, www.leparisien.fr/societe/les-francais-champions-du-monde-du-pessimisme-03-01-2011-1210951.php. More examples reinforce this idea in *The Economist* (2010). The redistribution of hope. 16

A last reading, different in its origin yet similar in its categorization, comes from China. In 2010,[43] Jiemian Yang, President of the Shanghai Institutes for International Studies, one of his country's main think-tanks, made quite a conclusive reading of the dynamics that operate on the planet. Yang holds that there are four main groups:

- Those who are on the way up: China, India, Brazil and South Africa

- Those who are on the defensive: USA, IMF and World Bank

- Those who are losing influence in the world: Europe, Russia and Japan; decadent demographically

- Those who have neither power nor influence: the rest

To what extent are the frameworks offered by the above authors more than just a quick diagnosis of what is happening in the international sphere? The changes brought about by the crisis, the current redistribution of roles and forces among the world's major powers; to what extent are they here to stay? To what degree do these changes that are already detected provide us with pointers that help us to interpret the changes that are yet to come? If we take a look at one of the main proponents of globalization, the UK *Financial Times*, and one of its star commentators, Martin Wolf, we can say without doubt that we are standing on the threshold of an age of sweeping transformations that will affect the model of globalization promoted up to this point by the West; the ways of understanding the market and the state and interactions between countries. Nor can we ignore the changes we will have to implement to remedy an economic system that still has a lot to learn from the string of crises it has experienced in recent years.[44] Now we need to understand how we got here.

December 2010, www.economist.com/node/17732859?fsrc=nwl. This time the source is surveys conducted by Pew.

43   Batalla X. (2010). Derechos. *La Vanguardia*. 10-10-2010.

44   See the series of articles Capitalism in Crisis (2012) in the *Financial Times*. By way of example: Wolf M. (2012). Seven ways to fix the system's flaws. *Financial Times*. 22 January 2012, www.ft.com/intl/cms/s/0/c80b0d2c-4377-11e1-8489-00144feab49a.html#axzz2dS2Xx7YS.

2
Social change, technology and collective identities

Why is globalization subject to disputes, debates and confrontations of all sorts? No doubt because to talk of globalization involves talking about how we should see the world and what tools we should use to try to run it. And also because we will come up with different answers depending on what ideological conceptual device we choose.

In this chapter we take a look at two of the most controversial aspects: the impact of globalization on the labour market and social change; and the effects of the development of technology on what some authors have regarded as the birth of the risk society.

2.1 Globalization and social change

Understanding the events that occur around us requires some sort of theoretical framework. From a sociological perspective[1] we talk of three spheres that affect and account for the existence of social phenomena. First of all there is the sphere of survival, understood as the series of techno-economic

---

[1] Here we use the following reference sources: K. Marx (1963). *Karl Marx: Selected Writings in Sociology and Social Philosophy. Edited with an Introduction and Notes by T.B. Bottomore and Maximilien Rubel*, Harmondsworth: Penguin; M. Weber (2005). *The Protestant Ethic and the Spirit of Capitalism*, London: Routledge; and G. Rocher (1972). *A General Introduction to Sociology: A Theoretical Perspective*, Canada: Macmillan. Especially Chapter 11, "Factors and conditions of social change".

Techno-economic (technical)
Area of survival
What can be done?

Cultural (values and ideals)
**Area of culture
and meaning**
What is good or accepted?

*Sociopolitical (structural
and institutional)*
Area of coexistence
What do social norms and
regulations say about it?

FIGURE 2.1 The triangle of social phenomena

Source: C. Comas & J. Miralles. Notes, Department of Social Sciences, ESADE[2]

components that enable this to happen. Then there is the sphere of co-existence, the set of politico-institutional factors with which societies equip themselves in order to regulate, execute or prevent certain human activities. Lastly there is the sphere of culture and meaning: the set of values and ideas that substantiate, justify or guard against specific aspects of our behaviour in society.

An example will help us to understand this better. Why do the world's countries show such a wide variety of assisted reproduction treatments and *in vitro* fertilization techniques, ranging from strict prohibition through stringent regulation to almost absolute freedom of activity? Precisely because societies are built on this differentiated social architecture. In the techno-economic sphere, technological developments have enabled what was unthinkable a few decades ago: to aid or prevent conception, on the basis of a series of breakthroughs developed by technology and driven by the market. In the sociopolitical sphere, the action of governments and

2   The above figure is based on the Marxian image of the edifice with an "invisible structure and a visible superstructure" but eschews the author's material determinism. This is achieved by assuming Weber's idea that the individual meanings we give to facts condition people's actions. The idea behind the triangle is the need felt by all societies to address three key issues: how to organize survival, how to co-exist, and the meaning we give to the facts around us.

parliaments has given rise to the appearance of regulations and has given this set of practices a broader or narrower field of development. And finally, in the cultural sphere, each country's historical background, morals or religion have provided an umbrella to veto, restrict or facilitate its expansion.

2.1.1 Agents and factors

So how has globalization come about? What agents and factors have encouraged its growth and allowed this leap forward in the interrelation of countries that we are grappling to comprehend and manage? The answer is, basically, the first two that we were discussing earlier: technology and the economy. As far as technology is concerned, we are talking about the birth of the information society and the knowledge society. As regards the economy, we are referring to the advent of what we call post-industrial society. Changes that, as we will see, will radically affect an important part of our behaviour in society and our way of understanding the world, with effects that will transform man's relationship with nature, society itself, politics and culture.

Since the end of the Second World War, the list of technological feats developed by man has not ceased to grow. Microelectronics, information and communication technologies and advances in biotechnology have resulted in personal computers, software, mobile telephone networks, robots for industrial and domestic use, surgical techniques that were unimaginable just a few years ago, new medicines and more efficient transport systems. These developments have lowered the cost of trade in goods and services and have made possible the displacement and migrations of masses of people from one side of the planet to the other. We live in an ongoing technological revolution, increasingly organized, directed and driven by both markets and states.

From 1945 onward, after a first stage of technological development led by scientific elites with an enterprising mind-set, the context of change at the end of the 1960s saw the progressive deployment of a veritable movement of cultural renewal marked by innovation, individualism and a growing sense of competitiveness. In this context, the West saw the appearance of the microchip (1958), the Internet (1969) and the birth of what is now Silicon Valley, while the East saw the development of the transistor (1955) and the Japanese technological revolution.[3] Subsequently, after the troubled

3   A summarized history of this process can be found in Castells M. (1996). *The Rise of the Network Society: The Information Age: Economy, Society, and Culture.* Volume I. Blackwell. Chapter 1.

1970s and the two oil crises, came the organizational changes that led companies to focus on improving their productivity and their competitiveness, taking advantage of innovations that gave rise to increasingly decentralized transnational corporations operating in different parts of the globe under efficient co-ordination.

2.1.2 Characteristics of societies undergoing globalization

The alteration of the social structures derived from the above changes has been radical, and has profoundly transformed our way of life. If we tried to sum up these social changes brought about by globalization we would find the following elements.

- **Multi-dimensionality**: globalized societies are affected across the board. Globalization has a techno-economic dimension (which translates as ecological impact and affects man's relationship with nature), a social dimension (which among other factors will transform the demographics of our societies), a political dimension, and a cultural dimension. This multi-dimensionality will have dominant centres or hubs (drivers of change) and dependent ones (more or less passive subjects of these transformations).

- **Interdependence** between societies and countries, the fate of all thus being bound together regardless of the will of each of the parts. To quote former British Prime Minister Tony Blair in a speech in Bangalore (2002), in today's globally interdependent world, foreign policy and domestic policy are part of the same thing.[4]

- **Asymmetry** (of this interdependence): not all societies, or all countries, or all levels of government, are transformed equally by the changes that go hand in hand with globalization. Different transformations in the techno-economic field, ecology, society, demographics, politics, culture and so on can involve different transformations at a global, macro-regional, state, national-regional, local or individual level.

- **Connectivity**: people, goods, capital and information all circulate, making us part of a whole, a society that is permanently interconnected in a huge network.

4   Domain-B (2002). Blair calls for global interdependence. 7 January 2002. www.
     domain-b.com/industry/associations/cii/20020107_blair.html.

- **Complexity**: the different types of transformation are linked and fed back, producing new transformations. Thus, migrations affect societies, make them multicultural and affect their identity. This transforms social structures, the demographics of our cities, our family make-up and the spectrum of social classes. Mobility will also affect companies and organizations, as it will alter their composition. Their action will transform the economic sectors (agriculture, industry and services) and will put new pressure on natural resources, energy and water. In turn, these changes will bring about the appearance of new social actors, new demands and new pressures on states, political frameworks, and state and supra-state institutional structures. New technologies, added to the above changes, will introduce successive alterations into the traditional media and the way citizens understand the events around them. The sum of all these changes affect movements once more, thus setting the transformational wheel in motion yet again. We are faced with an array of technological, economic, demographic and institutional forces that operate in different directions and interact with the rest of the forces, changing their make-up.[5]

2.1.3 A historical vision of the baselines: towards a new social model

Ultimately, all these phenomena are attributable to a particularly profound transformation of our societies that poses an interesting discussion: when we talk of globalization, are we not merely talking about changes in the capitalist system? Or, alternatively, about a series of alterations, now compressed in time and experienced everywhere to an increasing degree, caused by the shift from industrial or pre-industrial societies to post-industrial ones?

In pre-industrial societies, defined in the West as those existing prior to the Industrial Revolution, the resources that provided the basis for development were land and access to raw materials. The mode of production was extractive, the production technology was labour-intensive, and the type of transformation (from the ancient Greeks until the advent of industrial societies) consisted essentially in taming wild nature. Societies, then, were

---

5   One simple way of visualizing this permanent and complex interaction of forces is to take a look at the map of global risks produced annually by the World Economic Forum. See WEF (2013). *Global Risks Report 2013*: www.weforum.org/reports/global-risks-2013-eighth-edition.

	Pre-industrial society	**Industrial society**	**Post-industrial society**
Resources	Land	Machinery	Information
	Raw materials	Energy	Intellectual capital
Mode of production	Extractive	Manufacturing	Processing
Technology	Labour-intensive	Capital-intensive	Knowledge-intensive
Purpose	Interplay with nature	Interplay with man-made nature	Interplay between people

TABLE 2.1 Economic activity and social transformation

Source: Department of Social Sciences, ESADE

organized around the specific way in which their essential economic activities were performed.

The Industrial Revolution marked a radical change. Societies valued machinery and access to energy as the key resources. The mode of production was based on the manufacturing of goods: the necessary technology was capital-intensive and the focus was on management and the interrelation with this new "man-made nature". Lastly, in post-industrial societies the key resource is information and intellectual capital. The mode of production is based on the processing of this information. The technology is intensive in the use, handling and transformation of this information, and the ultimate purpose of this series of activities can be understood as interplay between people.

However, if we are talking about the Industrial Revolution in the Western world, historically we should distinguish at least three.[6] The first of these (A) began at the end of the 18th century, and revolved around coal, steel, the steam engine, the birth of the railway, the textile industry and chemistry. The second (B) started around the beginning of the 20th century and focused on the development of the combustion engine, organic chemistry, electricity, oil, automobiles, the new mechanical industry, air transport and the telephone. The last stage of development (C) got off the ground after the oil crisis with the rise of new energy sources (nuclear, biomass, marine energy, etc.), microelectronics, computer science and genetic engineering.

It is important to stress that this chronological sequence is a very rough sketch with a Western slant, and extrapolates to the rest of the planet only with a large pinch of salt. Some countries have experienced an aggressive

6   Bell, D. (1974). *The Coming of Post-Industrial Society*. New York: Harper Colophon Books.

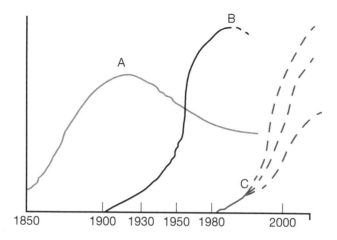

FIGURE 2.2 Cycles of the industrial revolutions

Source: A. Castiñeira. Notes, Department of Social Sciences, ESADE

transition from one stage to the next (China, Korea, Japan), while others have hardly started this transformation (much of Africa) and still others have skipped some of these phases and inserted themselves into the last stages of industrial transformation (some Arabian Peninsula countries and Singapore).

In any case, the idea of the omnipresence of transformations, the acceleration of cycles, is behind part of the anguish and unease with which different societies live and experience these changes. Leadership expert Peter Scholtes[7] wrote in 1997: "A young person today will witness four technological revolutions in his or her lifetime." How many did our great-grandparents see? One? Two at the most? If between 1785 and 1845 we needed 60 years to exploit the cycle of the birth and boom of hydraulic power, textiles or steel, for new technologies to successfully compete with or push out older ones, by the middle of the 20th century we needed only 40 years to complete the cycle of expansion of oil, electronics or aviation. Innovation cycles are therefore getting shorter and shorter.

The transformations of the dimensions considered here in the economic sphere inevitably involve profound changes in the structure of society. For the so-called developed countries, in a period of barely more than two centuries we have come to have a primary sector in clear decline (in fact, on the

7   Scholtes P. (1997). *The Leader's Handbook: Making Things Happen, Getting Things Done*. McGraw-Hill.

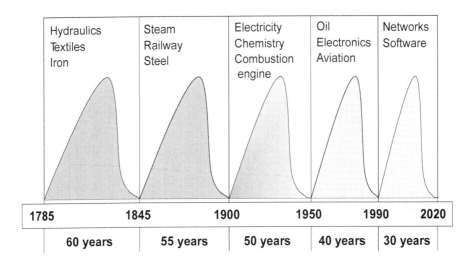

FIGURE 2.3 Innovation cycles

Source: Department of Social Sciences, ESADE, based on Scholtes, op. cit.

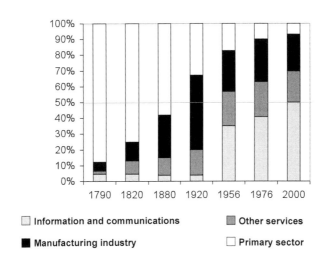

FIGURE 2.4 Population and economic activity

Source: Department of Social Sciences, ESADE

verge of disappearing, as today it accounts for less than 5% of the employed
population of the EU and around 2% of its GDP),[8] a population employed in

8   Eurostat data. For employment, data is for 2010. http://ec.europa.eu/agriculture/
     rural-area-economics/briefs/pdf/08_en.pdf. For contribution to the GDP, data

the industrial sector that is in a state of stagnation, and a services sector that is booming, especially in the information and communication industries.

The social transformation brought about in post-industrial societies has given rise to the appearance of the knowledge economy and the generation of a series of profound changes that have come to alter the way we work and organize our lives. Essentially the knowledge economy is based on the following characteristics:

- As we have already seen, the shift of key economic resources towards information and knowledge

- Increasing decentralization and flexibility in production

- Interconnection between companies in the form of networks, supply chains, clusters, etc.

- Establishment of new ways of generating synergies between groups and companies

- Intensive use of new technologies

- A new, more densely interactive relationship between the public and private sectors

- The reactive rise of the pro-sustainability and environmentalist movement

- The importance of encouraging creativity and innovation as business assets

Thus this post-industrialism features new businesses, new forms of organization and a new kind of business leader that values, hires and rewards knowledge at a premium. We will see this below.

2.1.4 The information society and changes in the labour market

Sociologist Manuel Castells coined the concept of the information society at the end of the 20th century. Castells[9] says:

is for 2012. http://epp.eurostat.ec.europa.eu/statistics_explained/index.php/National_accounts_-_main_GDP_aggregates_and_related_indicators.

9   Castells M. (1996). *The Rise of the Network Society: The Information Age: Economy, Society, and Culture.* Volume I. Blackwell. In brackets, we assign each of the dimensions analysed by Castells to the spheres of the triangle of social phenomena set out at the beginning of this chapter.

> The information technology revolution led to the introduction of informationalism as a material foundation of the new society. In informationalism, the generation of wealth [techno-economic sphere], the exercising of power [sociopolitical sphere] and the creation of cultural codes [sphere of culture and values] have come to depend on the technological capacity of societies and people, information technology being the core of this capacity.

We are witnessing the birth of a new model of society, the information society, which gives rise to a model of capitalism: informational capitalism.

The key issues of this new informational paradigm are as follows:

- **Information** as the raw material. Information processing and the generation of knowledge are the driving forces behind innovation and the transformation of production processes.

- The configuration of production agents in **networks**, making the system globally interconnected.

- **Flexibility** as a central value for agents' survival in an ongoing cycle of adaptation and readaptation of means and ends.

- **Convergence** of specific technologies into an integrated system.

- The enormous capacity of the new information and communication technologies to **penetrate** our social life.

The implications of the changes introduced by the information society into job profiles, especially in those sectors that are most closely linked to the rise of the knowledge economy, will alter the way worker productivity is measured. Workers will need to be increasingly oriented to the application of their knowledge, capable of making themselves understood to other experts, capable of integrating other specialized knowledge, capable of working in a team and accessing and transforming organizations in order to make them intelligent. Organizations will need to be capable of competing adequately in the new informational context, as described by Castells.

Obviously, not all of a society's workers will have to equip themselves with the skills and abilities discussed above, even in developed countries. The important point, however, is that for Castells the advent of the information society will bring about a change in *successful*[10] job profiles and will cause

---

10   Success understood from the economic and individual perspective, and thus reinforced by social patterns and media. In short, a type of success that is compatible with the existence of major social problems, as we will see presently.

ever deeper divisions within our societies. It comes as no surprise that the informational model requires on the one hand **self-programmable workers**: knowledge workers or "symbolic analysts". And that on the other hand it needs **generic workers**, employed in routine production or service tasks. Let's take a look at this.

As early as the beginning of the 1990s, in his classic *The Work of Nations*,[11] Robert Reich, former labour secretary in the Clinton administration, highlighted the changes that went hand in hand with this new economic model for societies that were open to globalization such as that of the United States. With the data available at that time, Reich judged that economic globalization would bring the appearance of three distinct job categories:

- That of **routine production workers**: these account for around 25% of the labour market, and are exposed to international competition. The job supply/demand ratio is very high (a huge supply of labour for a given demand) and the system of payment is based on hours worked. This category is increasingly threatened by the workforce of the emerging countries, and its importance in the economy is destined to diminish insofar as these tasks can to a large extent be relocated to other countries with lower labour costs.

- The category of **in-person service workers**: these amount to about 30% of the labour market. They are protected from international competition insofar as their functions cannot be relocated (hospital or retirement home attendants, home helps, etc.). As in the previous case, the supply/demand ratio is very high and wages are based on hours worked. The main competition comes from unemployment in the previous category and immigration.[12] This category shows a rising trend, parallel to the growth of the services sector.

- The category of **symbolic analysts**: some 20% of the labour market, they are exposed to international competition and show a lower supply/demand ratio (less supply for the existing demand or companies interested in employing them). Increasingly, they are paid

11 Reich R. (1991). *The Work of Nations: Preparing Ourselves for 21st Century Capitalism*. New York: Vintage Books.
12 Which nevertheless becomes necessary, particularly in declining demographic contexts such as Europe. The paradox today is to see massive unemployment in many countries alongside the need to take in these immigrants both to cover labour market needs and also to maintain the level of public spending, which calls for an increase in the taxpaying workforce.

JOB CATEGORY	PROPORTION OF THE LABOUR MARKET	INTERNATIONAL COMPETITION	SUPPLY/ DEMAND RATIO	SALARY
ROUTINE PRODUCTION	25% falling	YES	Very high	Hours worked
IN-PERSON SERVICES	30% rising	NO immigration	Very high	Hours worked
SYMBOLIC ANALYSTS	20% rising	YES	Low	Added value

TABLE 2.2 Population and economic activity

Source: ESADE. Department of Social Sciences based on Reich (1991)

on the basis of the added value provided by the worker. The trend is rising, insofar as the domestic and international market is growing in this direction.

It is important to insist on the impact of the change in labour structures on the entirety of societies affected by the phenomenon of globalization, i.e., practically all the countries in the world. Following Reich, we could talk of a veritable international division of labour between developed countries, emerging countries and developing countries. The common theme running through this division is provided by the relocation of production centres of goods and services on a worldwide scale, together with the appearance of new territorialized production centres in different regions of the planet. In the emerging or newly industrialized countries we find regions in which labour and social dynamics produce a clear reduction in poverty. However, as we will explain presently, this phenomenon is accompanied by a notable increase in internal inequality everywhere.

For the specific case of the developed countries, prior to the current crisis, we observe a twofold movement that advanced in parallel: the stagnation of social mobility and the slowing of the social elevator. This meant that in these countries people gradually ceased to be able to take a leap forward from their social class of origin or birth to their social class of destination once they reached adulthood. This marked the beginning of a stage of polarization of wealth that according to historian Tony Judt[13] originated in the new type of stark economic globalization that extended in the 1970s and especially the 1980s. In the so-called developed countries, this polarization was the starting point for the breakdown of social cohesion and the crisis of the welfare state that we are experiencing today.

The most notable element in the developed countries is the appearance of new areas of vulnerability and exclusion that are linked not to the specific economic context of the present but rather to the ocean swell caused by globalized markets. Thus, we are faced with a shrinking integration or comfort zone. This zone is comprised of individuals with a steady job, solid social relationships and a strong sense of having a meaningful existence.[14] Then there is a second group whose numbers are on the rise, formed by individuals who live in a zone of vulnerability, with a more or less precarious job, increasingly debilitated social relationships and a sphere of meaning that is dominated by fragility. And lastly there is a third group, also on the increase, who are excluded and marginalized. Excluded from the labour market; socially isolated in a society that still today takes employment as the starting point for organizing the other human facets; and with a strong feeling of insignificance in life, insofar as their personal contribution to the expectations generated by society as a whole is minor or nonexistent.[15]

For Bauman, the essential difference between these groups lies in the mobility of the labour factor: the winners in the globalization process will be those who are capable of offering their productive capacity all over the world, while the losers are those who are confined to a specific territory.[16]

Up to now we have traced the evolution of technology in historical terms and we have set out succinctly the force of innovation through market dynamics, together with its impact on the transformation of labour markets worldwide. Now it is time to turn our attention to its impact on the perception of risk and why it is that the globalization of the effects of technological development, far from reassuring us and giving us confidence in our ability to manage the present, has come to be a major cause for concern.

---

13   Judt T. & T. Snyder (2012). *Thinking the Twentieth Century*. The Penguin Press.

14   Here we again use the pyramid set out at the beginning of this chapter.

15   The author of this analysis is Castel R. (1995). *Les métamorphoses de la question social*, Paris: Fayard. See also García Roca J. (1998). *Exclusión social y contracultura de la solidaridad. Prácticas, discursos y narraciones*. Particularly Chapter VI. Madrid; Ediciones HOAC.

16   Bauman Z. (1998). *Globalization: The Human Consequences*. New York: Columbia University Press.

	TECHNO-ECONOMIC	SOCIO-POLITICAL	CULTURE
INTEGRATION ZONE	Steady job	Solid social relationships	Meaningful existence
VULNERABILITY ZONE	Precarious job	Fragile social relationships	Fragile convictions
EXCLUSION AND MARGINALIZATION ZONE	Exclusion from labour market	Social isolation	Insignificant existence

TABLE 2.3 New zones of vulnerability and exclusion

Source: Castel R. (1995). *Les métamorphoses de la question social*, Paris: Fayard.

2.2 Technological change and the risk society

We can define technology as the result of the relationship of human beings with each other and with nature in order to obtain services and products intended to meet human needs. We know that technology is based on premises, means and objectives or purposes, and seeks to bridge the gap between the purpose and the reality that surrounds it.[17] From the point of view of its attainments, the results achieved by technology over the last century can only be described as extraordinary. Technology is certainly responsible for a large part of humanity's successes. In the field of medicine, antibiotics and vaccines have diminished mortality and improved our quality of life. In the field of agriculture, the Green Revolution has enabled us to overcome the Malthusian trap: the growing gap between food production and population increase. In the industrial field too, notable progress has been made in productivity. In the social field, communication between individuals and across continents is instantaneous and almost free. The list of technological breakthroughs is endless.

However, the 20th century and the beginning of the 21st have also borne witness to the dark side of technological progress. The Manhattan Project made possible the appearance of nuclear power, but also its shadow side: Hiroshima and Nagasaki. And more recently, Chernobyl and Fukushima.

17   Hausman D.M. & M.S. McPherson (2006). *Economic Analysis and Moral Philosophy*. Cambridge University Press.

The urge to progress has also led to experiments with human beings, from medical research on prisoners in concentration camps to experiments with pharmaceutical products on convicts in the US, and pharmacological trials in Africa. On the environmental front, we find global warming: the melting of the polar ice caps and the increase of the greenhouse effect. The genetic engineering behind the Green Revolution has produced transgenics, the effects of which on human health are still unknown today.

From a historical perspective, this double-edged globalized technology takes us into a new age. Modernity, the long period that extends from the end of the Middle Ages notably until the Enlightenment, in both the West and the East represented the future, optimism and an increase in man's ability to predict and control his own destiny. Modernity, in short, was associated with an increase in security. The state was supposed to transfer this security to the social sphere, and science and technology were supposed to apply it to the individual's ability to control his own life in the face of nature.

Giddens[18] and Beck[19] talk of the advent of a New Modernity. However, far from providing security, this Second Modernity (a term coined in 1992), born of globalization and the spread of technology, generates an increase in potential dangers, an expansion of risk, uncertainty and, in short, insecurity. The great transformation that has occurred is in the notion of risk, a fundamental element that characterizes our life today. We now live in a risk society: a situation in which we find ourselves permanently engaged by threats and dangers caused by the process of modernization itself.

In the premodern age, threats were natural. Diseases, natural disasters and bad harvests cost lives and limited our ability to guard against the future. Our lack of knowledge about these dangers was almost absolute, and our ability either to control or anticipate them was nonexistent. All things considered, the impact of these risks on human life was great. Modernity, however, with technological and scientific development in pride of place, made it possible to advance in taming these risks. Certainly, new risks appeared as a result of technological progress (pollution, diseases related to new working conditions, etc.), but the delimitation and reduction of risks was a central aspect of modernity. Risks, then, were increasingly defined

18   Giddens A. (1991). *Modernity and Self-Identity: Self and Society in the Late Modern Age*. Cambridge: Polity. Other reflections by this author that complement this notion of New Modernity can be found in Giddens A. (1999). *Runaway World: How Globalization is Reshaping Our Lives*. London: Profile; and the earlier Giddens A. (1990). *The Consequences of Modernity*. Cambridge: Polity.
19   Beck U. (1992). *Risk Society: Towards a New Modernity*. London: Sage.

	THREATS	KNOWLEDGE	CONTROL	MAGNITUDE
PRE-MODERNITY	Natural hazards	Unknown	No control	Great
MODERNITY	Manufactured risks	Known	Control	Defined
2ND MODERNITY	Manufactured risks	Manufactured uncertainty	No control	Major catastrophes

TABLE 2.4 Risks and technological development

Source: Department of Social Sciences of ESADE, based on D. Bell: *The Cultural Contradictions of Capitalism* (1976)

and moreover could be managed, with new advances such as the establishment of insurance companies.[20]

Today the situation is different. Manufactured risks are huge and growing. They range from the use of nuclear power (the appearance of a new Fukushima) to the financial world (the effects of a potential breakdown in automatic investment systems),[21] food (do we really know what we eat?) and the products around us (does the proliferation of articles made of plastic, an oil derivative, have something to do with the increase in cancer cases, as several studies indicate?). These are all examples of man-made risks, the impact of which we know to be potentially great, and our control of which is very little or nonexistent.

For Ulrich Beck, behind this there is a transformation of the actual notion of technology, which we are forced to rethink. Technological development

20   Indeed, a good example of this attempt to limit and control risk is provided by the development of the insurance market with the birth of the British Lloyd's of London at the end of the 17th century. See Zelizer V. (1979): *Morals and Markets: The Development of Life Insurance in the United States.* Columbia University Press.

21   See Aldridge I. (2013). The Risks of High-Frequency Trading. *The Huffington Post.* 29 March 2013. www.huffingtonpost.com/irene-aldridge/the-risks-of-highfrequenc_b_2966242.html.

used to be directed at "taming nature", generating wealth and—at least potentially—becoming a tool to forecast and control our own future. However, now we see the proliferation of these new manufactured hazards, understood as the series of unwanted consequences of man's intervention in nature and/or society. Let us recall, although it is known well enough: the BP ecological disaster in the Gulf of Mexico, the Fukushima incident in Japan and the Lehman Brothers episode in the US were not natural disasters but were caused by the actions of man.

This transformation of the notion of risk implies its redefinition. If in the classic economistic vision risk was calculated as the probability of an event happening multiplied by the magnitude of the harm caused,[22] can we continue to use this definition when the harm is unknown or the "risky" event itself is unknown? The assumption that is dismantled is the ability of humans to forestall and anticipate future risks. Is this still possible nowadays? Particularly when we are dealing with risks that are taken thousands of miles away by actors unknown to us, such as computers engaged in automatic share trading in financial centres such as Shanghai, Singapore or Chicago?

This is the paradoxical nature of the new contemporary risk that sociologist Ulrich Beck is talking about. Sources of wealth in themselves become generators of risk. Risk is ubiquitous; it is everywhere and it surrounds us permanently. It is at the same time local and global, and often it is impossible to anticipate or verify; and this makes it impossible to tell when we are confronted with a risk and when it is just unnecessary alarmism. Let's take an example: the reaction to the H1N1 influenza pandemic in 2009, which was supposed to lay waste to the planet and which gave rise to multimillion-dollar vaccine purchases and prevention measures. Was there any real justification for the mass purchase of vaccines by Western governments and the orders that were given to vaccinate the weakest extremes of the health pyramid? In view of the mortality caused by the virus[23] the answer would have to be no. But could governments and international organizations—with the World Health Organization at the fore—have acted any other way? Risk means permanent exposure to catastrophe.

According to Giddens we are faced with the proliferation of areas of risk as a result of technological advances. We observe the expansion of industrial

22   This is the definition of risk still used today in the WEF Global Risks Report, op. cit.

23   Triggle N. (2009). Swine flu less lethal than feared. *BBC News*. 10 December 2009. http://news.bbc.co.uk/2/hi/health/8406723.stm.

interests but also their impact on ecosystems, today regressing almost without exception. We see the economic progress caused by new development, but also the increase in inequality and the appearance of new pockets of poverty. We see the deployment of financial globalization but also the impact of technology on the capacity to destabilize markets and countries. We see technological progress in ballistics, robotics and remote control systems, but also the danger of the "democratization" of the possession of weapons of mass destruction.

The new context forces us to rethink the notion of risk and how we relate to it. It means being aware of the limitations of science when it comes to saving us from the risks generated. It means realizing that we are surrounded by often unpredictable dangers of an unknown intensity, and contingent and threatening events. It means being conscious of the amplifying effect of the media in distorting risk and generating moments of mass hysteria. It means being aware of the omnipresence of risk and the breaking of the promise of modernity: in the face of global risk we are on our own, no one can save us.

Beck[24] emphasizes this individualization of risk. On the one hand it makes us all equal, but on the other it makes us different. On the side of equality he says: "Poverty is hierarchical, while smog is democratic." On the side of difference he notes how rich countries can transfer risks to poor countries (by the export of polluting or radioactive materials, by dumping scrapped ships or electronic apparatus, and so on). As individuals too, we can cover ourselves better against these risks depending on our income (private mutual funds, private insurance, moving house or changing country of residence, etc.).

All this heightens our awareness of the impact of our actions on the future, the unwanted effects of technological development and the inevitable impact of this form of progress on future generations. It forces us to wonder whether we might be involved in a particular form of trans-generational tyranny: we impose costs on those to come without their having any say in how they are managed, or in the profits thus made. What should be done in the face of all this? There are two answers: one ethical and the other political.

On the one hand, some call for the establishment of an ethics of risk, the application of a responsibility principle along the lines of philosopher of

---

24　Beck U. (2006). Living in the world risk society. A Hobhouse Memorial Public Lecture given on Wednesday 15 February 2006 at the London School of Economics. *Economy and Society*, 35 (3): 329-45.

ecology Hans Jonas: "Act so that the effects of your action are compatible with the permanence of genuine human life."[25] This responsibility principle should be applied not only in space but also in time: bearing in mind those who will be born in the future. This principle has a corollary in the form of the precautionary principle: we have to be able to make decisions even when scientific certainty is not conclusive, or to say the same thing differently, if an action or policy has a suspected risk of causing harm to the population or the environment. In the absence of scientific consensus on the harm caused, the burden of proof falls on those who are going to take a particular action and will have to demonstrate that there is no inherent risk. There are two insurmountable problems here: the strength of the scientific evidence currently available (is it sufficient to take an action?) and who should prove this risk (the company, governments or IOs, the scientific community?).

Anthony Giddens, erstwhile adviser to British Prime Minister Tony Blair, urges a return to politics:[26] the assumption of a "democratic utopia", the ability to take the risks around us publicly, consciously and through debate:

> Risks with far-reaching consequences show a utopia that nevertheless presents a very high dose of realism. It is a utopia of universal cooperation, which recognises unity in the diversity of human beings. Evils show us what we should try to avoid: negative utopias. The difficulties of a scientific and technological civilisation cannot be solved only by introducing more science and technology. It is necessary to deliberate, publicly and openly, on how social and environmental restoration can be linked to the quest for positive life values [...] guiding us in autonomy, solidarity and the search for happiness [for all].

2.3 Culture and its functions

Reactions for or against globalization cannot be understood solely from the perspective of technology, changes in the labour market or new forms of risk. It is true that technological change and its effect on labour markets, social restratification processes or the environment are a manifestation—the most visible one—of the transformations that are part and parcel of

---

25   Jonas H. (1984). *The Imperative of Responsibility: In Search of an Ethics for the Technological Age.* University of Chicago Press.

26   Giddens A. (1994). *Beyond Left and Right: The Future of Radical Politics.* Cambridge: Polity.

globalization. Yet there is a deeper level of transformation that has to do with the processes of invisible change that lurk beneath it. We are referring to culture. In this chapter we will explore the social transformation processes caused by globalization. We will strive to understand the relationship between technological, economic and cultural transformation. We will examine the origin of the underlying identity problems and we will explore their impact on relations between countries.

As a starting point, a definition of culture and its functions may help us to highlight the importance of the transformation processes we are dealing with. Culture is the set of ways of thinking, feeling and acting that are shared by a society. They allow our survival, provide identity and belonging, and give meaning to the members of a group. Cultures are made up of a second important concept: values. The function of these is to give meaning to the members of the group (whether it is a whole society, a group of individuals or a company). We can see the function of values in the case of an organization: the Danish services sector transnational corporation ISS.[27] On their website we find:

> ISS has an unmistakable set of values. ISS employees know them and act by them: these values guide behaviour among employees, customers and businesses. They are the foundation on which ISS was built. [...] Our values define who we are and serve as a key differentiator of what sets us apart in the market place.

This, then, is the function of values: to orient our behaviour, to motivate and guide our way of doing things, to identify us as belonging to a group in relation to the rest, and to provide a framework explaining the world and our role in it. The last of these elements is fundamental: culture is like the software that enables us to interpret and interact with our environment (or hardware). It is also important to understand that our vision of the world is thus initially reduced to the patterns of behaviour established by the culture in which we are immersed (country, nation, group of individuals or organization), which nourishes and feeds us constantly with the "right" way to see the world. This moral perspective is basic to understanding the identity shock that underlies globalization and the reason for the sometimes aggressive reactions it provokes.

So there are two ways of looking at how values work. The first, of a sociological nature, avoids making a normative interpretation of those values. It

---

27   ISS (2013). Corporate website (accessed 5 September 2013): www.issworld. com/about_iss/Strategy/Pages/Our_values.aspx.

shies away from any discussion regarding the "correctness" of values. It simply takes note of their function as a driving force for individuals; their ability to channel ways of doing things and behaving in society. For example, the statement that we live in a competitive world would mean simply describing this value of comparison and classification of individuals around the achievement of a goal. We would not discuss the "goodness" of competitiveness or its effects. Obviously, no one can doubt that these values are to the benefit of some (e.g., an employer who wants to take on a worker) and the detriment of others (those who lack this value), while at the same time guiding our way of being, doing and generating our personal ambitions. Thus, to carry on with our example, we understand competitiveness as the way to achieve our goals (whatever those goals may be), as the way to interact with our classmates or workmates.

Then on the other hand there is the moral or normative vision of values. This is the more widespread vision, and the one with the longer tradition. According to this reading, values are what, after the analysis, debate and evaluative reflection, is regarded as worthy of guiding the lives of individuals and the dynamics of societies.[28] Here there is indeed judgement of the "rightness" and "goodness" of the value in question. From this viewpoint, the statement that ours is a competitive society would mean that this is the right way to be and to act in this world; that it is a value we should defend and promote.

It is important to note the confusion that habitually surrounds the use of the two meanings of the term value. We can be either describing or judging. In everyday speech we mix the two meanings, thus making it difficult to be aware of when we are describing a personal attribute, a way of doing things (such as being competitive), and when we are fostering a correct way of interacting in society (through competitiveness). Thus we blur the two levels: what we are and what we should be.

According to sociologist Salvador Giner, the essential functions of culture are:

- To be a factor for cohesion: it enables us to belong to a group, to communicate and integrate with its members

- To be a tool for dominance and the legitimization of relations of power: as such, a mechanism of control and generation of countervalues (those values that we should reject)

---

28   I owe this definition to my ESADE colleague Raimon Ribera.

- To be a driving force for innovation and creativity: at its edges, it allows for social criticism and change, albeit at the expense of conflict[29]

Culture, then, should be understood as the glasses through which we see and feel the world. These glasses are not just cognitive (enabling us to understand what goes on around us) but evaluative too (enabling us to judge an event, and so to approve or reject it). The problem with culture lies in the invisibility of its influence, our unawareness of the extent to which our thoughts and behaviour are conditioned by these *cultural* glasses we wear. French historian Paul Veyne put it like this: "In every age, contemporaries are thus trapped in 'discourses' [cultures] as if in a deceptively transparent fishbowl, unaware of what those glass bowls are and even that they are there."[30] Dialogue with otherness, with cultural difference, therefore implies an effort to reformulate the world; it implies being capable of getting out of our fishbowl or, if necessary, changing our glasses. This is not always easy to achieve, in that this exercise forces us to take a step back from our own culture, relativizing it and putting it on a par with other different ones.

If after this theoretical digression we turn our attention back to the matter in hand—the discussion on the transforming impact of globalization on cultures—the first thing we will have to do is to acknowledge that economic and technological globalization involves a repositioning of the values of society, which must now be argued out, to oppose or embrace the values that go hand in hand with globalization. In other words, globalization is not culturally neutral.

2.4 The culture of the globalized market economy

Can markets themselves be the source of a society's values? Well, in fact they are, at least partly. As we have seen, globalization has this ability to spread values, to influence, contaminate or shift principles and guidelines for action that for years and indeed centuries had been considered as essential

---

29   Giner S. (1997). *Sociología*. Barcelona: Península. 96-101.
30   Veyne P. (2010). *Foucault. His Thought, His Character*. Cambridge: Polity, 14. In brackets, the reading of the sentence according to the methodological framework presented above.

for societies and cultures. What would be the key elements of the market system? To begin with, economic freedom (of enterprise and investment), private property, pursuit of maximum profit, capital accumulation (and reinvestment of part of the surplus generated), mass production, productive specialization, the conversion of all social interchange into a market with a price, supply and demand, wage labour, and mass consumption.[31]

What values are associated with these seemingly "neutral" phenomena? Values such as individualism, personal initiative, the desire to possess, success understood as economic success and purchasing power, competitiveness (or personal value measured in terms of contribution to the economic system), *value* understood as economic utility, effectiveness, efficiency, the idea that more is better than less, effort, consumerism as a path to personal fulfilment and happiness, and so on.

We should underline that this shift of values spreads with the phenomenon known as economic imperialism: the growing application of a model of interpretation of economics (now converted into a hard science) as explained by the neoclassical model. A discipline that has come to invade the rest of the academic fields and is used increasingly to account for each and every pattern of human behaviour in society. Behaviour that can be reduced to prices, utilities and incentives.[32] Sandel[33] recounts this change of direction in economics as of the 1970s, when it ceased to be a circumspect and restricted discipline (that sought to explain how depressions, unemployment and inflation could be prevented and to study productivity and the improvement of living standards) and became nothing less than a science to explain the behaviour of individuals.[34] This is the economics, or at least a large part of it, that is tending to expand around the world today.

31 Here I follow the analysis made by my colleague Ferran Macipe. Class notes.

32 The most notable example of this would be Gary S. Becker. See Becker G. (1976). *The Economic Approach to Human Behavior*. University of Chicago Press. A summarized version of his thought can be found in his Nobel Prize acceptance speech: Becker G. (1992). "The Economic Way of Looking at Life": www.nobelprize.org/nobel_prizes/economic-sciences/laureates/1992/becker-lecture.pdf.

33 Sandel M. (2012). *What Money Can't Buy: The Moral Limits of Markets*. New York: Farrar, Straus and Giroux. pp. 84 ff.

34 The recent proliferation of "freakonomics" texts would be an example of this trend: Levitt S. & S. Dubner (2005). *Freakonomics: A Rogue Economist Explores the Hidden Side of Everything*. William Morrow/HarperCollins. Note that Levitt, like Becker, is a professor at the University of Chicago.

The substratum of these *market* values that are spreading worldwide—individualism, personal initiative, ownership, success, consumption, competitiveness, etc.—force us to get down below the surface of the changes that are occurring. Below this model of globalization there lies a belief in progress, the inevitability of this progress when it is ingrained in economic development,[35] utility as the basis for market-dictated value (what is the utility of civility, or of respect for the aged?), and in the work ethos linked to one's job and measured in terms of the size of one's salary (but what of the effort of the amateur athlete, or the social activist striving to improve her home town?).

Consumerism, the mainstay of the system and driving force behind a large part of the values of globalization today, merits a place of its own. Some authors[36] trace its origins to the consumer revolution in the US in the 1920s. Others identify this revolution as occurring in the wake of the Second World War. The phenomenon owed much to the economic recovery of Europe, the technological advances of the time (TV, the transistor, the car, and so on) and the expansion of the purchasing power of both households and states in the heyday of Keynesianism. At its epicentre we find the transformation of the notion of desire, now the linchpin of new patterns of consumption, which will be stimulated to unsuspected and often irrational extremes in fields as varied as cosmetic surgery, luxury and health.

As individuals, consumption is an essential part of us. And to encourage this consumption, sellers have no compunction about exploiting human nature and our most basic instincts: fear (the insurance sector, the pharmaceutical industry), sexuality (drinks, fashion), social status (cars, watches) and so on. The media plays a crucial role in driving this, and advertising becomes omnipresent. Explicit advertising appears in the streets and spreads to prisons, schools, books, police cars and even the human body.[37] The cult of the new, the feeling of *not being able to live* without possessing

---

35   Obviously it could be otherwise. Our progress depends to a larger extent on respectful co-existence with the environment, and on the equity of this development in society.

36   The information that follows is taken from Albareda L. (2010). *Consum i valors. La mercantilització dels valors.* Fundació Lluís Carulla-ESADE. This text is based mainly on the references: Lipovetsky G. (2006). *Le bonheur paradoxal. Essai sur la société d'hyperconsommation*, Paris: éditions Gallimard; Bauman, Z. (2007). *Consuming Life.* Cambridge: Polity. And lastly: Cortina, A. (2003). *Por una ética del consumo.* Madrid: Taurus.

37   Sandel (op. cit.), especially p. 163 ff.

a particular good, is given double force by advertisers on the one hand and the pressure exerted on us by the rest of society on the other. It is important to emphasize that this is a way of life and of understanding the world that has come about. Just as it now *is*, for centuries it was not. Some cultures and countries are only now becoming integrated into these patterns established by consumerism.

And of course these values adapt to or clash with preexisting values. Values such as solidarity, the existence of communal goods, systems of equal participation, and different readings of the notions of happiness or value (use value rather than monetary value, for example) are often threatened and pushed out by prevailing values. So there is a reaction which, as we will see, can be manifested in different ways individually or collectively. At the end of the 19th century, Émile Durkheim published a classic sociological study linking the increase in suicides in France to the economic and cultural changes taking place at the time.[38] In his work, Durkheim highlights the notion of anomie as the process of breakdown of social ties between the individual and the community, in the face of changes that affect individual identity and prevailing social values. Thus, the globalization of consumerism, insofar as it transforms society, collides with traditional beliefs, religion, the family. It drives us towards a potential identity conflict and turns upside down essential features of Western modernity that require a strong sense of the collective: human rights, democracy and the welfare state.

The social repercussions of consumerism are deeper than we see at first glance. First, there is a disintegration of class consciousness—class being definable as the place we occupy in the system of production—which will gradually be replaced by individuals belonging to groups and lifestyles, and also patterns of consumption.[39] Second, a model of economic development appears that is based on credit and indebtedness in which household expenditure accounts for around 60% of the GDP of the respective states,[40] representing the root of the current global crisis. Lastly, individuals are reduced to the category of products in the labour market, with the resulting need to adapt and retrain in order to sell themselves.

38   Durkheim E. (2006, original 1897). *On Suicide*. London: Penguin.
39   Beck U. & E. Beck-Gernsheim (2002). *Individualization: Institutionalized Individualism and its Social and Political Consequences*. London: Sage.
40   See World Bank data (accessed September 2013): http://data.worldbank.org/ indicator/NE.CON.PETC.ZS/countries?display=graph.

2.5 Cultural globalization and conflict of identities

2.5.1 A tour of identities in a globalized world

So can we draw a direct line connecting this clash of values to, say, the anti-Erdoğan demonstrations in Taksim Square in Istanbul at the beginning of 2013? And to the earlier Arab revolutions at the beginning of 2011? And to 9/11? Many authors have attempted it, and some have done so by creating theoretical frameworks that have been quite influential in offering a way of seeing the world in order to promote concrete political action. However, let's go step by step. In order to take this leap from the cultural world to that of identity, and then to that of politics, first we need to gain greater insight into the cultural transformation that comes to us from the confluence of globalized markets with scientific and technological development.

At the deepest level of transformation we find the rise of innovation, the individual and organizational focus on scientific and technological learning. Patterns of study change, relations of power and influence within organizations shift in favour of those who can generate added value through new products. Furthermore, we observe the rise of a cosmopolitan culture which collides with local cultures. Market values clash with preexisting values, as we saw earlier. Then again, in the dawn of this new globalized and post-traditional society, everywhere we see a convergence towards a new kind of education and an individual adapted to the needs of globalized capitalism. Lifelong learning, the importance of creativity, communication, collaboration. These are all necessary factors for each of us to engage individually with global production chains and improve our position once we are inside them. Of course, these characteristics generate a new type of star worker with links to the group of symbolic analysts put forward by Reich: individualists with a strong, flexible, creative personality.

On a second visible level, globalized markets transform power dynamics. The mass media, under the impetus of globalized patterns of consumption, makes all-pervading the frame of reference of the winners of globalization and redefines ways of doing things and concepts. Ritzer calls this process the "McDonaldization" of society.[41] It is a form of American cultural imperialism that fosters the values of efficiency (at all costs), calculability (with the emphasis on quantity); predictability (leading to the worldwide homogenization of ways of doing things); control of the individual by means of

---

41   Ritzer G. (1993). *The McDonaldization of Society*. Thousand Oaks, CA: Pine Forges Press.

technology and the (irrational) rule of rationality (leading to the degradation and dehumanization of such basic life experiences as eating). The most visible values are those habitually found in the market: individualism, competition and consumerism. The added effect is that of the reconfiguration of relations of global economic and political power (following Wallerstein and Sklair above) in terms of winning societies (capable of advancing these values, which are their own) and losing societies (the rest). As we will see presently, there are two possible reactions:

- The accommodation of states to the (Western) values of globalization, as set out by Francis Fukuyama, a world increasingly marked by the values of liberal democracy; or

- The identity confrontation set out by Benjamin Barber, which ultimately erodes democracy itself under the aegis of the values of the globalized market

On the third level we find conflicts and the *identity* reaction, which cannot be understood without reference to the change in relations of power resulting from this clash between market culture and traditional culture. On the one hand, on an individual level, we recover the notion of anomie mentioned earlier: a new evaluative framework implies a new world-view, a different way of understanding the world around us. This is a shake-up that translates into the loss of reference frameworks (now replaced), the reshaping of identity, of the sense of belonging, the feeling of community; our certainties and existing hierarchies. We can take the example of the culture shock that must have been experienced by a peasant in the region of Shanghai on observing the radical transformation of his city. But on a collective level, too, there are reactive social movements involving those who some would see as the losers of the globalization process: a return to ethnocentrism (shutting oneself into one's own culture by rejecting outsiders), the rise of fundamentalisms, of exclusionary nationalisms, racism, xenophobia, and group withdrawal into subcultures and urban tribes.

Castells[42] defines identity as "the process whereby a social actor recognises himself and constructs meaning, above all by virtue of a particular cultural attribute (or set of attributes), disregarding other social structures such as power, wealth or status." The problem with parts of the above-mentioned "-isms", a problem that we will find presently and is shared

42   Castells M. (1997). *The Power of Identity. The Information Age: Economy, Society and Culture.* Vol. II. Cambridge, MA; Oxford, UK: Blackwell. Chapter 1.

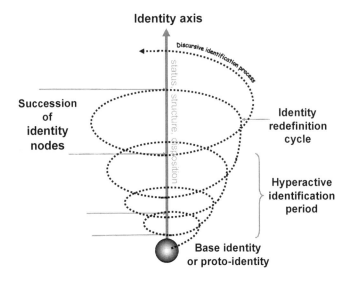

FIGURE 2.5 Evolution of personal identity

Source: Department of Social Sciences, ESADE. Adapted from Chebel M., 1998

by Western authors, is the fixing of identity as a stable entity rather than what it actually is: a process of configuration and reconfiguration of a self-representation around an axis that goes through moments of acceleration (during adolescence) and change (throughout one's life).

M. Chebel[43] talks of identification as a generally unconscious evolutionary process that develops throughout one's life and through which an individual acquires an identity. Identity, on the other hand, is a relatively stable and subjective structure that remains steady over time and is characterized by a complex, integral and coherent representation of the ego.

Castells[44] reminds us of the importance of observing what happens to identity in the globalization process. Globalization for many individuals implies lack of control over their own lives. It is also a search for immediate meaning, a redefinition of the community and the bonds of belonging. And the making and unmaking of our own identity and the society to which we belong.

43   Chebel M. (1998). *La formation de l'identité politique*. Paris: Payot.
44   Pascual M. (2006). ¿En qué mundo vivimos? *Conversaciones con Manuel Castells*. Madrid: Alianza Editorial. Chapter VII: "La fuerza de la identidad".

2.5.2 Globalization and conflict

To what extent do all the above changes in the cultural sphere provide us with a better understanding of international relations and conflicts between countries? In the West, several authors have given their interpretation of recent changes, taking as their starting point the world that opened up after the fall of the Berlin Wall (1989) and the dissolution of the USSR (1991). If we go further back in time, into the area of international relations, international conflict can be divided into a number of stages:

- From 1648 to 1789, in the period running from the Peace of Westphalia to the French Revolution, conflict is to be understood as a decision made among sovereign princes, still fought by mercenary troops and in the geographical region of the West.

- In the period between 1789 and the end of the First World War (1918) conflict was among nation-states, involving the civil population through conscription and the identification of the state with society. This conflict was still primarily among Western countries.

- From the end of the First World War until 1989, global conflict was mainly between ideologies: first between fascisms and liberal democracies, and later between communism and liberal democracies. The framework of conflict, although global geographically, from the cultural perspective was nevertheless between two worldviews of Western origin (fascism/communism and liberalism).

Since the 1990s, however, we have been confronted with the problem of understanding where we are heading, in the wake of the fall and unexpected dissolution of communism, and where future conflicts will come from. Two of the most successful interpretations, at least during the 1990s and well into the 21st century (with an end date located around 2004–2008 with the failure of President Bush's War on Terror and the financial crisis), have been those of Francis Fukuyama[45] and Samuel Huntington:[46]

- For Fukuyama, the world that started in 1989 is marked by **the end of history**: the ultimate victory of liberal market ideology over all

45   Fukuyama F. (1989). "The end of history?" *The National Interest*; Fukuyama F. (1992). *The End of History and the Last Man*. Free Press.

46   Huntington S. (1993). "The clash of civilizations?" *Foreign Affairs*, vol. 72, n. 3, Summer 1993, pp. 22-49; Huntington S. (1996). *The Clash of Civilizations and the Remaking of World Order*. New York: Simon & Schuster.

PERIOD	TYPE OF CONFLICT	AREA
Westphalia's Peace (1648) to French Revolution (1789)	Between sovereign princes	Western
French Revolution to World War I (1918)	Between nation-states	Western
World War I to 1989	Between ideologies	Western
Present (1989)	End of history	Western Global
Present (1993)	Clash of civilizations	Global

TABLE 2.5 Global conflict according to Fukuyama and Huntington

Source: A. Castiñeira based on Fukuyama and Huntington. Class notes

other alternatives (fascisms, communisms, tribalisms and religious fundamentalisms). This victory, originating in the West, now has a global framework, as it will impose itself everywhere, generating minor reactions of a religious or ethnic nature that are doomed to failure.

- For Huntington, we are experiencing not the end of conflict but rather its transformation. Ideologies will be replaced by ethnic conflicts (regarded as minor by Fukuyama) on religious grounds that will necessitate a new policy of affinities and animosities on the basis of cultural and civilizational alliances.

We need to get a good grasp of both these approaches. For Fukuyama, an American thinker indebted to the work of the German philosopher Hegel, the world of ideas (and ideologies) displaces other minor interests (the economy, consumption) that transform the epidermis of our world but not our way of interpreting it. Ideas clash in a process of confrontation, response and synthesis (thesis-antithesis, synthesis), in which victorious ideas push out the rest. This final stage which gives meaning to how we should live and relate to each other is called liberal democracy; that which *everyone* would choose if given the chance. This leads us to the end of history: the *victory* of liberalism everywhere. The only remaining opponents of liberalism are minor and negligible—religion and nationalism—although they are not

necessarily incompatible with liberalism. The consequence of this ideological convergence towards Western values is that we will live in a more
consumerist (and more boring) world, lacking great alternatives, in which
competitiveness and peaceful economic war will replace military conflict.

> What we may be witnessing is not just the end of the Cold War, or the
> passing of a particular period of post-war history, but the end of his-
> tory as such: that is, the end point of mankind's ideological evolution
> and the universalization of Western liberal democracy as the final
> form of human government.
>
>   We might summarize the content of the universal homogenous
> state as liberal democracy in the political sphere combined with easy
> access to VCRs and stereos in the economic. [...] The end of history
> will be a very sad time. The struggle for recognition, the willingness
> to risk one's life for a purely abstract goal, the worldwide ideological
> struggle that called forth daring, courage, imagination and ideal-
> ism, will be replaced by economic calculation, the endless solving of
> technical problems, environmental concerns, and the satisfaction of
> sophisticated consumer demands.[47]

For Huntington, on the other hand:

> culture and cultural identities [...] are shaping the patterns of cohe-
> sion, disintegration, and conflict in the post-Cold War world. [...] In
> the emerging era, clashes of civilizations are the greatest threat to
> world peace, and an international order based on civilizations is the
> surest safeguard against world war.[48]

According to this US thinker, world politics is truly multipolar and multi-
civilizational for the first time in history. There is neither Westernization nor
any universalization of liberalism. On the contrary, we are witnessing the
loss of Western influence. The Asian civilizations are increasing their economic, military and political strength; the Muslim countries are experiencing a population explosion. The end of the Cold War has brought above all
a reinforcement of cultural patterns, hidden up until then behind the clash
of ideologies.

   In Huntington, it is essential to grasp this reconfiguration of global order,
as it implies a new set of rules of the game. The key player in the new diplomacy will now be the civilization: the conglomerate resulting from the clus-
tering of countries and societies around their cultural and ethnic affinities.
New conflicts will arise on a twofold scale:

47   Fukuyama F. (1989). op. cit.
48   Huntington S. (1993). op. cit.

- Global, among civilizational blocs: the so-called clash of civilizations, the contenders of which will be the three blocs with universalist ambitions, namely the West, Islam and China

- On the other hand, local conflicts along cultural fault lines: small-scale civil wars in states torn apart by their ethnocultural differences (former Yugoslavia; Caucasian Russia)

From a Western angle, Huntington's recommendation is to prepare ourselves for a new kind of conflict. The survival of the West will depend on the conviction with which the US reaffirms, renews and preserves its Western identity with the support and union of the other Western powers. He continued to explore this thesis in subsequent work,[49] at the same time providing intellectual ammunition for certain political groups in the US: "When Osama bin Laden attacked America and killed several thousand people, he also did two other things. He filled the vacuum created by Gorbachev with an unmistakably dangerous new enemy, and he pinpointed America's identity as a Christian nation."

Criticism rained down on Huntington from all sides, particularly for his attempt to offer an essentially violent identity-based path, in fact a form of diplomacy, for leading international affairs. Indian economist and philosopher Amartya Sen is especially condemning of Huntington[50] for his violent use of identities, his reductionism in assigning an individual to a civilization and the fallacy of the homogeneity of cultures (Russian, Canadian, Australian, Bolivian, Indian or whatever). Sen criticizes the simplification and ignorance shown by Huntington, but above all the illusion of trying to comprehend people's destiny.

Nevertheless, from a radically different perspective, we would do well to note the evolution (also to be found in Fukuyama) undergone by Huntington from his original article ("The Clash of Civilizations?" in *Foreign Affairs*, of 1993) to his definitive book (*The Clash of Civilizations and the Remaking of World Order* of 1996). What in the first instance is a tentative title, *ending in a question mark*, three years on is a full-blown thesis. How did this transition happen? I would put forward two explanations here: first, a publishing industry that shuns toe dipping and weak theses and embraces cardinal concepts, forceful and preferably controversial

---

49   Huntington S. (2004). *Who Are We? The Challenges to America's National Identity*. New York: Simon & Schuster.

50   Sen A. (2006). *Identity and Violence: The Illusion of Destiny*. New York: Norton & Company. Chapter 3.

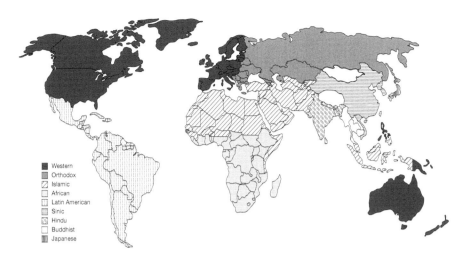

FIGURE 2.6 Huntington's map of civilizations

Source: Wikipedia (accessed 11th March 2014). The Clash of Civilizations Map, according to Huntington (1996)

statements; and second, a readership interested in anticipating conflicts and understanding what was to come after the fall of the Berlin Wall. In the academic world, particularly the Anglo-Saxon one, if you haven't got an interpretative thesis on how the world works you're nobody. So we also have to understand Huntington, and especially the unreserved nature of his statements, in the light of the clash of ideas in a period of considerable upheaval.

In a less prophetic and ideology-laden tone than Huntington, but along not dissimilar lines, we find Barber's thesis on the cultural conflict that lies behind the expansion of globalization.[51] For Barber, the revival of religious, ethnic and traditionalist movements is the flip side of globalization. The more progress made towards technicist modernity, the more the individual feels forced to seek refuge in his or her roots. The issue of identity comes to the forefront in politics. The outcome is always violent. The rise of the "global theme park" formed by MTV, McDonald's and Macintosh generates the violence that leads to the weakening of the state. The market's universal church triggers the retribalizing of politics at the service of particular identities. This tribal reaction, jihad, is just a sign of this eagerness to recover identity and, according to Barber, is no truer of Muslims than of Christians; of Arabs than of Germans. In the short term the tension between Jihad and

51   Barber B. (1995). *Jihad vs. McWorld*. New York: Crown, Introduction, pp. 3-20.

McWorld will bring chaos and anarchy; in the long run, homogenization and Westernization.[52]

Which reading should we take of this contact between cultures, heightened by globalization: that of co-existence, that of assimilation, or that of conflict? The most sensible interpretation is simply to note the existence of all three types of relationship, together with that of a growing *syncretism* that defends the hybridization of the different cultures in contact (Western and Chinese; Chinese and Philippine; Latin American and European, and so on). However, we should not ignore some of the serious problems involved in these culturalist interpretations, particularly when they portend culture shocks or even go so far as to defend a diplomatic strategy with the aim of *civilizing*.

First of all, we should emphasize the patent oversimplification involved in establishing relationships of equivalence between geography and culture. In such cosmopolitan and culturally and ethnically diverse societies as those of America, India or France, what is the sense in putting them all in the same cultural sack? Geert Hofstede, for example, gives a portrayal of different cultures depending on what he calls cultural dimensions: a snapshot of diversity that enables him to present the patchwork of cultural differences by groups of countries.[53] Thus, the acceptance of an unequal distribution of power, a sense of community and a long-term orientation of one's actions would be cultural attributes inherent in societies considered as Confucian (this would include Japan, Korea, China and Singapore), whereas individualism and immediate enjoyment of the returns yielded by a particular action would be characteristics of Western societies.

Lewis[54] performs a similar exercise that enables him to find associations between cultures on the basis of three poles of affinity: countries with

---

52   It should be noted here that Jihad and McWorld are broader concepts than their names suggest. Jihad, for example, goes beyond the political reading given to jihadism in the West, to which we referred earlier, and can quite easily be applied to other fundamentalisms such as Christian ones, and even some urban tribes.

53   These would be variables that explain how individuals and communities respond to various cultural manifestations. Hofstede enumerates the following variables: power distance, individualism, masculinity, uncertainty avoidance, long-term orientation, and indulgence vs. restraint. See Hofstede G. (1980). *Culture's Consequences: International Differences in Work-Related Values.* Beverly Hills CA: Sage Publications.

54   Lewis R. (1996). *When Cultures Collide: Leading Across Cultures.* Nicholas Brealey Pub.

linear-active culture (Germany, Switzerland, GB, USA), multi-active culture (much of Latin America) and reactive culture (Vietnam, Japan, China). Without going into the conceptualization that the author makes of these three categories, here we address only the ultimate meaning of Lewis's classification. For this author, the degree of emotion in discourse, confrontation (or avoidance of it), the value given to the written or spoken word and the degree of task orientation are, roughly speaking, differentiating attributes of each of these cultures.

The problem with the culturalist options is the across-the-board, over-simplifying nature of their portrayal. Any attempt to squeeze supposedly homogenous cultures into the pigeonhole of a nation-state conceals the diversity and complexity that exist. To quote Amartya Sen, is India, with its more than 100 million Muslims, a Hindu country? Is the lay republican France of today a Catholic country? Can the China of cosmopolitan Shanghai be understood using the same parameters as the equally Chinese but ethnically Turkic province of Xinjiang, inhabited by proud, rebellious Uyghurs? Within this same risk of oversimplification we find the effort made by authors such as Hofstede to try to understand cultures through supposedly quantifiable indicators (dimensions). Are we not leaving out the most important attributes of a culture, precisely when we reduce them to such rigid parameters? From an operational and analytical perspective, other questions we could ask ourselves might include: are the studies carried out on these categories replicable? Do they really throw light on this social entity formed by nation-states? Are we not falling into sweeping stereotypes that in an attempt to explain everything ultimately explain nothing? Are cultures not by definition blurred, fickle concepts that are constantly subject to the ebb and flow of outside influences?

So why do we have to mention attempts such as those above to understand and interpret cultural diversity in the framework of a globalized world? Well, because generalizations (by Huntington, Hofstede, Lewis or anyone else) do in fact convey *a certain degree* of truth. They are intended to grasp a series of essences, patterns that would work as cultural averages but would not necessarily enable us to anticipate behaviour, still less to take for granted political proposals such as those ventured by Huntington. Aside from the political and often economic use that is made of them, in the present context these sorts of generalization should be seen as an intellectual attempt to simplify the cultural complexity of the moment in which we live by means of comparison. One important virtue of them is to remedy some of the mistakes made by early anthropologists at the beginning of the 20th century: excessive particularization (each culture is different) and relativism (there are no global points of understanding, precisely because we are different). Simplification and generalization offer patterns, albeit weak ones, to allow contact and communication between cultures once considered remote and now rendered close at hand.

3
Economic globalization

3.1 A sociological approach to economics: definitions and concepts

If there is one single issue that usually predominates in the debate on globalization it is that of the economy. Its central role is due to the fact that it is considered to be the main driving force of change and the foundation on which lie the whole series of technological, cultural and political changes that help to describe the phenomenon of globalization. This said, we need to bear in mind that the present economic analysis of globalization in recent decades has developed characteristics of its own, different from those of previous decades, that force us to analyse it from two angles: first that of the productive economy, and then that of finance, which we will address in the next chapter. In the following pages we aim to arrive at an understanding of the specific nature of economic globalization, lending special attention to its most recent historical development: its phases and the elements that characterize it. We will then go on to explore its consequences from the viewpoint of the redistribution of political and economic power, particularly with regard to large corporations and states. Lastly, we will examine its impacts and reactions to it on a global scale, and tackle one of the key discussions at present: its impact on planetary inequality.

The approach that interests us, however, is not that taken by economists but for the most part that which is defended by economic sociology. The chief difference between these two disciplines lies in the methodology used and the importance of the role of institutions in accounting for a particular economic phenomenon.[1] Economics tends to proceed *deductively*, on the basis of premises that explain human behaviour. In neoclassical economics, currently predominant in universities, these premises are erected around an abstraction, the economic anthropology of *Homo economicus*, according to which, broadly speaking, all individuals are selfish, materialistic, individualistic, rational and out to maximize our preferences in a market (of goods and services) in which there are suppliers and demanders. This abstraction may be accompanied by others, such as the notion of perfectly competitive markets or the efficient market hypothesis. We will discuss this later on, but not yet. All we are interested in here is to point out the deductive approach of economics and alongside this the disdain this discipline shows for the effects of theories on the world around us. In the words of Nobel economics prize laureate Milton Friedman, the interest of a theory lies not in the goodness or veracity of its assumptions but in its ability to predict the outcome of a particular action.[2] The theory itself is neutral.

Thus, economics traces a downward path from ideas to reality. In contrast, sociology usually proceeds by induction, from the bottom up. It analyses how agents' economic behaviour varies over time—or from country to country—and depending on the social context. On this basis, it draws conclusions. A key concept of sociology is that it denies Friedman's statement above. When social scientists, including economists, describe the world, at the same time we are creating it. This phenomenon is known as performativity. According to this idea, axioms, premises and theories are not neutral but rather are interrelated with the world they are attempting to describe, and make it possible in a particular way.[3] So-called scientific theories, at least in the field of the social sciences, thus include an ideological component that is unacknowledged by economists such as Friedman. As US sociologist W.I. Thomas put it, if men define situations as real, they are real in their consequences.[4]

1　Here I follow Dobbin F. (2005). "Comparative and Historical Approaches to Economic Sociology." In Smelser N.J. & R. Swedberg: *The Handbook of Economic Sociology: Second Edition*. New York: Princeton University Press.

2　Friedman M. (1953). *Essays in Positive Economics*. Chicago: The University of Chicago Press.

3　See Mackenzie D. (2004). "The big, bad wolf and the rational market: portfolio insurance, the 1987 crash and the performativity of economics." *Economy and Society*, 33(3), 303-34.

4　Merton R.K. (1995). "The Thomas Theorem and the Matthew Effect." *Social Forces*, 74(2), 379-424.

So the sociological approach takes into account three basic social processes that are usually regarded as secondary by economics:

- **Relations of power** model agents' economic behaviour. In all societies there are groups who foster specific practices and public policies that are in *their* interest but which they manage to get the majority of society to perceive as being in the common interest.

- The **existence of institutions** that shape economic action and are defined as systems of collective beliefs, norms and feelings, according to Durkheim.

- The existence of **social networks**: social groups that establish patterns of behaviour, sanction behaviours, confer a sense of belonging and identity and configure what sort of action is socially acceptable.

For the case in hand, sociology is contextual; it does not seek to expound a single way of understanding the reality around us but instead erects interpretations on the basis of a reality that can be interpreted in different ways.[5] This first methodological digression will enable the reader to understand the approach to economic globalization that we set out below.

3.2 Economic globalization: concepts, phases and characteristics

After this brief tour of the world of comparative methodology, we are now in a position to observe the globalized economy from an institutional

---

5   As Bourdieu shows in a classic sociological study on 1960s Algeria, the explanation of the economic rationale of having few children—from our Western perspective, a burden that limits the capacity to maximize the utility of the various family members—is eclipsed in different economic, cultural and institutional contexts, in which the survival of the family actually depends on having as many children as possible and hoping that one or more of them will be able to guarantee the future of the rest. Thus, the same economic rationale is multiple and depends on cultural and institutional factors. See Bourdieu P. (2005). *The Social Structures of the Economy*. Polity. We can contrast this vision with the all-explaining account provided by the Chicago school of economics, for example in Gary S. Becker (1976). *The Economic Approach to Human Behavior*. University of Chicago Press.

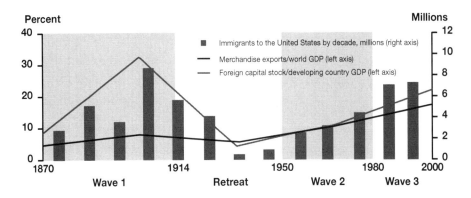

FIGURE 3.1 Three waves of globalization

Source: Collier, P.; Dollar, D. (2002). Globalization, Growth, and Poverty: Building an Inclusive World Economy. Oxford: World Bank Policy Research Report, p.23. © World Bank.

perspective, which is what we will be concerned with here. Collier and Dollar[6] talk of the unprecedented expansion of the economy as of the 1980s, and explain it in terms of three key variables: migrations, international capital flows, and flows of goods.

The authors hold that there have been three main waves of globalization: that which began around the year 1870 and continued until the First World War; that which started after the Second World War and extended until the 1970s; and the present one, which began in the 1980s. In the middle there was a period of retreat that lasted from 1914 to 1945. O'Rourke and Williamson[7] provide a broader historical perspective by examining the increase in world trade over the period 1500 to 1992. If the annual growth in trade in the 16th century was 1.26%, a century later it was only half this figure. Trade picked up again in the 18th century, and then boomed extraordinarily in the 19th century, the great age of European colonization, when growth reached an annual average of 3.85%, three times greater than in the previous century. This growth figure was almost repeated in the 20th century, despite the lull between the Wars.

If we take world trade as our yardstick, there is good reason to point to the change of cycle that began in the 19th century and was built on the expansion of mercantilism and the great trading companies, predecessors of

6   Collier P. & D. Dollar (2002). *Globalization, Growth, and Poverty: Building an Inclusive World Economy*. Oxford: World Bank Policy Research Report.

7   O'Rourke K. & J. Williamson (2004). "Once more: When did globalisation begin?" *European Review of Economic History* 8, 109-17.

Period (Century)	Annual growth in %
XVI	1.3
XVII	0.7
XVIII	1.3
XIX	3.9
XX (until 1992)	3.7

TABLE 3.1 European and intercontinental trade growth, 1500–1992

Source: Author, based on O'Rourke and Williamson (2004)

today's big transnational corporations. Rodrik[8] sets forth the changes that appeared with the rise of the great trade monopolies at the service of the European monarchies. We are talking about the British East India Company, the Dutch East and West India Companies and the Hudson's Bay Company, a corporation created at the end of the 18th century and which by 1870 had become de facto administrator of a geographical area of present-day Canada six times larger than France.

The Hudson's Bay Company began as a British monopoly for the trading of fur for the home market, but eventually it came to perform within its territory a long list of functions that nowadays would belong in the hands of the state. These would include waging wars, passing laws, administering justice, creating transport systems and providing public education. According to Rodrik, the core idea in the period of expansion of trade was to use the economy as a tool for international and domestic policy. However, this was still a pre-liberal stage that only started to get off the ground in the second half of the 18th century, especially with the publication and dissemination of the work of the Scottish moral philosopher and economist Adam Smith.

In the 19th century, with the rise of ideological liberalism, the essential economic idea was to create open markets to replace state monopolies and allow the appearance of competition. Competition, Smith tells us, favours small producers, traders and consumers, freeing them from the oppression of the great state-authorized monopolies. Rodrik, however, makes an unusual interpretation of the changes brought by Adam Smith. He claims that the economy did not in fact shift away from the state and towards the market; rather, what happened was an instance of delimitation. Markets

8   From this point on, in this chapter our key source will be Rodrik D. (2011): *The Globalization Paradox: Democracy and the Future of the World Economy*. New York: W.W. Norton & Company.

needed and continue to need institutions that are not governed by the market, among them laws and regulations. The changes that took place over the 18th and 19th centuries for the benefit of the market feature a seldom observed characteristic: role switching between enterprise and the state, whereby the former generate private profit in exchange for paying taxes—and therefore sharing their wealth—and generating institutions.

This reading that takes into account the institutional underpinnings of the economy is fundamental for an economist such as Rodrik. The market needs institutions to reduce transaction costs, i.e., the costs of operating in the market, and so allow it to function. Rodrik underscores the three types of institution created parallel to the development of these large enterprises:

- Long-term relationships based on reciprocity and trust among agents—relationships without which, it must be understood, trade would not occur

- A system of beliefs with widely shared values and principles of action allowing for predictable trade relations

- A system of enforcement to ensure compliance with commercial agreements

Rodrik goes still further, insisting on the importance of the development of institutions to understand economic growth. His thesis is that the larger an economy is, the larger its public sector needs to be. In other words, markets and governments are not substitutes but complements. They necessarily go hand in hand. Why is this so? Precisely because larger, more complex economies require a larger number of institutions that are not provided by the market in order to function correctly. The greater the exposure to trade, the greater the need for institutions enabling the market to work and protecting the citizen from the malfunctions of the market—market failures, in economic language.

If in 1870 the role of the state in the economy of countries considered to be advanced was equivalent to 11% of their GDP on average, by 1920 it accounted for 20%, by 1960 for 28% and by the 1970s for 40%. In the new century we are now beginning, the planet's economic powerhouses have a GDP in the hands of the public sector that ranges from 35% to 60% of the total. Indeed, using World Bank data,[9] if we compare the level of state spending in developed and developing countries, we can observe the correlation

9   Gill, I.; Raiser, M. (2012). Golden Growth: Restoring the Lustre of the European Economic Model. Washington: The World Bank.© World Bank.

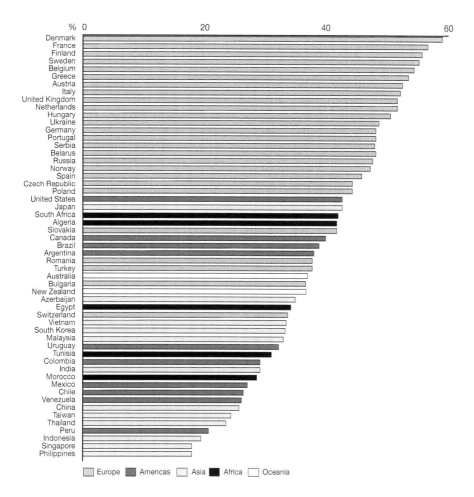

FIGURE 3.2 Public spending as a percentage of GDP, 2004–2009

Source: Gill, I.; Raiser, M. (2012). Golden Growth: Restoring the Lustre of the European Economic Model. Washington: The World Bank. © World Bank.

between development and the size of the public sector measured in percentage of public expenditure (pensions, unemployment benefit, education and health).

The list of institutions required to keep the economy working is huge, Rodrik tells us. Economic development occurs parallel to their evolution and consolidation. Over the years, this institutional deployment has been manifested in the existence of property rights, courts to enforce agreements, commercial regulations to protect trade, police forces, macroeconomic policies to correct the economic cycle, prudential and supervisory standards to guarantee financial stability, the idea of the need for a lender of last resort for moments of financial panic … Also appearing on the scene are health standards, safety standards, labour standards, environmental standards, and subsequently income redistribution systems to compensate those who lose out from globalization. There are social safety nets and, of course, taxes to fund all the above. Let there be no doubt about this: for decades, the overwhelming majority of academics, citizens and politicians took it for granted that without the above institutional systems the market would be unable to function. It was not until the 1970s that this interpretation of the fruitful co-existence of institutions with markets was brought into question; a historically novel phenomenon that hides behind the arguments for and against globalization.

Rodrik sets the first main stage of globalization in the period from 1800 to 1914. In a historical perspective, the worldwide growth of trade (measured as a percentage increase) was unprecedented. If in the 17th and 18th centuries trade increased by around 1% on average, in the 19th century and up until the First World War this figure was 4%. Trade plummeted by no less than half in absolute volume between the two world wars and up until the end of the Second World War. Subsequently it rose by 7% a year until the 1990s. The first lesson to be learned, questionable but not without its reasons, was to link the global trade increase with economic growth. And on the other side of the coin, to equate economic autarky (Spain in the 1940s and 1950s, China until 1979, Albania during the Cold War or North Korea today) and protectionism with war and loss of living standards.

This reading of the effect of trade on economic development—and world peace—gave rise in 1944 to the Bretton Woods system, the new world order in the wake of the Second World War and the embryo of today's European Union. And so the link was made between peace, globalized trade, world integration and progress. Some took this thesis to its ultimate consequences, but it was not until the oil crises of the 1970s that this select intellectual minority came to win political favour. What changes have come out of this globalization of the economy and its resulting social transformation? If we look back a couple of centuries, in the techno-economic sphere we can point to the appearance of steamships, railways, canals and telegraphy. In the cultural sphere we find, inevitably, the rise of liberal and market ideology. And in the political and institutional sphere, the establishment of the gold standard, liberalizing economic policies and the expansion of colonialism.

The second wave of globalization, says Rodrik, started with the so-called Bretton Woods consensus and lasted until the 1970s. Rodrik labels this as globalization with *respect* for difference; globalization that had learned from the interwar period. The Bretton Woods model was based on liberalizing trade but at the same time granting state governments plenty of space to implement differentiated social and economic policy. This was, then, a moderate kind of globalization in which the policies of states usually overrode international agreements, with rare exceptions. In the framework of the new post-war international organizations we find the International Monetary Fund (IMF), the World Bank (WB) and the GATT agreements (as of 1995 subsumed within the World Trade Organization, WTO), bodies aimed respectively at supervising global financial stability, fighting poverty, and defending free trade and solving commercial disputes.

The central idea of this new order was to equip the international community with a set of operating rules for the global economy, to be supervised by the above organizations. These organizations were created multilaterally around the powers that won the Second World War, and therefore enjoyed a high degree of international legitimacy, born out of a war. As an umbrella institution, the old dream of US President Woodrow Wilson (1913–21) to avail ourselves of a worldwide organization to foster global peace and co-operation was given new energy. The birth of the United Nations in 1945 marked the arrival of an improved version of the League of Nations, which was born lame and incomplete after the First World War. This time the winning powers in the worldwide conflict (USA, France, UK, USSR and China) would occupy permanent seats in its highest governing body, the Security Council, and maintain an effective power of veto over the resolutions passed by the rest of the member states. As regards international organizations, this is the scenario that still today helps us to understand how the world works.

From an economic perspective it is important to emphasize the moderation of the objectives of this second wave of globalization. This moderation lasted until the 1970s and resulted, as had been intended, in the growth of global trade, equality, security and stability. The different GATT rounds worked from the starting point of the extension of the most favoured nation clause in transnational trade agreements. The key idea was to lower trade barriers, reduce protectionism and liberalize many economic sectors. This must be made clear: the intention was not to maximize global trade, but merely to extend sectors where possible. Notwithstanding, it was acknowledged that certain sectors and areas such as agriculture, finance and public services would be safeguarded from international competition. Among the difficulties encountered by the GATT to perform its function we find its limited supervisory capacity, which was weak and often inapplicable. But it's an ill wind that blows no good, and this weakness allowed a range of globalizing strategies depending on the ideology and level of economic development of each country.

In Western countries this globalization with respect for the idiosyncrasies of different states gave rise to different types of capitalism: the more deregulated Anglo-Saxon model of the US and the UK, the robust welfare state of the Scandinavian countries, and the French indicative planning system, for example. As historian Tony Judt points out in his book *Thinking the Twentieth Century*, the action of the state in the economy had not yet been discredited by the neoliberal wave that was soon to come. Culturally quite homogeneous countries, at least in Europe, with a vivid memory of the human cost of world wars, legitimized the varied institutional deployment described above.

The difficulties arrived with the deterioration of the Western economies, increasing inflation and unemployment, which came hand in hand with the Yom Kippur War (1973), rising oil prices and the feeling, particularly in the US, that the trade war with Japan was being lost. The America of the late 1970s saw the appearance of the bestselling essay *Japan As Number One*, which cites the prowess of the Japanese model of production. In the eyes of some, there were more efficient ways of producing and managing the economy. The neoliberal revolution was about to start.

This new globalization that began in the 1980s was led on a political level by the conservatives Ronald Reagan (1981–89) in the USA and Margaret Thatcher (1979–90) in Britain. Alongside economists such as Milton Friedman, Friedrich Hayek and the Chicago school of economics, their influence spread everywhere, across countries, academic disciplines and political leanings. And so was born a new way of looking at the economy, and a new way of understanding the role of the state and institutions. Also, a different way of understanding globalization and how to steer it.

This was the advent of hyper-globalization, when globalization becomes *an end* in itself and the range of domestic policies of individual countries give way to the boom in international trade and finance. It was not until the beginning of the 1990s that this set of recipes would have a single format liable to be extrapolated to any part of the globe. It was named the Washington Consensus (1990) and one of its main features was that it turned its back on the different routes towards progress taken until then by such widely varying countries as South Korea, China, Japan and Singapore. The protection of national economies was no longer possible as a recommendation; it was necessary to open up to international markets, particularly the capital market, *to a maximum degree*. The Washington Consensus demanded a favourable economic environment for setting up multinational companies, low corporate tax, a tight fiscal policy, regulatory "disarmament" and less power for the unions in the business sphere. The key word was homogenization of the world economy: a single recipe for a single growth model.

Under the aegis of this new hyper-globalization, in 1995 the GATT was replaced by its more belligerent and active version, the World Trade Organization (WTO), which was to go far beyond the GATT agreements in areas such as agriculture, intellectual property, patents and other services (tax systems, food safety standards, environmental regulations, industrial promotion policies, etc.). The WTO's role as arbitrator had now become mandatory and binding, over and above state regulations. The aim was formally well-meaning: to stop protectionism and to prevent national economic policies from being subverted by partisan interests, corruption and clientelism. The real added impact was to weaken democracy; citizens' ability to fix, through their parliaments, the economic rules by which they live. Hyper-globalized globalization imposed its law. Everywhere.

Increasingly, the real economic battles took place within the WTO, with sanctions, threats and counterattacks. In 1998 the EU was forced to accept hormone-treated meat, when judged to be attempting an internal market protection manoeuvre. Something similar happened in the US when they had to rule out establishing standards for CO_2 emission from fuel combustion. Brazil had to backpedal on credit subsidies for its aeronautical industry. India, Indonesia and China were forced to do the same with the promotion of their automobile sector. Obviously, as the saying goes, every (global) law has its (local) loophole, but the international framework for global trade was in place.

As time passed, the failure of the hyper-liberalizing operation in countries such as Argentina,[10] one of the main defenders and standard-bearers of the cause of the Washington Consensus, represented the failure of the hyper-globalization option. Nobel economics prize-winner and former WB chief economist Joseph Stiglitz criticized the neoliberal shift head-on. At least from an intellectual standpoint, hyper-globalization seemed to be crumbling. Furthermore, in the area of the major international organizations, the new waves of trade liberalization came up against growing obstacles. The Doha Round (2001) was proof of the stagnation of the liberalizing impetus:

10   Stiglitz J. (2002). *Globalization and Its Discontents*. W.W. Norton & Company.

for the first time the emerging countries blocked any new move towards the opening up of new markets unless the same was done in the area of agriculture. After that, talks were to remain practically at a stalemate.

3.3 Economic globalization at the beginning of the 21st century

How is globalization starting off this 21st century? In a word, disorientated. With no clear guiding star and an obvious crisis regarding which model to follow, which has only got worse up to the time of writing. In 2001 the Chinese giant stormed into the WTO and flooded global markets with its products. Production started to relocate away from Western countries. Value-added was concentrated and the intellectual, economic and political consensus surrounding the hyper-globalizing and—we can now use the term with full knowledge of what it entails—neoliberal wave of the 1980s was broken, but no clear alternatives could be identified. The crisis of 2001 and especially that of 2008 hammered home this disorientation.

The decadence and stagnation of the West deepened this trend. Over the years, the expansion of trade at any cost had rallied against itself a group of affected parties large enough to strip down the great liberalizing thesis and reduce it to the category of ideology—indeed, to the extent of bringing into doubt even the positive elements of the expansion of free trade. The current economic globalization will see more and more opponents in the West. Even in China and the rest of Asia, the economic growth that engenders hope is accompanied by an increasingly critical analysis of the consequences of this growth in terms of inequality, corruption, environmental problems and so on … The marginal gains of each new opening up of markets to global trade will get smaller and smaller. The number of countries opposed to such moves will get larger and larger—not just underdeveloped countries, as used to be the case until the 1980s. In the age of the WTO, international rules have become our rules. Economically speaking, at least.

In this stage of hyper-globalization debates such as those we identified in Chapter 1 appear or resurface. In *The Paradox of Globalization* Rodrik makes a considerable list of them. Is it really possible to establish a general equivalence between free trade and economic progress? Is it always so? For everyone? Might it not also mean a reduction in social rights, health, environmental conditions and trade union rights? Furthermore, isn't the argument that protectionism is backwardness tantamount to ignoring the economic history of many countries, including liberal Britain?

Can't the journey along the road to progress also start from the protection of more vulnerable industries and sectors in order to put them on a truly competitive level globally, as several Asian countries have shown us?[11] Isn't protectionism also a legitimate defence for those who are unskilled and uneducated and therefore have little labour mobility? Doesn't drawing a parallel between the development of free trade and technological progress (remember the question: who can stand in its way?) require turning a blind eye to the impact on wealth redistribution both globally and locally? If we address its more neglected side—for example when we see the association between the mass distribution of junk food, poverty and obesity—mightn't less trade actually be better than more trade?[12]

These debates serve to problematize economic development as we know it, and especially the idea of maximizing trade as the Holy Grail of world progress. Society and academics are gradually beginning to problematize the commitment to hyper-globalization. They are discussing the relationship (or lack of it) between inequality and the stability of institutions; the relationship between equality and democracy; and the relationship between democracy and power groups. Other debates of a methodological nature refer to the system of *beliefs* (a human construct like any other) built around the *myth* of GDP; or indeed the very *cult* of international trade.[13]

11   Schuman M. (2009). *The Miracle: The Epic Story of Asia's Quest for Wealth*. New York: HarperCollins Publishers.

12   According to ILO and UNICEF data, between 2% and 14% of the GDP of countries such as Indonesia, Malaysia, the Philippines and Thailand is generated by child sex tourism. The collateral cost of this "growth" (!?) is that 1.8 million children enter this "market" every year in order to contribute to the so-called economic "development" of the country. Is this really progress, even economic? What does this fact tell us about GDP as an indicator of development? For the context of the article in question, see: www.adnargentina.com/argentina/turismo/turismo_sexual_infantil_sureste_asiatico_tu_5092009.html.

13   After all, as an indicator, international trade often captures movements of goods and services within the same large business conglomerates. Such movements of goods and services are of very questionable value beyond the walls of these multinationals; especially when they can be replaced by local goods and services, which as such place a lighter burden on the environment and, above all, do not conceal a way of avoiding or shifting the tax burden from one country to the other in an attempt to pay as little tax as possible on profits. We will see this in the next chapter.

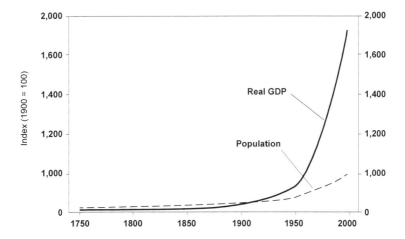

FIGURE 3.3 Comparative growth of global GDP and population, taking 1900
as base year

Source: IMF World Economic Outlook. October, 2000. Washington

As we can see in Figure 3.3, if we compare the trend in the growth of global
GDP with that of population[14] we find that up until the beginning of the 20th
century these two variables evolved in parallel. This side-by-side development was broken around 1900 and the gap got steadily wider. The Malthusian nightmare of an overpopulated Earth without resources seemed to be
averted, but another was created: that of the struggle to appropriate this
surplus and in particular that of the never-ending race between states to
gain competitiveness.[15]

In a highly influential essay,[16] Thomas Friedman anticipated the Flat
World idea on which this hyper-globalization rests. How did we get here?
Well:

> the Cold War world has been replaced by the globalisation world,
> understood as the integration of markets, finance and technology, in
> such a way as to make the world shrink from medium-sized to small
> and enable any of us to stretch out our arm to any point on the planet,
> further, faster and cheaper than ever before.

14   IMF (2000). *IMF World Economic Outlook. October 2000.* Washington.
15   Productivity is usually measured as a ratio between resources generated and
      inputs.
16   Friedman T. (1999). *The Lexus and the Olive Tree: Understanding Globalization.*
      Farrar, Straus and Giroux.

A number of elements have brought us to this present stage of economic globalization. First, the self-destruction of socialism and the planned economy as an alternative. Second, as we mentioned earlier, the acceleration of the rate of economic openness and exchanges of services, goods and investments led by capital markets. At the same level we find the computer and telecommunications revolution, which has made it possible to reduce costs and increase the crucial indicator: productivity. We are in the midst of the global informational capitalism expounded by sociologist Manuel Castells.

3.3.1 Global production chains and changes in the world production structure

It is interesting to see how this new hyper-globalized capitalism has impacted on production chains. If we take a look at the account given by Peter Dicken[17] of the globalization of the automobile industry in the 1980s, we will see where the parts for the European model of Ford Escort were made: the carburettor and oil tank in the UK; parts of the exhaust pipe and the bodywork in Sweden; the ignition key and gearbox in Germany; the brakes in France; the speedometer in Switzerland; the electrical system in Spain. The list is considerably longer, of course. What we want to draw attention to here is that the only non-European countries that supplied parts for this model were Canada (windows and the radio), the US (wheel studs, hydraulic pump and windows) and Japan (ignition key, windscreen wipers and fuel tank). Yet an examination of the concentration of the automobile sector today amounts to a leap not only in time but in space too. The dispersion and extension of the chain is extraordinary, spreading throughout the geography of the planet and going way beyond the framework of production of the once eminently European Ford Escort.

Sociologist Ulrich Beck[18] explains the impact of technological transformation in favour of productivity increases in German airports:

> after six p.m. Berlin time Tegel's announcement service is provided online from California. The reasons are as simple as they are understandable: in California, no extra payment has to be made for late working because it is still daytime; and indirect labour costs for the same activity are considerably lower than in Germany.

---

17   Dicken P. (1986). *Global Shift: Industrial Change in a Turbulent World*. London: Harper & Row, p. 304.

18   Beck U. (1999). *What Is Globalization?* Cambridge: Polity Press.

Another interesting example is that of Barbie dolls, made by the American firm Mattel, who in 2009 celebrated the 50th anniversary of their first appearance. Nowadays the raw materials for making the Barbie doll (plastic and hair) are obtained from Taiwan and Japan. The dolls are assembled in Indonesia, Malaysia and China. The moulds come from the US, as do the paints for decorating the dolls. China supplies the cotton cloth for the dresses. The dolls are exported from Hong Kong at a unit price of $2, of which 35¢ covers Chinese labour costs, 65¢ the cost of materials, and the rest transport costs, administration and profit.

The dolls are shipped to the US, where they are sold at $10, of which the designer (Mattel) gets $1 and the rest covers the cost of freight, marketing and distribution. Despite relocation and disintegration, most of the added value is created in the US. The dolls are sold all over the world at a rate of two dolls per second. Some curiosities worth mentioning: more than 500 million Barbies had been sold worldwide up to 2009. Over the last 40 years, 90% of American girls have owned at least one Barbie. An American girl aged 3–11 owns on average ten Barbies. The bestselling Barbie in history was Totally Hair, released in 1992, which sold 10 million dolls.[19]

Another more controversial and in many ways paradoxical production chain is that of the iPhone. Controversial because of the implications of the seasonal nature of iPhone sales—around Christmas—on working conditions in subcontracting companies. Paradoxical because of what it reveals about the implicit association made between innovation, consumer goods and contribution to a country's GDP. Using data for 2010,[20] the value of the parts and the labour that go into Apple's star product would be $178.96, which can be broken down as follows: Japan 34%, Germany 17%, South Korea 13%, China 3.6%, and other countries 27%. Most of the innovation is generated at the headquarters in Cupertino, California. In spite of all this, the iPhone enters the US economy as a Chinese product because that is where it is assembled. Quite apart from other side-effects for the US economy—in terms of its impact on local firms, tax revenue, or research and development—paradoxically this import is computed *against* America's GDP.

19   See   http://dolldiaries.com/50-fun-barbie-facts/;   www.buzzfeed.com/
     briangalindo/18-surprising-things-you-dont-know-about-barbie;   www.
     barbie.com/.
20   Batson A. (2010). "Not really 'Made in China': The iPhone's complex sup-
     ply chain highlights problems with trade statistics." *The Wall Street Journal.*
     December 15, 2010.

As the above examples show, we are in the midst of a veritable globalization of production and trade. An investment is made anywhere in the world to manufacture anywhere in the world in order to then sell anywhere in the world. The race run by states and companies in pursuit of the ethereal concepts of productivity and competitiveness is now a global race. Traditional economic activities such as investment, production, distribution and consumption have now transformed the planet into a single market.

For companies, these changes have in turn spelt changes in the ways they themselves are managed. If in the 1980s Japanese influence caused firms to concentrate on obtaining improvements in quality and production process re-engineering, in the 1990s we saw the rise of subcontracting processes, process outsourcing and companies focusing on their core activities. According to strategy gurus such as Michael Porter, the idea is to improve companies' positioning by reducing non-essential activities to a minimum.[21] Or as Mintzberg, another management guru, put it, the rise of "lean and mean" organizations.[22]

In the 2000s, large corporations aimed to take advantage of differences in operational costs by relocating the value chain (production centres, R&D centres, logistics centres and corporate headquarters). The distribution of internal costs and profits, and the emergence of taxes among subsidiaries came to be carefully calculated with the objective of *optimizing* their result—maximizing profit. Decisions about the location of company offices, subsidiaries and research departments were also reached through strategic planning. The first consequences of all this were that Europe was to lose industrial capability and possibilities of generating added value; developed states had less revenue-raising capacity in the face of rising tax avoidance. At the same time, we saw how companies exerted their power to condition legislation and pressurize political power. Increasingly, the economic power of big business was transformed into political power.

From a more basic perspective, the problem is the dematerialization of corporations. They used to be defined as four walls, a workforce and a team to manage the available resources, all pinpointed geographically. What is a

21   For example: should a university have its own cleaning, catering, reception and security staff, or can it outsource these services? Where should it place its management priorities? If we follow the organizational dynamic derived from this obsession with productivity, we will have to say solely on its core activity: teaching and research.

22   Mintzberg H., R. Simons & K. Basu (2002). "Beyond selfishness." *MIT Sloan Management Review* 44 (1), 66-74.

corporation today? Very often, just the idea of a product, a sometimes minimal material infrastructure for generating that product or service, and a sales system that may be entirely virtual. To this we should add an organization and a certain amount of funding. Ascribing nationality to these large transnational corporations is another added difficulty, as we will see presently. And this denationalization of corporations is accompanied by the denationalization of products: the "made in" label is increasingly meaningless. We saw this earlier in the case of the iPhone, although we could say the same about most of the clothes we wear: the whole manufacturing process is outsourced, usually to South-East Asia, but the logistics and design centres are in either Europe or North America.

With economic globalization, the economic system itself is also transformed. We shift from stable markets, a competitive environment usually restricted to the domestic scale, and hierarchical and bureaucratic forms of business organization, to increasingly changing and dynamic markets, companies that compete in local markets but also globally, and networked systems of organization, with a high degree of interrelation and dependence with subcontracting companies—the paradigmatic case here being the automobile sector.

We are beginning to leave behind the kind of industry that is focused on mass production, in which capital and labour are the essential production factors; in which mechanization is the key competitive factor; in which competitive advantages are achieved through cost reduction and economies of scale; and in which intra-company relations are primarily on an individual basis (separate, *vis-à-vis*). We are now advancing increasingly in the direction of flexible production models, with short and long cycles; in which knowledge—obtained through access to information—is the essential production factor; in which digitization is the key competitive factor. Innovation, quality and low cost are the sources of differentiation and competitive advantage. Relationships are complex, and are built in the framework of alliances and collaborative systems that go beyond the old one-way business relationships.

In the old economy, the goal of states in labour issues was to reach full employment, by promoting training in specific well-defined skills. Degrees and diplomas certified a person's educational level. People management was based on control and command. Jobs were stable. In the New Economy the most important factor is permanent adaptability to the job; the acquisition of a range of skills that enables the individual and the job to fit into a flexible environment. Education no longer has an end date (18 or 23 years of age) and instead has become continuing education. Personnel management gains complexity: the interplay of motivation, incentives, tensions and collaboration is also the reflection of adaptation to a flexible environment.

In this context, states can no longer be content to just regulate. The growth patterns and economic dynamics of the global economy overwhelm them on all sides. They are limited to encouraging growth. Increasingly, top-down regulation is giving way to a patchwork of interactions in which lobbies, corporations (either on their own or in association) and international regulatory initiatives gain more and more importance.

In order to find their place in the new global economy of the 21st century, countries aspire to be capable of attracting the symbolic analysts that Reich wrote about in his 1991 book *The Work of Nations*. Developed countries are seeking to generate their own Silicon Valleys and their own Seattles. Richard Florida[23] defined this new class on which innovation and growth rest as the creative class; and he made some specific recommendations for governments. The crux for attracting human capital—these highly innovative and creative individuals, generators of ideas and new technologies, according to Florida the sorts of worker all companies and all countries should want to have—is to think what they are like and what they want.

The characteristics of this group of individuals are as follows: they are well educated, with strong personal skills and a set of values that can be understood as *progressive*: individualism (freedom of action), meritocracy (anti-authoritarianism and defence of the government of the best), diversity and tolerance. The author's central thesis is that it is essential to foster contexts that are creative and multicultural (even bohemian), *progressive* contexts in which these highly skilled workers feel comfortable. He argues that we have already gone from an industrial society to one of services, and that now we need to move on to the creative society. According to Florida, not only are these individuals the driving force behind worldwide progress, innovation and creativity; they also attract the highest income and set trends and patterns of consumption.[24]

Pressure on states will therefore be channelled towards attracting human capital but also and especially investment, capital inflows. Here we will have to watch out for the wish-list of big business. Along macroeconomic lines, if the recipes of the Washington Consensus enabled us to see one part of

---

23   Florida R. (2002). *The Rise of the Creative Class: And How It's Transforming Work, Leisure, Community and Everyday Life*. New York: Perseus Book Group.

24   See www.creativeclass.com/.

recommended public policies, a report by IE and Kreab Gavin Anderson[25] gives us insight into the specific demands large corporations make of states, and how the latter try to accommodate them.

Corporations will invest depending on a country's strengths: a large domestic market, access to necessary raw materials, an interesting location that is well connected and close to major national and global trade routes. The fact that the country has signed free trade agreements with other countries will also be a plus, as will competitive production factors and access to a skilled workforce. On the side of risks and threats to avoid, we find political and economic instability, legal uncertainty (non-compliance with the agreements signed), high citizen insecurity, an unpredictable exchange rate, and lack of infrastructure and logistics to produce, import or export goods. In order to play a leading role in the economic scenario of globalization, it will be necessary to meet the demands of businesses and adjust the country's attributes—make it attractive—to the needs of global production chains. We are shifting, then, from a state that regulates the economy to a state that is increasingly subject to the dictates of the global economy.

3.4 Economic globalization: strategies and reactions

3.4.1 The rise of geo-economics: geo-economic strategies

Submitted to pressure from markets and businesses, the difficulty for states will be to calibrate the right weapons to use in order to compete in the international sphere. However, before we descend to this level of economic diplomacy we should collate the main agents of economic globalization in this second decade of the 21st century. To begin with, there are the IMF, WB and WTO, which we have already discussed. But alongside these we find a new intellectual driver of this hyper-globalization, the World Economic Forum (WEF). This meeting of business leaders, heads of state, heads of government, academics and intellectuals has been held every January since the 1970s in the Swiss town of Davos. From there they sound out globalization, diagnose its problems and discuss solutions … of a neoliberal nature.

Other leading players on the economic stage include the large corporations themselves, which in the post-Keynesian age that opened up in the

---

25   IE Business School & Kreab Gavin Anderson (2011). IV Informe. Panorama de Inversión Española en Latinoamérica.

1970s have taken on the role of key actors, and two important groups of countries, one in decline and the other on the rise: the G8 and the G20. The former comprises Canada, France, Germany, Japan, Italy, the USA, the UK and Russia, and is the image of the countries considered to be most developed from the 1970s to the 1990s. It meets annually, is equipped with a permanent working structure and prepares reports on key issues of world economic policy to be discussed by the respective heads of government.

Inevitably, with the changing economic weight of the great powers, especially since the 2008 crisis, a new platform for dialogue gathered momentum, consisting of the G8 countries plus Argentina, Australia, Brazil, China, India, Indonesia, South Korea, Mexico, Saudi Arabia, South Africa and Turkey. Together with these countries, the European Union President, the European Central Bank, the IMF and the WB all occupy a permanent seat in this forum. The aim of this new bloc is to gain representativeness over the old G8. The costs of this enlargement are also evident: fragmentation of interests and perspectives, lack of stable administrative structures and, in short, the irrelevance of its conclusions. All in all, an interesting touchstone highlighting the difficulties involved in any progress towards an increase in world governance. We will come back to this later.

In the meantime we would do well to recover the role that globalization reserves for states in the economy. Historian and essayist Edward Luttwak in his book *Turbo-Capitalism*[26] describes the changes brought about in the economic sphere in the wake of the disappearance of the USSR, and explains the reasons for these changes:

> As soon as the Cold War ended, economic rivalries visibly intensified. No longer forced into a compulsory solidarity by a common fear of the Soviet Union, Americans, Europeans and Japanese started a whole series of new quarrels over trading rules and industrial leadership in sectors that were revealingly labelled "strategic" from aerospace to TV serials. […] The era of geo-economics was upon us. […] In a global environment, the economic interests of nations (based on policies for controlling those sectors of activity considered to be strategic) override their geopolitical interests (based on the control of territories). This shift marks the era of *geo-economics* [emphasis mine].[27]

According to Luttwak we are leaving behind the great era of empires and territorial control and entering a new historical moment in which economic

26   Luttwak E. (1999). *Turbo-Capitalism: Winners and Losers in the Global Economy*. New York: Harper Collins.
27   Luttwak E. (1999). op. cit. Chapter 7. p.127.

and political roles merge in the framework of international economic competition.

> In traditional world politics, the goals are to secure and extend the physical control of territory, and to gain diplomatic influence over foreign governments. The corresponding geo-economic goal is [...] the conquest or protection of *desirable* roles in the world economy. Who will develop the next generation of jet airliners, computers, bio-technology products, advanced materials, financial services [...]? Will the designers, technologists, managers and financiers be Americans, Europeans or East Asians? The winners will have those highly reward-ing and controlling roles, while the losers will have only assembly lines—if their home markets are large enough [my italics].[28]

The geo-economic strategies of states will consist of helping large corpo-rations—so-called **national champions**—to conquer segments of the world market relating to the production or marketing of a product; to strengthen their economic potential and acquire technological and commercial supremacy. The role of states will therefore be to engage in active or even aggressive economic diplomacy at the service of the interests of corpora-tions that are considered to be key. The objective: to go out and conquer those economic sectors that are regarded as having strategic importance and high added value. Nonetheless, this is no different from what govern-ments of countries such as Japan, Taiwan, South Korea, China and Singa-pore have been doing for some decades with a variety of public tools.[29]

Turning our attention to corporations, Luttwak notes that they will become increasingly inclined to invest in high-risk R&D; they will make major investments in order to enter the various national markets, even using aggressive pricing strategies such as dumping.[30] They will also overin-vest in productive capacity to force the state to take protective action to the benefit of the company and in defence of the jobs it has created (although often neither the domestic nor the international market can absorb the stock generated).

---

28   Luttwak E. (1999). op. cit. Chapter 7. p.133.
29   Schuman M. (2009). op. cit.
30   Selling below cost price, and therefore at a loss. As a commercial practice it is banned because it centres the competitive arena not on the intrinsic qualities of the product but rather on the financial muscle of the company involved; the company that is capable of sustaining these losses for a longer period of time than its competitors do. Under normal conditions this practice leads to the elimination of competition and the establishment of a monopolistic market.

For their part, states will seek to establish tariffs and quotas, and to install regulatory barriers disguised as administrative regulations or quality standards (e.g., packaging format, minimum quality requirements for public health, conditions for recycling a good, etc.). They will go out of their way to provide financial support for exports and to help technology programmes—primary research on which to build the applied research that interests business—aligned with the interests of the national production structure. They will strive to generate techno-economic intelligence, ranging from the gathering and generation of information of business interest to out-and-out industrial espionage. Sectors such as computers, biotechnology, aircraft, cars and telecommunications will thus come to be seen as strategic sectors and to enjoy public support for private interests.

A glance at the newspaper archives of recent years reveals just how relevant Luttwak's theses still are today. Business trips by heads of government are commonplace: Western leaders travel to Japan to ensure the maintenance of jobs in European manufacturing plants; Asian leaders travel to Latin America to clinch deals for the supply of raw materials. In 2010 Wiki-Leaks made public the "implacable" pressure exerted by the US embassy in Panama to guarantee that the enlargement work on the canal that connects the two oceans would be awarded to the American firm Bechtel and not the Spanish one Sacyr.[31] Then again, Chinese President Hu Jintao's official visit to the US at the beginning of 2011 concluded with the signing of an agreement to export products to China to the value of $45,000 million. The package included a commitment to purchase 200 Boeing aircraft valued at $19,000 million.[32] Economic relations are becoming one of the linchpins of a country's diplomacy.[33]

As we mentioned earlier, identifying the nationality of these large corporations will be increasingly problematic. What is the determining factor

---

31 See Jiménez M. (2010): "US tried to block bid for Panama job." *El País*. 19 December 2010. http://elpais.com/elpais/2010/12/19/inenglish/1292739643_850210. html. Also: http://wikileaks.org/cable/2009/07/09PANAMA550.html.

32 BBC News (2011): "China to buy 200 Boeing aircraft." 19 January 2011. www. bbc.co.uk/news/business-12229585.

33 In this context, it hardly comes as a surprise that none other than the US ambassador in Madrid described himself as "head salesman" of American companies in Spain. He made this statement at the event organized by CIDOB and ESADE-geo in February 2013: *War & Peace in the 21st Century. The foreign policy of the United States: Transatlantic Perspectives*: www.cidob.org/en/news/security_ and_world_politics/is_the_us_still_interested_in_europe_an_assessment_of_ the_transatlantic_relations_and_obama_s_foreign_policy_agenda.

in attributing nationality to a corporation? The location of its headquarters? That of its production plants? Where it pays taxes? Amazon Spain and Google Spain, for example, pay their taxes in Ireland. What stance should Spanish diplomacy take on these two companies? If, in spite of their name, we agree that these are not Spanish companies, to what extent are other large enterprises, such as Banco Santander?

According to Santander's corporate website,[34] at the end of 2012 the bank had 186,763 employees, only 31,428 (16%) of which worked in Spain. Spain accounted for a mere 15% of its consolidated profit, as opposed to Brazil's 26%, for example. Spain provided 28% of the group's assets. Exactly the same figure as Britain. So, is Santander a Spanish company? On what basis would we define it as such? In any event, one thing is for sure: if in the past what was good for Santander was good for Spain, this maxim no longer necessarily holds. The bank's interests and business focus have clearly outgrown its original framework of action, namely Spanish territory. The nationality of a large corporation such as Santander gives us very little information about the allegiances and objectives of that company.

Deutsche Bank, once a veritable de facto power of German commercial banking, paints an even more complicated picture. Its present CEO is the British citizen of Indian origin Anshu Jain—who took over from the Swiss Josef Ackermann in 2012—together with co-chairman Jürgen Fitschen, who is about to retire. When Jain took the job, his knowledge of German was pretty scanty. Deutsche Bank is now one of the planet's main investment banks, operating in 74 countries, although first and foremost in the City of London. It has employees of 120 different nationalities.[35] The days when a former CEO of Deutsche Bank could stand in for the economy minister in a cabinet meeting seem to be over for good. Justifying the adjective "Deutsche" (German) in this bank's name is an increasingly tricky exercise.

At the beginning of the 21st century the planet is knitted together in networks where states have a considerably lower profile than they had in the past. APEC, EU, ASEAN and Mercosur are just some of the regional economic groupings that seek to encourage production and domestic consumption by granting preferential trade conditions to its member states. Unequal in scope

34   Santander. Investor information. www.santander.com/csgs/Satellite?pagename=CFWCSancomQP01%2FPage%2FCFQP01_PageResultados_PT23&cidSel=1278684289572&appID=santander.wc.CFWCSancomQP01&canal=CSCORP&empr=CFWCSancomQP01&leng=en_GB&cid=1278677300268.

35   http://topics.nytimes.com/top/news/business/companies/deutsche_bank_ag/index.html.

and size, today they constitute a powerful tool to drive and channel the interests of the great economic champions of states in the global geography. In February 2013, President Barack Obama announced the beginning of talks with a view to creating a free trade area between the USA and the EU. If this plan succeeds, it will be the biggest free trade zone ever.[36] And there is nothing to suggest that this road to economic and trade union has come to an end. Quite the opposite. Similar initiatives are extending all over the planet.

3.4.2 Reactions against neoliberal globalization

How have the planet's different societies experienced this hyper-globalization? At least with regard to some of its variables, such as the increase in inequality, with concern.[37] We have to look back at what happened in the early 1990s to understand the beginning of this erosion of globalization's public image. The Washington Consensus[38] was a package of macroeconomic proposals drawn up in the early 1990s in order to inform the general public about *ideal* policies for fostering development. The *single* recipe we were talking about earlier. It comprised a series of measures initially intended for Latin American countries but subsequently converted into a general programme of political and institutional reform. A programme that was to benefit from the ideological buzz resulting from the fall of the Berlin Wall and the discussion surrounding the "End of History" and the existence of a single victorious economic model: capitalism. The ten main points of the Consensus were as follows:

- **Fiscal discipline**: large sustained fiscal deficits contribute to inflation and capital flight. A trend towards balanced budgets should be pursued.

- **Public spending** priorities should change. Subsidies should be reduced or removed. Public spending should be redirected towards education, health and the development of infrastructure.

36   Kanter J. & Ewing Jack (2013). A Running Start for a U.S.-Europe Trade Pact. *New York Times*. 13 February 2013: www.nytimes.com/2013/02/14/business/global/obama-pledges-trade-pact-talks-with-eu.html?_r=0.

37   Simmons K. (2013). "World worried about inequality." *Special to CNN*. 28 May 2013. http://globalpublicsquare.blogs.cnn.com/2013/05/28/world-worried-about-inequality/.

38   Williamson J. (1990). "What Washington means by policy reform." *Latin American Adjustment: How Much Has Happened?* Washington: Peterson Institute for International Economics, 1990.

- **Tax reform**: the tax base should be broad and marginal tax rates should be moderate.

- **Interest rates**: national financial markets should determine the interest rates of each country. Real interest rates should be positive in order to discourage capital flight and encourage saving.

- **Exchange rates**: developing countries should adopt a "competitive" rate to boost exports.

- **Trade liberalization**: tariffs and duties should be reduced to a minimum and should never be applied to intermediate goods necessary to produce exports.

- **Foreign direct investment**: foreign investment can provide capital and skills, and therefore should be encouraged.

- **Privatization**: private enterprise operates more efficiently than public enterprise. State-owned companies should be privatized.

- **Deregulation**: excessive government regulation can lead to corruption and work to the detriment of small and medium-sized enterprises. Governments should liberalize the economy.

- **Property rights**: property rights should be respected. Weak laws and justice systems without resources reduce incentives to save and accumulate wealth.

To what extent has recent history corroborated the suitability of these proposals? Former WB chief economist Joseph Stiglitz has been one of their fiercest critics. Significantly, Williamson himself tried more than once to correct the above decalogue to adapt it to the failed experiences of the 1990s: the crises in Mexico, South-East Asia, Russia. And later on, the dot.com technology bubble. Moisés Naím[39] underlined the disagreement that existed even among economists when it came to defining and supporting the ten points, and the intellectual naivety of assuming that a model for economic reform is the path towards development, when in fact it could only be a necessary condition for this development. Thus, problems appear in relation to: its applicability; the unforgivable omission of the role of institutions in making growth possible; and the underestimation of the destabilizing effects of globalized markets, particularly the financial market. Honest governments,

---

39   Naím M. (2000). "Fads and fashion in economic reforms: Washington Consensus or Washington Confusion?" *Third World Quarterly*. June 2000; 21, 3; 505-28.

an impartial legal system, professional and well-paid civil servants and transparent regulatory systems are also conditions for growth. But in spite of everything, to a large extent still today the world seems to turn at the rate dictated by this ill-named Consensus.

This said, it was the Argentine case that gave most ammunition to the critics of the globalization preached by the Washington Consensus. Argentina, one of the showcase countries in the application of the IMF and World Bank criteria set out in the Washington Consensus, was one of the hardest hit by the crisis at the beginning of this century. A dismantled economy, rampant capital flight, the *corralito* or bank freeze and political instability were the outcome. Its role as the exponent of the virtues of the theses of neoliberalism was taken up by Ireland, at that time called the Celtic Tiger, which likewise achieved dazzling socioeconomic indicators until it blew up during the 2008 crisis, leaving behind one of the most damaged and indebted economies. This result was only logical after more than a decade of aggressive property and financial speculation that paradoxically went undetected by the blinkered gaze of the Washington Consensus indicators. Incidentally, the cost of the public bailout of the Irish banks was equivalent to 40% of its GDP, the biggest bailout in history[40] for another star pupil of deregulated markets. Quite a record.

It is hardly surprising, then, that in recent years voices have been raised in growing criticism of the orthodox globalization presented under the auspices of the international organizations. The demonstration in Seattle in 1999 against the WTO paved the way for the legitimation of the World Social Forum, envisioned since its beginnings in 2001 as a counterforce to the World Economic Forum (WEF). The WSF, held on approximately the same dates as the WEF, is intended as an open and democratic arena bringing together the wide spectrum of alter-globalization movements. In short, the antithesis of the WEF, protected by sophisticated accreditation systems and police surveillance. The first WSF was held in Porto Alegre (Brazil) and was jointly organized by the French Association for the Taxation of Financial Transactions and Aid to Citizens (ATTAC) and the Brazilian Workers' Party.

The proposals discussed at the Second WSF, in January 2002,[41] were as follows:

---

40   Robinson A. (2013). *Un reportero en la montaña mágica. Cómo la élite económica de Davos hundió el mundo.* Barcelona: Ariel, p. 108.

41   Tintoré E. (2002). "Foro Social Mundial. Las propuestas alternativas." *La Vanguardia.* 31 January 2002.

- To impose a tax on flows of speculative capital of between 0.001% and 0.025%.

- To impose a tax on foreign investment, to be collected by the ILO, in compensation for the fiscal dumping practised by countries interested in attracting this investment.

- To levy a tax on the profits of multinationals.

- To abolish tax havens.

- To cancel the foreign debt of the poorest countries.

- To promote worldwide land reform guaranteeing countries' food sovereignty. To exclude agricultural liberalization from WTO agreements and prohibit export subsidies for food products.[42]

- To work for a new system of world governance in which organizations of an economic nature (WB, IMF and WTO) do not overrule those of a social or public health nature (WHO, ILO).

- To foster citizen involvement in social and political debate.

It is interesting to note that some of the proposals set out in that second edition of the Forum are still being discussed today and in some cases have come to occupy a prominent place in the political agendas of governments, the EU, and in particular recent G20 meetings. The crux, then, is not so much in the goodness of many of its proposals or in the consensus surrounding them, but rather in how to implement them and the capacity to confront the real power wielded by the major economic players.

3.4.3 The relationship between globalization and inequality

The relationship between inequality and economic globalization has long been under the scrutiny of economists and social scientists. However, it has been analysed in a great variety of ways, and it is only in recent years that this wide spectrum of readings has come to converge into something resembling critical consensus, as we mentioned at the beginning of the previous section. One of the defenders of the idea that the development associated with globalization brings equality was the editor of the *Financial Times*, Martin Wolf. In 2004 Wolf addressed the impact of globalization

---

42   For example, such measures have caused small farmers in Haiti to be ruined by massive imports of subsidized rice from the US.

on equality.[43] In his opinion, world inequality had been reduced thanks to globalization.

Wolf highlighted three conclusions reached by the World Bank on the relationship between inequality and globalization. First, the number of people living in extreme poverty (according to the WB definition) had dropped from 1,800 million in 1987 to 1,170 million in 1999. Second, most of those who lived in situations of extreme poverty did so in East Asia, a region still at an incipient stage of economic development. Wolf admitted that the exception to this trend was Eastern Europe, Central Asia and sub-Saharan Africa, where the number of poor increased from 217 million in 1987 to 315 million in 1999.

For Wolf, however, life expectancy had continued to rise since 1970. Child mortality rates had diminished. Education (measured in terms of the literacy rate) had improved; fertility rates had also fallen; as had the number of people with chronic malnutrition (as defined by the United Nations). Lastly, the percentage of children aged 10–14 who worked had also dropped by the end of the 20th century. In short, all these indicators would appear to show that globalization has a positive socioeconomic impact on society.

In contrast with this initial positive reading of globalization, in recent years, as we were saying, a considerable number of research papers and studies have appeared that point to a less optimistic conclusion. The OECD report *Growing Unequal?*,[44] prepared with data prior to the 2008 crisis for the OECD member countries, dealt with the factors that have brought about changes in income inequality and poverty. First of all, the wage gap between the highest and lowest earners was getting wider and wider. Furthermore, capital income and income from self-employment were found to be very unevenly distributed. Although work is indeed an effective instrument in the fight against poverty, in itself it is not enough to ward off poverty, as more than half of the poor belong to households with some earnings. The new working poor work at the multinational Walmart, on German production chains or in the fast food chains of southern Europe. Access to work no longer guarantees a decent standard of living, yet it does guarantee a more unequal society.

Among the lessons to be learned, according to the report, we find the following: public services offset income inequality. Consumption taxes widen

43 Wolf M. (2004). *Why Globalisation Works*. Chapter 9 (Incensed about Inequality). Yale University Press.
44 OECD (2008). *Growing Unequal? Income Distribution in OECD Countries*. Paris: OECD Publishing. Available at www.oecd.org/els/soc/41527936.pdf.

inequality. Entry into poverty mainly reflects family- and/or work-related events (such as losing one's job), and social mobility is usually higher in countries with less income inequality and vice versa. Precisely the sorts of event (erosion of the welfare state, increase in consumption taxes, mass unemployment, etc.) that have hit many of the countries this report focused on. In short, the gap between the richest and poorest levels of our societies is getting wider: the rich concentrate an increasingly large part of new income, and they do so at the expense of the lowest levels of society.

Another OECD report, published in 2011,[45] shows how inequality, measured from the 1980s to 2008 using the Gini index, grew in 17 of the 27 countries that make up the OECD, including two of the three countries that were already most unequal: Mexico and the US. It remained steady in three countries (France, Hungary and Belgium) and diminished slightly in Turkey and Greece prior to the intervention by the Troika (IMF, ECB and EC) of 2010. As well as problematizing what we actually mean by inequality and how to measure it—more difficult to pin down than would appear at first sight— the report provides some significant data.

For all the OECD countries analysed, between 1990 and 2007, the richest 1% of the population either maintained or increased their slice of the total cake of disposable income. The case of the US is notable: the most privileged 1% went from having 13% to having 18% of all income. The UK followed at some distance, with 14%. From 1980 to 2011, in the US the weight of wages as a percentage of GDP dropped from 69% to 61%. In the UK, from 65% to 53%. The salaries of CEOs of American corporations are four or five times higher than their Asian counterparts, despite the fact that American companies are usually less competitive and profitable than their Asian competitors.[46] The tax rate applied to America's highest-earning elite, the richest 0.1%, went from 60% in the 1960s to under 30% in 2000. Many cleaners who work in the mansions of Connecticut hedge fund managers, Robinson tell us, pay more tax than those who contract them.[47]

Even the Global Risk Reports issued by the WEF[48] constantly warn of the problems brought by this increase in inequality. These include the end of

45   OECD (2011). *Divided We Stand: Why Inequality Keeps Rising*. Paris: OECD Publishing. Available at www.oecd.org/els/soc/dividedwestandwhyinequalitykeepsrising.htm.

46   Robinson A. op. cit. p. 87.

47   Robinson A. op. cit. p. 93.

48   WEF (2013). Global Risk Report: www3.weforum.org/docs/WEF_GlobalRisks_Report_2013.pdf.

mass consumption targeting the increasingly impoverished and indebted middle and lower classes. As we have already seen, capitalism needs consumerism, but for a growing sector of the population—at least in the so-called developed countries—inequality is making this consumption an increasingly difficult mission.

In her article "The rise of a new global elite", published just days before the 2011 summit in the prestigious magazine *The Atlantic*, Chrystia Freeland,[49] a regular at the WEF meetings in Davos, tried to justify the rise of the new class of multimillionaire income-hogging executives by making a particular use of the notion of meritocracy. According to Freeland, this new elite is made up of highly educated individuals who work long hours, veritable workaholics. These **working rich**, she holds, have benefited from the information technology revolution and the liberalization of world trade but, unlike the old inherited fortunes, they owe their weath to hard work. As Andy Robinson[50] points out in his essay on the Davos summits, *Un reportero en la montaña mágica* (*A Reporter on the Magic Mountain*), two unknowns prey on the mind of the sceptical reader of Freeland's theses: do the working poor work less hard than the working rich—with the added grievance of having to do so for a wage that does not even get them to the end of the month? Second, if we compare the above-mentioned increase in the salary of this wealthiest 1% with the increase in their dedication to their job, did American multimillionaires work 40% more in 2007 than in 1990? The comparison hardly seems possible, or very justifiable. It is not meritocracy that has put this elite in the position it now holds; it's something else.

None other than Dominique Strauss-Kahn, managing director of the IMF, admitted in 2011, shortly before falling into disgrace, that the reports that were circulating on the worldwide economic recovery could be deceiving. Indicators showing a constant rise—in income, trade, stock markets or employment—are based on averages, and conceal the growing division between rich and poor, said Strauss-Kahn. Both between and within states. A recovery built on "unstable foundations" could "sow the seeds of the next crisis. [...] tensions [...] may ultimately set off civil wars in deeply unequal countries."[51] In its report entitled *Inequality, Leverage and Crises*, the IMF

49   Freeland C. (2011). "The rise of the new global elite." *The Atlantic*. January/February 2011, www.theatlantic.com/magazine/archive/2011/01/the-rise-of-the-new-global-elite/308343/.

50   Robinson A. op. cit.

51   Evans-Pritchard A. (2011). IMF raises spectre of civil wars as global inequalities worsen. *The Telegraph*. 1 February 2011. www.telegraph.co.uk/finance/

noted that the extreme difference between the rich and the poor was one of the underlying causes of the Great Recession of 2008–2009.[52] As we can see, the growing accumulation of data casts doubt on an over-optimistic reading of the redistributive impact of economic globalization.

In a speech in Singapore, Strauss-Kahn set out the economic consequences of inequality:

> Inequality can dampen economic opportunity, since the poor have less access to credit. It can divert people toward unproductive activities. It can also make countries more prone to shocks—where fewer people have savings for a rainy day, more will suffer when the storm hits. Inequality can even make it harder to recover from shocks: more equal societies tend to grow for longer.[53]

Inevitably, though, if we are to understand what lies behind this increase in inequalities we will have to turn away from the so-called productive economy and delve into one of the key phenomena for comprehending this polarization of income: the financialization of the economy. And this analysis demands a whole chapter.

globalbusiness/8296987/IMF-raises-spectre-of-civil-wars-as-global-inequalities-worsen.html.

52   Kumhof M. & R. Rancière (2010). *Inequality, Leverage and Crises*. International Monetary Fund. WP/10/268. IMF Working Paper. Research Department.

53   IMF (2011). *The Right Kind of Global Recovery*. Speech given by Dominique Strauss-Kahn, IMF MD, 1 February 2011. www.imf.org/external/np/speeches/2011/020111.htm.

4
Financial globalization

If globalization has become a synonym for capitalism to the extent that globalization is converted into a province of the world economy, in recent decades the economy itself must be seen as a province of capital flows and the global financial system. The key concept that accounts for this alteration is that of financialization: the profound transformation of economic structures through the progressive deployment of an increasingly autonomous, globalized and deregulated financial system. We must therefore conduct an in-depth examination of this concept of financialization and its scope. We will also need to understand the economic changes associated with financialization and its impact on social and political structures, and we must do so without losing sight of the current crisis and its relationship with the expansion of the global financial system.

4.1 Macroeconomic imbalances and financial imbalances

Economics provides a quite descriptive account of the relationship between the theoretical construct we call the current account deficit and the behaviour of states. Stated simply, the current account balance is just one of the three balances that make up the balance of payments,[1] albeit the main one,

---

[1] A definition of balance of payments: "The total of all the money coming into a country from abroad less all of the money going out of the country during the same period." See *The Economist* dictionary of economics: www.economist.com/economics-a-to-z.

alongside the capital account and financial account balances. It represents the sum of the exchange of goods and merchandise, services and current transfers that a given country makes with the rest of the world. When a country has a current account deficit, it needs money from abroad to offset the difference with the savings generated. This is what happened over the period 1999–2007 in many of the countries that are still now struggling to overcome the crisis.[2] For years and years, countries such as the US, Spain, the UK and Italy gave up saving and embarked on the mass consumerism intrinsic to globalization, financing themselves with cheap and seemingly infinite loaned money coming from abroad. This situation led to a money shortage which in turn resulted in a rise in the interest rate (the main indicator of money shortage or surplus in a closed economy).

Macroeconomically speaking, then, we can describe what happened as an increase in inequalities in the balance of payments of the world's countries. There was a group of principal capital-exporting countries (China, German, Japan, Saudi Arabia, Kuwait, Switzerland and Russia), from which funds were directed towards countries in need of capital. For the first time, countries considered to be poor such as China, with a GDP ten times smaller than that of the US, were financing the rich countries. There are several explanations for this phenomenon. First of all we should highlight the authoritarian system of government of many of these countries, which prevents the channelling of proposals in such a way as to enable these resources to be invested domestically. Then we find the existence of more profitable investment opportunities outside these countries than inside them, a fact that we can attribute to financialization and the way trade or energy resource surpluses are used. Lastly, there is the existence of new mechanisms of foreign investment: the sovereign wealth funds that we will analyse presently.

However, if neoclassical orthodoxy has seen the liberalization of capital as an efficient way of putting funds where they are profitable and necessary, in short, as an opportunity for a country's development, recent history shows us that financial liberalization has also given rise to the formation of huge bubbles of abundant credit, followed by periods of abrupt contraction.

Economist Irving Fisher[3] talked of the debt disease to expound this tendency towards the generation of economic peaks and troughs with serious consequences. With loaned money, he held, we are more reckless than we

2   Tugores J. (2010). *El lado oscuro de la economía.* Ed. Gestión 2000. Chapter 5: "Finanzas y crisis".
3   Tugores J. (2010). Op. cit.

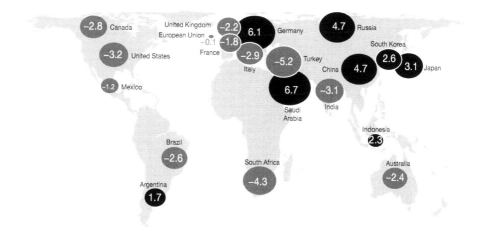

FIGURE 4.1 Balance of payments of the G20 countries, October 2010

Source: IMF, 2010; World Bank, 2010

are with money we have earned. Investors' behaviour is therefore based
more on patterns of behaviour and attitudes to risk than on any rationality
of the agents, as orthodox economics would have it. Liquidity bubbles originate from the investor's gradual progression towards increasingly aggressive speculative practices. When considering a potential investment, the
investor starts by studying the possibilities facing him or her on the basis
of the analysis of future returns, applying rationality and studying the time
required for the investment to reach maturity; in other words, by observing
the mid- and long term. When the flow of liquidity continues, this makes
prices rise. Investment decision-making processes change and begin to
be built on the premise of selling soon and making a quick profit. Unwise
deals (involving real estate, production capacity and the like) resting on
irrationally optimistic perspectives become more and more fashionable.
Ultimately, situations of outright fraud are reached, feeding off the transformation of the general public into a public that is gullible and accustomed to
a bullish economic cycle.

Studying the inherent instability of the financial system didn't save Fisher
from being personally ruined in the 1929 crash. We find an identical reflection in the English financier Sir Thomas Gresham. According to what we call
Gresham's Law,[4] bad and harmful (rash or aggressive) behaviour replaces

---

4   Historically this attribution to Gresham has been questioned, but the law as
     such continues to bear his name.

good (careful, sensible) behaviour: "Bad money drives out good." If we introduce counterfeit money and valid currency into a community at the same time, which will circulate and which will be hoarded? Obviously, says Gresham, we will try to get rid of the bad money and keep the good money. The same thing happens with the investor's mood. Bad practice, moral hazard, pushes out good, sensible investment behaviour.[5] In the case that concerns us here, we will invest thinking about the future price increase, rather than about the real capacity of that investment to generate value. Here the confusion of value with price, habitual in all speculative processes, is clearly exposed.

Heterodox economist Hyman Minsky theorized about the inherent instability of the capitalist system by attacking one of the basic premises of the Chicago school, the stability of financial markets. Minsky postulated the hypothesis of the "financial *instability*" of the system. Again, this explanation is based on irrational moods and behaviour. According to Minsky, financial optimism causes the investor to forget the possibility of failure and the upsetting of the economic cycle. In fact, all financial economies have three types of investor agents. First there are the careful, stalwart investors who are the central players in stable periods and avoid speculative peaks. Alongside them we find speculative borrowers, whose investments only enable them to cover the interests on the debt owed, but not to return the principal. Lastly, Ponzi borrowers form pyramidal structures of pure speculators in which the investment has no interest in itself, as its return makes it impossible to repay not only the borrowed capital but also the interests on the loan. The continued existence of this third group of investors, more properly called fraudsters, is explained by the fact that it allows the entry of new investors or lenders to ensure the withdrawal of assets[6] or the payment of interests to those involved.[7]

---

5   The idea of the socialization of bad practice can extend well beyond this: if a professor repeatedly turns up late for lectures, hitherto punctual students will stop coming on time. The bad practice of lack of punctuality will spread and we will have driven out good behaviour and rewarded bad behaviour.

6   According to *The Economist* dictionary of economics: Things that have earning power or some other value to their owner. www.economist.com/economics-a-to-z/a.

7   The best-known case of pyramidal fraud in recent years is that of Bernard Madoff, with losses amounting to $10–17 billion. See Shamir S. (2009). "Extent of Madoff fraud now estimated at far below $50b." *Haaretz*. Associated Press. 6 March 2009. www.haaretz.com/news/extent-of-madoff-fraud-now-estimated-at-far-below-50b-1.271672.

When one of these speculative pyramids fails, it generates an instance of panic, a "Minsky moment", which marks the beginning of a spiral of mistrust that takes the form of the massive sale of assets, falling prices and the extension of the crisis of the financial economy to the real economy and rational investors. Minsky's message is not encouraging: the capitalist system leads us inevitably to cycles of permanent instability. The role of central banks, as Keynes had urged long before, should be to provide the necessary liquidity, i.e., to act as lenders of last resort to prevent businesses in the real economy from succumbing to the speculative cycle.[8] Minsky, who died in 1996, fully anticipated the reaction of the US Federal Reserve and the US Secretary of the Treasury, Hank Paulson, when the crisis broke in September 2008.[9] The conclusions of Minsky's thesis on the instability of the financial system are still far from having been fully assimilated and corrected. Again, here we are interested in highlighting the fact that agents' behaviour is irrational and that economic globalization is conditioned by these waves of instability coming from the financial system.

4.2 Lessons from the recent financial crises

So it comes as no surprise that, as Rodrik states in *The Globalization Paradox*, the process of liberalization of capital markets has been greeted with little enthusiasm. Never since 1929 have crises been either so unremitting or so devastating as they have since the advent of the hyper-globalization process initiated in the 1980s. The first major global crash since the Second World War occurred in 1987 following the collapse of the New York Stock Exchange, in October of the same year, while the Japanese property and banking crisis broke out in 1990, and is still dragging on today. In 1992 there was the economic and monetary union crisis and the speculative attacks on the pound sterling and the Spanish peseta. The Mexican crisis came next, in 1994–95. Then in 1997–98 that of South-East Asia as a result of massive capital flight from the region. In 1998, the Russian crisis. In 2000–2002, the

---

8   Mihm S. (2009). "Why capitalism fails. The man who saw the meltdown coming had another troubling insight: it will happen again." *The Boston Globe*. 13 September 2009.

9   The effect of the injection of liquidity into the system carried out by the central banks of the EU, USA and Japan, among others, was to keep the credit circuit alive, but at the expense of costs that are still unknown today.

bursting of the technology and dot.com bubble. In 2001 the Argentine crisis broke out. After that period came several years of low interest rates, sponsored by the US Federal Reserve, then chaired by the conservative libertarian Alan Greenspan. Until the 2008 crisis. Since then a series of bank and government failures, accompanied by financial rescue plans, have loomed over many EU countries.[10] As Nobel Prize winner Krugman tells us, the harsh reality is that the best predictor of future financial crises is mass entry of foreign capital.[11]

According to Rodrik, the lessons learned since the Asian crisis of 1997 are as follows: the shadow banking system[12] generates crises; financial markets are prone to bubbles, as Minsky warned; financial leverage[13] generates systemic risks; and lack of transparency increases global risk. In short, for Rodrik, recipient countries of international financial capital are among those most disappointed with globalization. Following Beck's thesis on the risk society, the amount of risk—this time financial—accumulated in investment firms all over the world, in a variety of financial instruments or operating from unregulated regions such as tax havens, makes the possibility of a

---

10   A differential and far from minor crisis occurred on 6 May 2010, the 2010 Flash Crash, which caused the New York Stock Exchange to plunge 9% for a few minutes, as a result of a series of operations carried out by automatic high-frequency trading (HFT) software. See U.S. Securities and Exchange Commission and the Commodity Futures Trading Commission (30 September 2010). "Findings Regarding the Market Events of May 6, 2010": www.sec.gov/news/studies/2010/marketevents-report.pdf.

11   Krugman P. (2013). "Hot Money Blues." *The New York Times*. 24 March 2013: www.nytimes.com/2013/03/25/opinion/krugman-hot-money-blues.html?_r=2.

12   Para-banking activities that escape the supervision of regulators and are conducted by, among others, investment banks and hedge funds. See Schiller R. (2012). *Finance and the Good Society*, Princeton University, pp. 42-3.

13   Investment operations based on loaned resources, with little own capital, the credit of which can only be returned using the revenues generated by that investment. A recent example of a leveraged operation is that of the Spanish construction company Sacyr and its long struggle to gain control over Repsol. This control was to enable it, by increasing share dividends, to repay the abundant outstanding debts from the times of uncontrolled expansion. See Rathbone J. & A. Thomson (2011). "Pemex and Sacyr team up over Repsol." *Financial Times*. 30 August 2011: "Sacyr bought its 20 per cent stake in Repsol in 2006 for €6.5bn, using debt to fund the purchase. It has often struggled with the investment's financing since." www.ft.com/intl/cms/s/0/95f9fa12-d290-11e0-a409-00144feab49a.html#axzz2fuy84Ly2.

new global financial meltdown a constant presence.[14] Furthermore, from an economic perspective, as the saying goes, international capital lends you an umbrella when it's sunny and takes it back when it starts to rain. It is hardly surprising, then, that financial globalization is increasingly experienced as more of a threat than an opportunity.

The profound change in the economic system in recent years and its progressive destabilization should be understood as the result of unrelenting pressure from agents and organizations to liberalize global capital. In the times of the Bretton Woods consensus, says Rodrik, there were controls over loans and cross-border indebtedness, limits on firms' and banks' capacity for foreign indebtedness; and hot money was globally perceived as a danger. With the hyper-globalization of the 1980s a new chapter was added to the Bretton Woods agreement and the objective was imposed of liberalizing capital in order to allocate international savings more efficiently.

The core problem with this shift in the perception of financial markets is to be found not only in relation to their efficiency (does deregulation really contribute towards a more solid and stable global economy?) but above all, according to Rodrik, in two serious conceptual shortcomings. First, it is assumed that financial markets are *rational and far-sighted*. Recent history has shown that the degree of rationality of markets and their predictive capability are much more modest than their defenders think. And second, as we saw earlier, financial markets also require *institutional frameworks*, global regulations and standards, monitoring mechanisms, enforcement of this supra-regulation, and an organization to act as a lender of last resort for countries in a liquidity crisis. And a deregulated market cannot provide this kind of action.

The questions asked by Rodrik tend to cast doubt on much of this false consensus reached around the role of the market in the global economy. Are markets always efficient? Is financial innovation always good? Does self-regulation work better? Is all government intervention ineffective and harmful? The problem that lies before us, then, is how to correct these imbalances: what platforms and institutions and what theoretical model we

---

14   We could quote the simile used by the investor Warren Buffett when he said that derivatives were the new weapons of mass destruction of the financial system. We know that some of our neighbours (investors) in this neighbourhood (planet) have weapons but we don't know whether they are knives, guns or nuclear bombs. What we do know for sure is that, thanks to the liberalization of financial markets and the continuous flow of international big capital, the risk potential of the neighbourhood is constantly increasing.

should use to start to retrace our steps along the road to hyper-globalization. According to Rodrik, as we will see, the road to follow will be to recover the Bretton Woods type model of moderate globalization.

Then why is it so difficult to put right what's wrong with our deregulated economic system? Because unlike in the orthodox theoretical models of the economy, in the real world there are two key elements, essential to the sociological approach to the economy, that make it rather difficult for actions to transform reality. We are talking about the existence of power, on the one hand, and the role of culture, on the other. We discussed the latter concept earlier from the perspective of ideologies.

First we have to take into account the weakening of the state in parallel with the increase in the power of the large corporations, particularly those in the financial sector. There has been a shift in power that has benefited from the following mechanisms:

- Lobbying conducted by corporate interests around the centres of political decision-making (Brussels, London, Washington, etc.)

- Influence exerted by these large corporations on the media, through two channels, namely by conditioning its income (through advertising) and by acquiring its share capital[15]

- Direct funding of political parties, either legally or illegally, in order to condition their policies

- The mechanism of the revolving door: companies taking on politicians (prime ministers, ministers) or senior civil servants (public prosecutors, judges, directors-general, state secretaries) in order to capture intellectual capacities and knowledge of the functioning of government agencies, regulation mechanisms and the enforcement of laws and regulations, and also as networks of contact and influence; and no less importantly

- The support of various intellectuals, economists, think-tanks and academic centres who have sustained this intellectual status quo in exchange for funding for chairs, research, publications or career

15 Examples of interrelation between finance, the media and political power are legion. Amazon bought up the prestigious *Washington Post* in 2013. The US fund Liberty Acquisition Holdings did the same with Spain's largest newspaper, *El País*, in 2010. But the most paradigmatic case is that of Silvio Berlusconi and his group Mediaset, from which he entered Italian politics in the 1990s, to condition it incessantly ever since.

opportunities in academia, or else in exchange for consultancy revenue, or just status or prestige.[16]

This debilitation of the state has been accompanied by an unprecedented transfer of economic sovereignty towards supra-state bodies such as the European Union, through the various regional free trade agreements (ASEAN, NAFTA, Mercosur, etc.) and also towards international bodies such as the World Trade Organization, the International Labour Organization, and so on. We have also witnessed a progressive deregulation that has advanced greatly in spheres such as finance, in which a host of agents operate, often with very little transparency (in their investments, their corporate governance models, their risk management systems, their investment tools), out of vast twilight zones that become veritable black holes for the regulator. But above all we are confronted with a new culture of the financial sector (values, standards, languages) that has permeated business as a whole, not just the sector, and can hardly be made to change overnight.

Nonetheless, we can at least highlight the advanced state of erosion of the intellectual model that paved the way for the deregulation of the financial sector over the last few decades. In October 2008, during his appearance before the Congressional Committee that investigated the responsibilities surrounding the fall of Lehman Brothers, Alan Greenspan, former Chairman of the Federal Reserve and leading light of neoliberal orthodoxy, admitted the flaw in his theoretical model and expressed his *intellectual* concern at this unexpected discovery[17] which at the outset was to leave the US taxpayer out of pocket to the tune of $700 billion. A year later, on 19 February 2010, the front page of the influential *Wall Street Journal* featured the surprising 180° turn in the recommendations of the International Monetary Fund, which now called for capital controls.[18]

---

16 On this last point, it is worthwhile reading about the interconnection between academia and the World Economic Forum in Robinson A. (2013). Op. cit.

17 "Yes, I've found a flaw. I don't know how significant or permanent it is. But I've been very distressed by that fact." See Andrews E. (2008a). "Greenspan Concedes Error on Regulation." *The New York Times*. 23 October 2008.

18 Davis B. "IMF, reversing course, urges capital controls." *Wall Street Journal*. 19 February 2010. http://online.wsj.com/article/SB40001424052748704269004575073610075698010.html. Along the same lines, another sample of the debate among economists in favour of heeding the lessons of recent history can be found here: Grabel I. & Chang H.-J. (2010). "Why capital controls are not all bad." *Financial Times*. 25 October 2010. www.ft.com/intl/cms/s/0/4d0e3e34-e02f-11df-9482-00144feabdc0.html#axzz2gMQEzT3e.

However, despite the dilapidation that threatens the intellectual apparatus of the unfettered deregulation of financial markets, it turns out that there is a wide gap between this erosion and the enforcement and implementation of policies aimed at reversing the damage done over the last 30 years. To understand this paralysis in practical terms, underneath the veneer of confessions, proclamations and apologies, we should go back again to the previous section concerning the power of states *vis-à-vis* the great business and financial frameworks at the turn of the 21st century. This requires a more in-depth exploration of a concept we presented earlier on: financialization.

4.3 An introduction to financialization

4.3.1 Basic concepts

Let us recap the basic elements we have mentioned so far under the label of financial globalization. In the globalized world, information is now the most valuable product in the global economy. The driving force behind this economy is freely moving capital, beyond the control of governments. Of these movements, 90% of the money in circulation is in the form of transactions made in less than a week and does not correspond to movements of goods, services or productive investments. This is *hot* money: money that is not intended to buy or sell goods or services; it is just money in pursuit of money, return.[19] Power is shifting from governments to markets and it is a power that has a huge destabilizing potential.

One of the best-known examples of these transfers of "hot money" with counterproductive results for local economies is that of the famous Asian crisis of the second half of the 1990s. In 1996, inflows of international capital into the region comprising Indonesia, South Korea, Thailand, Hong Kong, Malaysia, Laos and Philippines totalled $93 billion. One year later, there were capital outflows to the value of $105 billion. This was when financial globalization was still in its infancy. The shake-up for economies, businesses, budgets and public policies was overwhelming. The world's savings flooded into Asia, and when they receded they left the region's whole financial system

---

19 The typical example of hot money is that of cash and carry trading: international capital flow operations that are often carried out for very brief periods of time and are intended to take advantage of minor variations in exchange and interest rates between currencies.

high and dry.[20] Now we are acquainted with the mechanism, we are interested in finding out what lies behind this sudden disappearance of capital.

Let's take a more recent case: the fall of Spain before the financial markets at the beginning of 2010. At the time, Spain, under Rodríguez Zapatero's Socialist government, boasted that it had one of the least indebted economies in the Western world (this was true of public indebtedness, but not private) and one of the sturdiest banking systems in the world (true as far as the balance sheets were concerned, but not when it came to the huge risks involved in the credit and property bubble, which by then had already burst). The year before, Spain had even embarked on an expansive policy, the E Plan (at an estimated cost of some €13 billion),[21] which was immediately criticized by the markets as ineffective. The Keynesian orthodoxy was about to lose the day irreversibly. The financial markets homed in on Spain. In what was considered to be a major communication error, Zapatero agreed to attend the annual meeting of the World Economic Forum at the beginning of 2010 in Davos, the epicentre of world economic power, and to share a panel with the likewise Socialist President Papandreu of Greece, a country that was at the eye of the financial hurricane, with massive withdrawals of capital, processes under way for a public bailout and on the threshold of a Draconian tax realignment process.

The photo of Zapatero with Papandreu was seen all over the world, and put the two countries in the same boat. On 7 February, Spain's largest newspaper, *El País*, reproduced the photo alongside a headline that revealed what many were thinking: "They're after Spain. Markets target possible fiscal crisis." We should point out that in 2010 the Spanish public debt (what the state owes to its creditors) was equivalent to 59% of the GDP, a long way off the 77% of the UK, Germany's 81% and Japan's 198%.[22] Seemingly, the markets anticipated the profound fracturing of the Spanish economic model, the lack of growth and the unsustainability of its banks which, sure enough, soon had to be rescued. On 9 February, *La Vanguardia*, the largest newspaper in Catalonia, published the following headline: "Campa [Secretary of State for the Economy] defends the solvency of the Spanish economy

---

20   See IMF (1998). "The Asian Crisis: Causes and Cures." *Finance and Development.* June 1998, 35 (2). www.imf.org/external/pubs/ft/fandd/1998/06/imfstaff.htm.

21   www.publico.es/dinero/263326/el-gobierno-pone-en-marcha-el-segundo-plan-c-para-crear-200-000-empleos-duraderos.

22   *The Economist.* "The global debt clock." www.economist.com/content/global_debt_clock.

before the City." Note where this senior Ministry official went to defend the solidity of the Spanish economy: Europe's main financial centre, and one of the most important in the world, the City of London.

Within days, the vice president of the Spanish Government had a meeting with the editorial board of the *Financial Times*, who accused the government of paranoia. In September, months after the policy change that was to cause Spain to follow in Greece's footsteps, the Spanish Prime Minister travelled to New York to sell the virtues of the reform processes initiated and met for talks with the same Wall Street operators he had called *speculators*.[23] These included managers of large pension funds, institutional funds and investment banks, and the director of the *Wall Street Journal*. In short, those operators responsible for issuing the Spanish public debt, which started to plummet and accrue exorbitant costs.[24] Names such as Citigroup, Prudential, BlackRock, Paulson & Co., Morgan Stanley, Bridgewater Associates and Goldman Sachs were just some of the corporations to which the Spanish government was required to be economically *accountable*.

We need a theoretical framework to understand what has happened. Palley[25] defines financialization as the process whereby capital markets, institutions and financial elites gain influence over economic policy and economic outcomes. Financialization transforms the functioning of economic systems at both micro and macro levels and its principal impacts are:

- To elevate the significance of the financial sector relative to the real economy

23   www.diariocritico.com/noticias/228291.

24   The price of issuing public debt, measured through the risk premium—the extra return that investors require to hold a risky asset instead of a risk-free one; see *The Economist* dictionary of economics: www.economist.com/economics-a-to-z—for Spain went from 100 basis points (where 100 points is equivalent to a 1% extra cost) at the beginning of 2010 to 600 in mid-2012. This meant an additional cost of 6% for the funding of Spanish sovereign bonds. Parallel to this, the rating agencies lowered Spain's country risk to the level of junk or purely speculative bonds. This makes sense considering that such a high cost of borrowing in a country with such a large deficit in practice spells a country in risk of default. (Note: "A bond is an interest-bearing security issued by governments, companies and some other organizations." *The Economist* dictionary of economics).

25   Palley T. (2007). "Financialization: What It Is and Why It Matters." Working Paper No. 525. The Levy Economics Institute and Economics for Democratic and Open Societies. Washington, D.C. December 2007. www.levyinstitute.org/pubs/wp_525.pdf.

- To transfer income from the real economy to the financial sector

- To increase income inequality and contribute to wage stagnation

It is the economic system itself that has been transformed under the rise of the financial sector.

Financialization works through three conduits:

- Changes in the structure and operation of financial markets

- Changes in the behaviour of nonfinancial corporations (which mimic the behavioural patterns of the financial sector)

- Changes in economic policy

The financial sector is made up of a much broader spectrum of organizations than just traditional commercial banks. It consists of companies engaged in financial intermediation, among which we also find trade finance, savings and housing institutions, leasing companies and insurance companies—with the specific difficulty that actions of a financial nature that used to be performed by specialist institutions can now be performed by a variety of business groups or by individuals with a certain amount of equity.

Torres López offers an analysis of the gradual trend reversal that has transformed practices and mentalities:

> What happened was that hitherto superfluous means of payment and others that joined them subsequently, attracted to global money and financial asset markets by such quick and high profits, grew incessantly, performing purely speculative operations and getting further and further away from the creation of productive businesses, the production of goods and services and job creation. Who was going to dedicate all their resources to this, when they could make much more money in financial investment? [...] The main reason why capital moved from the sphere of the productive economy to the financial sphere is that much larger relative gains can be achieved in the latter than in the former.[26]

4.3.2 Causes, consequences and the new investment culture

The manufacturing sector has progressively lost profitability in relation to the financial sector, especially in a large number of Western countries. Manufacturers look on as production moves abroad and the sale of foreign

---

26   Torres López J. (2009). *La crisis financiera. Guía para entenderla y explicarla.* Attac.

products increases while the domestic market stagnates or at best grows slowly. Opening up to external markets, although indispensable, implies entering into fierce competition with foreign producers. The financial sector, in contrast, shows an increase in instruments (derivatives),[27] numbers of customers (investors, savers) and the internationalization of its operations. It is hardly surprising, then, that shortly before the crisis General Motors, soon to be bailed out by the US government, based a very large part of its corporate revenue on activities far removed from car production and closer to sales of financial assets.

The socioeconomic impact of this shift of resources towards the financial sector is therefore important. This process transforms the production model, the types of activity in which companies are involved independently of the sector, and the system of remunerations. This is particularly the case in the financial sector, which provides employment for far fewer people of a much higher educational profile than manufacturing or other nonfinancial services. If we add to the above what we already know—the larger the financial sector the greater the risk—the question we have to ask ourselves is: what is the right size for the financial sector in an economy? The recent crisis has shown us the risk involved in overexposure to the financial sector. Thus, if we compare the data of two of the countries most seriously affected by the crisis, Ireland and Spain, we find that just when the property bubble was bursting (in 2008) the weight of bank assets in relation to the country's GDP was 1,016% and 294% respectively. The cost of a potential bailout of the financial sector, as has actually happened in both countries, entails the nationalization of the private debt and indebtedness for several generations to come. At the top of the table, Luxembourg has bank assets that represent 22 times its GDP.[28]

Another manifestation of the oversizing of the financial sector can be seen in the historical comparison between the market capitalization[29] of listed companies and the GDP of the country. Taking data for the New York

---

27 Derivatives: "Financial assets that 'derive' their value from other assets. For example, an option to buy a share is derived from the share." *The Economist* dictionary of economics.

28 Data from *The Economist* and Bruegel Institute: www.bruegel.org/nc/blog/detail/article/1062-large-banks-relative-to-gdp-is-there-a-risk-beyond-cyprus/.

29 Market capitalization: "The market value of a company's shares: the quoted share price multiplied by the total number of shares that the company has issued." *The Economist* dictionary of economics. www.economist.com/economics-a-to-z/m.

Stock Exchange (NYSE) since 1925 and comparing the market capitalization of listed companies with the nominal GDP of the USA, we find that the historic average since records began has been slightly over 60%. In the crash of 1929 a record was reached of 88%. Thus the market value of listed companies represented nearly 90% of the wealth generated by the whole country in that year. On 31 March 2000 the figure hit an all-time peak of 180%, having climbed steadily from the 49% of October 1990. At the worst moment following the 2008 crisis, the market value of companies on the NYSE fell to 72% of the GDP. By February 2013 the ratio had picked up again to 110%, thus exceeding the value of all the goods and services produced in the country that year.[30]

Turning our attention now to the growth in the volume of transactions in international capital markets from 1990 to 2006, according to International Monetary Fund data,[31] we find that world GDP doubled in that period. The foreign exchange market tripled, as did world trade (the usual indicator of globalization, remember), while the bonds and derivatives market multiplied by four and the equity market by nine. The increase in the circulation of these assets occurred at the same time as the above-mentioned financial crises were happening. If in 1981 institutional investors in the US owned financial assets corresponding to 70.5% of their country's GDP, by 2004 the figure was 182.9%. In the UK in the same period they went from 48.8% to 209.3%; in France, from 10.7% to 165.4%. In the US alone, assets held by pension funds, insurance companies, investment funds and the like stood at nearly $45 trillion ($45,000,000,000,000) in 2004. One of these was the insurance corporation AIG, rescued in 2008 after the fall of Lehman Brothers with an $85 billion loan.[32] The problem with such huge organizations so strongly linked to the rest of the financial sector and the real economy is their systemic risk. They cannot fall without causing widespread panic and the failure of the financial system as a whole.

Among the problems derived from the systemic risk of these organizations (insurance companies, commercial and investment banks, investment

---

30   www.ritholtz.com/blog/2013/02/market-capitalization-as-a-percentage-of-gdp-4/.

31   Here we will use the data provided by UCM professors Medialdea B. & Álvarez N. (2009). *Liberalización financiera internacional, inversores institucionales y gobierno corporativo de la empresa.* WP07/08. http://eprints.ucm.es/9031/1/WP07-08.pdf.

32   Andrews E. (2008b). "Fed's $85 billion loan rescues insurer". *New York Times.* 16 September 2008.

funds, etc.) we find, first, its cost (private profits and public costs) and second, moral hazard: if these organizations know that they are indispensable and will therefore be rescued in the event of failure, what will the cost of bad risk management be? What expectations can society have, not only of recovering the lavish rescue plans carried out with public money but also of seeing any improvements in their management in order to avoid future debacles?

It is estimated, using 2009 data,[33] that the financial economy (derivatives, foreign exchange markets and stock markets) are capable of mobilizing some $5.5 trillion a day. Overall GDP stands at around $150 billion a day (35 times less) and the volume of world trade about 100 times less: some $55 billion. It is estimated that $3.11 trillion of foreign exchange was traded every day in 2009 (20% more than in 2007). The City of London accounted for 36.7% of these operations. The USA, the second financial centre, 17.9%.[34] According to the data available at the time of writing,[35] total world financial assets stand at $209 trillion, an all-time high that beats the $197 trillion of the precrisis period (2007) and is equivalent to 293% of the world GDP. These assets correspond to the shareholder value of listed companies, public debt, loans to the private sector and others; a much greater volume, therefore, than printed money, which represents only a tiny part of the total of the means of payment we use: between 7% and 10%, a far cry from the 60–70% of bank money, consisting of the deposits that economic operators place in banks.[36]

An article in the *Financial Times* entitled "Ways to take stock of it all"[37] helps us to understand the changes financialization has brought about in the way people invest:

- The historical difference in returns between equity and fixed income (i.e., stocks versus bonds), overwhelmingly favourable to the former, lead investors to prefer to invest in stock rather than in public treasury bonds.

33   Torres López J. (2009). Op. cit.
34   Data supplied by the Bank for International Settlements. Estapé M. (2010). "Los mercados de divisas negocian 3,11 billones diarios." *La Vanguardia*. 2 September 2010.
35   Keohane D. (2013). "Global financial assets, there are lots." *Financial Times*. 13 February 2013.
36   Data for 2009, Torres López J. (2009). Op. cit.
37   Authers J. (2009). "Ways to take stock of it all." *Financial Times*. 15 October 2009.

- Fifty years ago, the average investor in a mature financial market such as the US was a wealthy man who invested on his own account. The growth of institutional investment led by investment fund and hedge fund managers[38] has replaced the individual investor and at the same time has assimilated the strategies and tools used by the professional managers of these funds, whose ways of investing become more and more similar.[39]

- From 2010 to 2050 it is estimated that the proportion of the population over 65 in Japan will rise from 22.6% to 37.8%. In the USA, from 13% to 21.6%. In Western Europe, from 18.4% to 28.9%; in China from 8.2% to 23.3%. With the increasing life expectancy of developed countries, private pension funds are gaining in importance in the face of the growing perception of the inability of states to provide an adequate public retirement pension. Much of these savings are channelled through institutional investment.

- With globalization, equity is shifting increasingly towards emerging markets. Thus, in 1990 the Japanese market represented 45% of all the planet's financial markets, while the US accounted for less than 25% and emerging markets less than 5%. Now Japan represents 10%, the US over 30% (but well under the 40% of a decade ago) and the so-called emerging countries total nearly 20%. Investments are made everywhere, and increasingly so in developing countries.

In *Liquidated: An Ethnography of Wall Street*[40] anthropologist Karen Ho sets forth how the financial sector has succeeded in creating, on the basis of the example set by Wall Street, an *elitist* culture perceived as such

38   Investment fund: "A collective investment scheme is a way of investing money alongside other investors." Presently we will provide a generic definition of a hedge fund. For the time being, here is the definition given by *The Economist*: "There is no simple definition of a hedge fund [...] but they all aim to maximise their absolute returns rather than relative ones; that is, they concentrate on making as much money as possible."

39   As we will explain below, this shows the importance of the herd effect in investors' behaviour. Taking the example of a shepherd in the mountains, if a thunderclap makes one sheep run towards a cliff, the rest will follow behind. This herd behaviour, based on theoretical models, investment strategies and tools, causes conduct to be reproduced and greatly increases the possibility that the boat of the financial system will end up capsizing and sinking, just because all the passengers rush to one side of the deck.

40   Ho K. (2009). *Liquidated: An Ethnography of Wall Street*. Duke University Press.

by society. According to Ho, Wall Street screens its new managers by only taking on graduates of the best American universities (the Ivy League). Neither previous experience nor any great knowledge of finance is necessary. The message to the markets is clear: to seek the brand association between the university of origin and the target firm, the legitimacy of Wall Street firms thus being built on their apparent meritocracy. Their way of presenting themselves is to say: we recruit the *best* and the *brightest*, so we are the *best*.

Once the entrance filter is overcome, a feat that few accomplish, internal competition, the linking of the variable part of each employee's salary to the performance of the portfolio he or she manages, translates as acute job insecurity yet high pay (extremely high during bullish market cycles). It is important to stress that the bonus is linked to the number of operations closed, not the long-term prospect of returns. In other words, the date on which the bonus is paid determines the investment horizon. With the bloating of the financial sector and the rise of institutional investment, globalization was to cause this particular investment culture and target-based remuneration (targets usually being measured in the short term) to extend first to the rest of the financial sector (commercial banks, insurance) and then to the rest of the sectors in the economy. If, as Ho argues, we are in fact dealing with an investment culture that takes the form of a culture of risk, the problem will be how to dismantle a whole culture with its values, ways of doing things, frameworks of interpretation, tools and rewards.

From a more clearly Marxist position, economists John Bellamy Foster and Fred Magdoff seek the origins of financialization[41] in an evolution that is specific to monopoly capitalism. According to the authors, economic stagnation is the prelude to financialization. In the face of the shortage of profitable investment opportunities to absorb international savings and capital flight from emerging countries to safer ones, these resources are channelled towards the financial sector. However, the problem does not lie in the lack of productivity of these potential investments but rather the pattern of accumulation that comes naturally to monopolistic financial capitalism. The concentration of enterprises and their huge size induces the formation of oligopolistic markets led by corporate giants. These yield an unprecedented increase in surpluses (business profits), together with the problem of where to put them. The outcome is the supremacy of finance as

---

41 Foster J.B. & Magdoff F. (2009). *The Great Financial Crisis: Causes and Consequences.* New York: Monthly Review Press.

a placement agent for this surplus, and as the predominant economic activity, even in nonfinancial sectors, which are subordinated to it.

In the field of financial sociology, Neil Fligstein[42] seems to agree with the Marxist reading of financial crises. According to this American sociologist, the rise of the great diversified conglomerates that invested in multiple sectors and industries, bestowing formal independence on each business unit, caused the investment mentality of the main fund managers to start to be applied to these large corporations. The new theory of the firm wrought by up-and-coming financial specialists meant that these large corporations had to act with their units in the same way as an investor would do with his or her diversified investment portfolio. According to the modern portfolio theory put forward by who was subsequently awarded the 1990 Nobel Prize for Economics, Harry Markowitz, companies should diversify their risk and invest their profits in industries with a high growth potential.

What happened, says Fligstein, was that the finance specialists who held key positions in corporations took over the discourse on *investment* in the company, pushing aside other managers of areas such as operations, sales and quality, in many cases to the extent that they gained control of the highest management posts (managing director, CEO) of these major groups. This replacement of business elites was not only to mark the dynamics of corporate acquisitions, mergers and sales as of the 1990s but was also to determine what sort of investment behaviour was considered right and even the very concept of economic rationality, as we have mentioned above.[43] Once again, we are dealing with a particular management culture, along the lines of that set out by Karen Ho for the case of Wall Street, but now applied to business as a whole and not just the financial sector.

The real power that investment analysts wield through their valuations of companies transformed the way these companies act, altered remuneration systems to align them with the expectations of institutional investors, and rewarded the achievement of targets based on share performance on the capital market rather than the usual indicator of profit. As we saw earlier with ideologies, new management theory, once socialized and accepted as true, thus altered the way companies were managed and fostered the financialization of the whole economic system. Such a diffuse or specific form of

42   Fligstein N. (1990). *The Transformation of Corporate Control.* Harvard University Press.

43   Fligstein N. & L. Markowitz (1993). "Financial reorganization of American corporations in the 1980s." In William J. Wilson, ed.: *Sociology and the Public Agenda.* Newbury Park, CA: Sage Publications, pp. 185-206.

power as the management model ultimately transformed the rules of the economic game.

Although this change of culture is not restricted to the business level, in 2000 another behavioural economist who has worked extensively on the financial sector, Robert Shiller, published the book *Irrational Exuberance*,[44] on the changes in cultural and economic patterns that paved the way for the rise of a veritable speculative culture in American society and prepared the ground for the formation and bursting of bubbles. The following points, he held, were new:

- Speculative capitalism is based on promising uninterrupted growth in earnings. This caused an essential confusion in savers: saving is not equivalent to speculation. The distinction between one and the other should be based on the perceived risk of the operation. This distinction was no longer always clear.

- The height of one of the essential foundations of our economic culture: materialism. The realization of citizens' aspirations and desires increasingly depended on consuming, and therefore this objective of the ongoing acquisition of material goods forced us to feed on permanent and growing income.

- The spread of gambling culture to the economy; it was common to say "gambling on the stock exchange" to talk about *investing* or *speculating* on the stock exchange. Thus, patterns of indifference to risk, chance or irrationality interfered with the rational investment patterns that, according to the market hypothesis, should explain the functioning of financial markets.

- Overestimation of the impact of new technologies on the market, which made us think, just like in any other previous speculative bubble (from the tulip crisis of 1637 to the Internet bubble of 2000–2001), that it was possible for new business opportunities to generate extraordinary profits.[45]

---

44   Shiller R. (2000). *Irrational Exuberance*. Princeton University Press.

45   A typical yet seldom remembered case is that of Terra Networks, the first Spanish Internet company, which went public on 17 November 1999 with a quoted market price of €11.81. In just three months its value surged to over €157, with daily rises of 10% or even 20%. Its value was soon to plummet to €5.25 during Telefónica's buy-back offer in May 2003. The day before it came off the stock market and merged with Telefónica it was listed at €2.90. See: *El País* (2005).

- The belief that financial managers would manage our savings better than we ourselves would, insofar as they had the best and best-trained specialists (recall Karen Ho and her ethnography of Wall Street), who applied the best and most rational investment methods.[46]

- The low interest rate monetary policy, which led to household indebtedness and made possible the apparently stable and cheap recourse to consumer credit.

- Private pension plans that had become an interested party in rising asset prices and therefore also in spreading optimistic messages to the effect that there were no speculative bubbles in sight.

- The popularization of business information of a speculative kind, which now fills several pages of our leading newspapers, the economic information available on the Internet and the advertising we receive through the media.

- Lastly, a reflection on the positive bias of the information we receive: historical information on market rates is not discounted for inflation, and therefore shows better results than is really the case. This comes on top of the well-known super-optimism of the financial

"Evolución bursátil de Terra." 15 July 2005. http://economia.elpais.com/economia/2005/07/15/actualidad/1121412773_850215.html.

46   The gap between the perception of their professionalism and the rationality of their methods has given rise to a host of articles and references. Let us mention just some of them. In an article in *El País*, "El mono, los dardos y el sonrojo de Wall Street" (2007), the columnist drew attention to Burton Gordon Malkiel's work on the predictive capabilities of a monkey throwing darts in comparison with those of stock market analysts, with the resulting embarrassing defeat of the latter by the former in 85% of funds. In "Credit crunch causes analysts to rethink rational market theory" (2008), *Financial Times* assistant editor Gillian Tett tells how two-thirds of analysts no longer believe in the hypothesis of the efficiency of financial markets and 77% even deny the rationality of the financial market. The best quote, however, is to be found in Thaler and Sunstein's book *Nudge* (2008: 125), in reference to the above-mentioned Nobel economics laureate Harry Markowitz: "When asked about how he allocated his retirement account, he confessed: 'I should have computed the historic covariances of the asset classes and drawn an efficient frontier. Instead ... I split my contributions fifty–fifty between bonds and equities.'" Not even the architect of modern portfolio theory would follow his own recipes.

analysts whose job it is to sell the stock of permanent investment opportunities.[47]

One last point to illustrate the importance of financialization is in reference to the impact of increasingly unequal societies on capital markets. Whereas in the 1950s, 1960s and 1970s, middle and lower class individuals dedicated part of their income surplus to buying goods in the real economy, these same savings, now concentrated in the hands of few, are directed towards luxury goods and in particular speculative activities via capital markets. As the meetings of the world's capitalist elite in Davos agree and acknowledge,[48] a more unequal society means a greater channelling of this *saving* towards the financial market and a greater marginal propensity to speculate, which encourages the recurrent appearance of bubbles in any sector or good (raw materials, foodstuffs, gold, property and so on).

Thus we have seen how financialization feeds on a series of changes that profoundly affect the economic system. On the management side, we have seen the transformation of the theoretical models of the firm, the rise of an eminently financial management profile and a management system designed to keep market analysts happy. On the systemic side, the Marxist analysis has placed the emphasis on the over-accumulation of capital that arises out of the concentration of capital in a handful of large corporations and the channelling of these resources towards the financial sector and the reaping of fast, short-term profits. From a macroeconomic perspective, we find the confluence of foreign trade imbalances, capital flow towards countries with prospects for investment (or speculation), and processes of advanced deregulation of capital markets under the aegis of the Washington Consensus.

---

47   This super-optimism camouflages the imparting of supposedly professional information with the pure perpetuation of their business model. In the piece "Why analysts keep telling investors to buy", published at the worst moment of the post-Lehman fall of the financial markets, at the beginning of 2009, we are shown how recommendations to sell stock remained below 10% as of 2007 and throughout the crisis. In any event, well below recommendations to hold on to stock (60%) or even buy (30%), which from sheer common sense would appear inappropriate at a time of steadily declining markets. Healy J. & M. Grynbaum (2009). "Why analysts keep telling investors to buy." *The New York Times*, 8 February 2009. Along the same lines, see McClellan S. (2009). "Decoding Wall Street's well-kept secrets." *Financial Times*. 23 June 2009.

48   Robinson A. (2013). Op. cit. Chapter 4.

We should also add, on this institutional political level, capture of public policies, the confluence of the activities of investment banks with those of commercial banks, until recently considered conservative and less prone to risk-taking, and the continued existence of major deregulated loopholes in the global financial system such as tax havens. On the last level, the new investment culture has transformed the way we as citizens relate to capital markets and the way we perceive investment banks as forming a meritocratic elite. The growing inequality of the planet has only reinforced the effect of financialization.

4.4 Main agents of financialization

Who are the markets? Economics tells us that they are the sum of the suppliers and demanders who exchange goods and services in a particular sector or industry. Individual savers and states with excess capital as a result of their trade surpluses, who seek ways of obtaining a return and do so by means of a set of specialized instruments and agents that make it possible.[49] In a fresh attempt to grasp the scope of financialization, we can focus on four main agents in this intermediation in the early 21st century: hedge funds, sovereign wealth funds, rating agencies and tax havens. Their role, as we will see, is vital in enabling us to understand both the dissemination of a particular culture of financialization and the spread of financialization itself to the corners of the Earth.[50]

[49]   Lacalle D. (2013). *Nosotros los mercados. Qué son, cómo funcionan y por qué resultan imprescindibles.* Barcelona: Deusto, pp. 26ff.

[50]   It is true that other actors such as central banks, especially in countries such as the US, Japan and indeed the EU, and major asset managers could be included in the above list for their decisive role in the financialization of the economic system. Since the crisis broke, the central banks of these countries have flooded their economies with liquidity, thus generating new resources in search of investment opportunities. Trillions of euros and dollars have made it possible, for example, for the financial sector firms that collapsed only five years ago to recover their profits. They have also enabled record levels to be reached on the New York Stock Exchange. As far as the big asset managers are concerned, we should bear in mind that the largest of them, BlackRock, with only 10,000 employees, manages assets worth more than $3 trillion. See *The Economist* (2011). "BlackRock: Goliath. The world's largest asset manager has done well out of the crisis. What now?" *The Economist.* 3 September 2011.

4.4.1 Hedge funds

Recall the photograph that exemplified the change in direction by the Zapatero government in 2010. When the Socialist Prime Minister travelled to the US he set up what we might call a road show to sing the praises of his new economic policy (aimed, remember, in the opposite direction to that which he had been practising only months earlier). One of the meetings in Wall Street brought together leading lights in investment banking and managers of hedge funds, including J.P. Morgan, Goldman Sachs, Deutsche Bank, BlackRock, Quantum and Paulson & Co. At the end of 2010, the assets managed by the 25 largest hedge funds were estimated at around €400 billion.[51] And in the second third of 2010, the top ten alone were able to generate $28 billion in profits for their clients, $2 billion more than the combined profits of the six big banks: Goldman Sachs, J.P. Morgan, Citigroup, Morgan Stanley, Barclays and HSBC.[52] Their main appeal obviously lies in their profitability, which is regularly higher than the average market return.

These hedge funds, some of them managed by banks, are characterized by having a workforce of barely a few hundred employees and being located in one of just three major global hubs: New York, London and Connecticut. The tax domicile of a large number of their activities is often in tax havens; they seek short-term increases in value, by changing their investment strategy and adapting it repeatedly to market fluctuations[53] and a wide variety of sectors and geographical regions. They can also invest in high-risk sectors

---

51   Agustina L. (2010). "El mercado baila al son de banca y 'hedge funds'." *La Vanguardia*. 14 November 2010.

52   Mackintosh J. (2011). "Top 10 hedge funds make $28bn." *Financial Times*. 1 March 2011. www.ft.com/intl/cms/s/0/24193cbe-4433-11e0-931d-00144feab49a.html?siteedition=intl.

53   Typical investment strategies include short selling (sale of a security that the seller does not own and will buy back in the future at a low price), arbitrage (simultaneously buying and selling a financial instrument on different markets to take advantage of the price difference), anticipation (investing ahead of a specific operation or event: merger, hostile takeover, spin-off, bankruptcy, etc.), leverage (borrowing money to invest it in stock of firms that are below market value, about to get into or out of financial difficulties, or bankrupt) and hedging (buying or selling a security to offset a potential loss on an investment). The principal characteristic of these *advanced* investment strategies is that they benefit from investing in markets that *a priori* are not correlated with each other. Nevertheless, in times of systemic financial crisis such as the events of 2008, this investment model may have worse results than others.

thanks to the use of financial derivatives, and for this reason can generate positive returns in markets with negative indicators.

The Achilles heel of these funds is their contribution to society. It is often said in their defence that they supply liquidity in markets where liquidity is low (i.e., they facilitate purchases and sales where such operations are scarce), but they pay little tax by setting up their registered offices in areas with little or no tax burden, and they generate little employment. In comparison with traditional investment funds, hedge funds can, due to their lack of regulation, contribute to the destabilization of markets by causing sudden massive capital inflows and outflows that affect, for example, prices of raw materials and foods. Their widespread use of derivatives in bear markets and currency speculation cause them to be perceived as a destabilizing agent for global finance.[54]

Using City UK data for 2010, we know that in 2009 around 60% of all hedge funds were registered in tax havens. The Cayman Islands are the most popular tax domicile and account for 39% of the overall number of funds, followed by Delaware (USA) with 27%, British Virgin Islands with 7%, and Bermuda with 5%. Five per cent of funds are registered in the EU, mostly in Ireland and Luxembourg. We also know that academic research reveals that hedge funds have higher profitability and lower overall risk than traditional investment funds and that "hedge funds provide an ideal long-term investment solution, eliminating the need to correctly time entry and exit from markets."[55]

---

54 George Soros, philanthropist, speculator and leading figure in Quantum, based in the Cayman Islands for tax purposes, became famous in 1992 for speculating against the pound and forcing it to leave the European Monetary System, having first played a dangerous multimillion wager on the markets that led to the intervention of the Bank of England and losses for the British taxpayer of a hefty £3.3 billion. See: Tempest M. (2005). "Treasury papers reveal cost of Black Wednesday." *The Guardian* (London). 9 February 2005. More recently we have seen the speculation against the euro and Greek bonds. The latter case involved Goldman Sachs, the same financial institution that advised Greece in its unexpected *compliance* with the single currency requirements and as such the possessor of in-depth knowledge of the actual state of the country's finances. See: Story L., L. Thomas & N. Schwartz. "Wall St. helped to mask debt fueling Europe's crisis." *The New York Times*. 13 February 2010.

55 Information taken from the City UK website. Note that many of the tax havens mentioned are British overseas territories and operate from London: www.thecityuk.com/media/2358/Hedge_Funds_2010.pdf.

4.4.2 Sovereign wealth funds

If hedge funds are one of the main agents of financialization at the advent of the new century, sovereign wealth funds are another sort of newcomer, although some of them have been operating for decades. Sovereign wealth funds are major investment funds usually owned by states, and they are commonly generated through the accumulation of capital originating from trading surpluses or exports of raw materials. They make it possible to invest in such a wide variety of assets as Spanish property, American ports, football clubs, or indeed the London Stock Exchange. What makes them special, however, is that they are veritable elephants within the financial system, as their actions can have major diplomatic and geopolitical impact.

Imagine the inflow of Chinese public capital into the private pension funds of a Latin American country; or into a large part of the energy sector of a country that is dependent on importing energy from abroad; or into the acquisition of large areas of arable land in sub-Saharan Africa, or key technological sectors of the Western arms industry. Nowadays this is a possibility to be considered. One of the main problems with this sort of fund is that many of them lack transparency, and as such are capable of generating systemic risks similar to those observed in the case of hedge funds.[56]

If we look at the list of sovereign wealth funds in terms of their size, in first place we find the Norwegian pension fund, with assets amounting to $737.2 billion, followed by that of Saudi Arabia, with assets valued at $675.9 billion. Next comes the fund of the United Arab Emirates, worth $627 billion. In fourth and fifth place there are two Chinese sovereign wealth funds, with assets valued at $575.2 and $567.9 billion respectively. Further down the list appear countries such as Russia, Singapore and Kuwait. Behind these we find some Latin American countries. Most sovereign wealth funds are located in Asia and the Middle East, which account for 76% of funds, followed at some distance by Europe, consisting basically of Norway. As far as the origin of the resources is concerned, 57% comes from gas and oil exports, and it is calculated that the total funds managed in these financial instruments exceeds $5.85 trillion.[57]

Let's take a standard example of a sovereign wealth fund: the Abu Dhabi Investment Authority. It was set up in 1976 using excess oil revenues, and is

---

56 DealBook (2007). "Sovereign wealth funds: the new hedge fund?" *The New York Times*. 1 August 2007.

57 *Global Finance* (2012). www.gfmag.com/tools/global-database/economic-data/12146-largest-sovereign-wealth-funds.html#axzz2gjprGdTK.

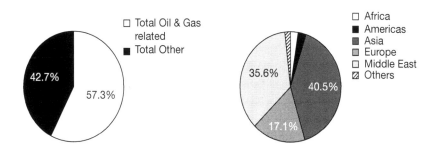

SWFs by Funding Source

SWFs by Region

□ Total Oil & Gas related
■ Total Other

□ Africa
■ Americas
■ Asia
■ Europe
□ Middle East
▨ Others

42.7%   57.3%

35.6%   40.5%   17.1%

FIGURE 4.2 Distribution of sovereign wealth funds by funding source and region

Source: *Global Finance*, 2012. © Global Finance

domiciled for tax purposes in a tax haven, the Cayman Islands. This allows it to have little regulation, little supervision and a smaller tax burden. In fact, its transparency index is very low: three out of ten. With data for 2011, this fund invests in a wide variety of assets and indices, from MSCI to the S&P 500. It invests in assets in both developed and emerging markets, hedge funds, futures, both public and private debt, property (in Europe, for example), private equity and infrastructures. It is neither a very aggressive fund nor a very conservative one.[58]

It is interesting to note that more than 60% of the 50 sovereign wealth funds recognized as such were founded during the first decade of the 21st century. One of these is the sovereign wealth fund of Brazil, created with $250 billion of capital in 2010. As regards the diversity of investment strategies, we see that the strategic fund of the United Arab Emirates (Mubadala) acts differently from those of Malaysia (Khazanah) and Singapore (Temasek). The first takes shareholdings in foreign multinationals in order to subsequently promote industrial plants within the country, whereas the two Asian countries opt to give support directly to the rise of what Luttwak calls **national champions**.[59]

[58]   See *Black Capital* (2011). "Abu Dhabi Investment Authority." http://black-capital.com/news/2011/03/abu-dhabi-investment-authority/?lang=en.

[59]   Santiso J. (2011). "Fondos soberanos latinos." *El País*. 3 July 2011.

4.4.3 Rating agencies

Rating agencies went unnoticed for years, until the 2008 crisis arrived. Since then, they have been discredited, denounced and accused the world over, yet their services continue to be in demand. How did all this happen? First of all, it is important to know how they work. Rating agencies live off what they are paid by the companies and institutions (states, regions, town councils, etc.) that request their services. Their function is to assess the risk and the reliability of debt issuance operations. Furthermore, these ratings are compulsory for all companies listed on stock markets. Their income depends, then, on the initial issuance rating and how it is revised in view of variations in market conditions. Traditionally, their main customers have been financial institutions, who needed an agent to rate their debt securities, many of which in the period 2000–2007 involved the securitization[60] of extremely high-risk financial assets (typically, a low-quality, high-risk sub-prime mortgage).[61]

Essentially, the quality rating of a bond (AAA or Aaa to CCC or Caa, depending on the agency concerned) enables us to grade it as prime, high, medium, speculative or junk. Thus, its influence is proportional to the opacity of a financial sector dominated by surprising offers, information that is not always either trustworthy or understandable, and largely or completely unknown issuers. The rating agencies therefore sell trust and security to the public. The risk premium paid by a state to place its debt on the markets or the success of a potential private debt issuance depends on their expert opinion. The worse the rating, the higher the interest rate to be paid to reward the investor prepared to run that risk.

At this point we come up against two major problems. First, the fact of being paid by the same player who requests the rating creates a conflict of interest, insofar as it is an incentive to make the picture look prettier than it should, depending on the importance of the client.[62] Second, the three main

---

60   Securitization: "Turning a future cashflow into tradable, bond-like securities." *The Economist* dictionary of economics.

61   Palau J. (2011). "Las agencias de rating. Viven de bancos y empresas." *La Vanguardia*. 14 July 2011.

62   This problem of conflict of interest has existed for decades between auditors and their clients. In the past it has made it necessary to impose regulations affecting the types of service that can be purchased from the same supplier, or the rotation of the auditor after a certain period. The scandal that hit Arthur Andersen in 2001 as a result of its repeated accounting manipulation of the accounts of Enron highlighted the potential dangers of conflicts of interest.

agencies—Moody's, Fitch and Standard & Poor's—form a quasi-monopoly cornering 90% of the ratings market. However, the hardest blow to the agencies' credibility was dealt in September 2008 by the collapse of Lehman Brothers, just one of many firms in the financial sector that were assigned the best risk ratings for their new issue only days before going bankrupt or being bailed out with public funds.

In a memorable article entitled "The uses and abuses of mathematical models,"[63] *The Economist* evinced the real capacity for anticipation of these rating agencies by taking the risk ratings issued during the period 2005–2007 for one of the derivatives that figured prominently in the crisis, collateralized debt obligations or CDOs (packages of mortgage debt formed according to the borrowers' risk profile) and putting them side-by-side with their actual outcome with 2010 data. The result is a margin of error 100 to 1,000 times greater than expected. For a *good investment* A, with an estimated risk of 0.09%, the actual outcome was that 29 out of 100 *investors* lost their money.[64] For a *risky* BBB grade investment in which it was estimated that one in 200 investors would lose their money, in fact one in two did. The magnitude of the error is plain to see if we resort to analogy and instead of ratings of financial assets we think of doctors advising a patient on the possibilities of complication involved in a surgical intervention. Errors such as these would inevitably lead to their being struck off the medical register.

Two new problems, just as bad as the above if not worse, derived from the action of the rating agencies, enable us to grasp the extent of the risk involved in our hyper-globalized financial system. First, there is the essential problem of the solidity of their analysis. In an increasingly technified financial world in which mathematicians take the place of financial strategists, the use and abuse of numerical models—to follow the terminology used by *The Economist*—forces us to rely on the services of a professional body that is capable of getting across to the uninitiated the merits of a particular asset. The question posed by *The Economist* was: what's better—to have a compass that doesn't work, or to have no compass at all?

The other serious problem with rating agencies is their performativity, which we have referred to before and will come back to again later. The

---

63   *The Economist* (2010). "The uses and abuses of mathematical models". 11 February 2010.

64   We talk of *losing one's money* in the sense that defaults occurred in that particular product. In fact, the asset in question may have been insured, resold or renegotiated before or after the default, so the amount or cost of this default may be lower or much lower than the initial value of the asset.

	Estimated 3-year default rate	Actual default rate
AAA	0.001	0.10
AA+	0.01	1.68
AA	0.04	8.16
AA−	0.05	12.03
A+	0.06	20.96
A	0.09	29.21
A−	0.12	36.65
BBB+	0.34	48.73
BBB	0.49	56.10
BBB−	0.88	66.67

TABLE 4.1 CDOs of subprime-mortgage-backed securities issued in 2005–2007, %

Source: MacKenzie, D. (2011), "The Credit Crisis as a Problem in the Sociology of Knowledge", American Journal of Sociology, 116:6 (2011), pp. 1778-41. © University of Chicago Press

opinions of this select group of three agencies do not have a neutral effect on the world they claim to describe. They trigger actions, and bestow or snatch away confidence and legitimacy. To say that a country's public debt, with which it pays pensions, civil servants and social services, is a junk bond is to automatically immerse that country into a debt crisis such as those we have witnessed since 2010 in countries such as Greece, Portugal, Ireland, Spain and Italy. Rightly or wrongly, the rating agencies certify that a particular country has global pariah status, and effectively pushes it into the abyss of closed markets, astronomical interest rates and the potential prospect of public service closures, pension cuts and the fracturing of the welfare state.

The rating agencies defend themselves against all this by saying that all they do is make judgements, give opinions; that they have no crystal ball to tell the future, and that their activities are conditioned by the demand for their services. In view of the major problems derived from the way they operate, their functioning clearly involves an increase in the global risk and once again focuses attention on the incapacity of states and supra-state organizations to correct these problems.

4.4.4 Tax havens

The last of the agents—the most significant and complex of all—serves to illustrate the extent of financialization and the powerlessness of states to limit its effects. The first thing to note is that there is no single definition of a tax haven. We talk of *characteristics* of tax havens (or offshore territories) to encompass particular features to be found not only in countries such as Liechtenstein, the Cayman Islands, Bermuda, Switzerland and Singapore but even the Netherlands, Ireland, the UK, Spain and the USA. Some are active in their role as black holes or uncharted territory of the world economy, and it is their intention to remain in that category. The rest allow or encourage, by means of more benevolent regulation, the transfer of capital towards other countries on the dark side of world regulation and incorporate characteristics of the first group. The list of tax havens therefore cannot be seen in terms of black and white; rather, they display a range of hues from light grey through shady to darkest black.

According to the OECD, we can define a tax haven on the basis of the following characteristics.[65] They are territories that:

- Host the registered offices of a large number of financial institutions that do business with non-resident individuals and institutions.[66]

- Have much deeper and more complex levels of business than would be necessary to maintain their domestic economies, which are very small.[67]

- Have a tax system that enables the organizations based there to pay very little or no tax.

- Have legal restrictions on the transfer of financial information to third countries.

---

65   OECD (1998). *Harmful Tax Competition. An Emerging Global Issue.* Paris: Organization for Economic Cooperation and Development.

66   Luxembourg, with 540,000 inhabitants, has $2.5 trillion in financial assets, a figure equivalent to the GDP of the United Kingdom. Robinson A. (2013). Op. cit., p. 170.

67   Liechtenstein and Zug would appear to hold the world record for entrepreneurship. The first has 40,000 companies and 30,000 inhabitants (Torres López, 2009. Op. cit.). For its part, the Swiss canton of Zug, with 19,000 inhabitants, has 29,000 companies and is head office for 500 multinational corporations, including Coca-Cola, Glencore and Burger King. It is also the headquarters of 17 subsidiaries of the German multinational Siemens. Out of this list of companies, 3,400 are letterbox companies, with no activity and no employees (Robinson, 2013. Op. cit., pp. 151ff).

These territories live off banking secrecy, the opacity of the operations carried out within their borders. This is their distinctive factor in the global economy: to become champions of global fiscal selfishness. Tax havens drain a large part of the financial resources of the world's states insofar as they propitiate changes of residence of high-income natural and legal persons in exchange for security, opacity and low taxation. With the help of investment banks or subsidiaries of commercial banks, famous opera singers, sport stars, bankers and executives of multinationals change their residence to tax havens or open accounts there to dodge taxation in their own countries, without actually living there.[68] Apple, Amazon, Google and the Irish group U2 are just some of the names to have undergone widespread public exposure for their indecent use of tax evasion. According to the Tax Justice Network, an independent organization that combats financial opacity and tax havens, the volume of capital estimated to be held in tax havens ranges from $21 to $32 trillion.[69]

Furthermore, these countries play a fundamental role in what is known as the *criminal economy*: money made from trafficking in arms, drugs and humans, together with resources of dictators (Gaddafi, Mubarak, Ben Ali and others) and corrupt officials from all over the world, mingle with others of lawful origin and are reinjected into the global financial system through a variety of investment funds, shareholdings in large corporations and even philanthropic or charitable causes. This is nothing that hasn't existed throughout history, although now it is increasingly channelled through these territories that act as the sewers of the global financial system, veritable specialists in planetary-scale regulatory and tax dumping techniques.[70]

---

68   In the open world of the Internet, it is starting to be common to find lists compiled by informers or whistle-blowers who, when still in their job in one of the major banks who operate in tax havens or after having left it, publish a list of tax evaders and sent it to the media. The fleeting presence of this information in the press or its disappearance should be read in the light of the relations between the media and big business, as mentioned earlier. By way of example, see the so-called Falciani list, which has enabled the Spanish treasury to recover €260 million from more than 600 tax dodgers, including the president of Banco Santander. Carvajal D. & R. Minder (2013). "A whistle-blower who can name names of Swiss bank account holders." *The New York Times*. 6 August 2013.

69   Tax Justice Network (2010): www.taxjustice.net/cms/front_content. php?idcat=148.

70   What percentage of these funds originates from illegal activities is a matter that, for want of information, can only give rise to conjecture. One item of

With the aim of seeking shelter from the supposed fiscal greed of states (this being the *rationale* of tax avoidance), 60% of hedge funds are based in a tax haven. In addition, 80% of the trading of derivative financial products takes place in these countries. The social problem arises when the individual rationale is established at the expense of the collective rationale and we observe the magnitude of the fiscal erosion caused by the competitive strategy of imitating tax haven behaviour in order to attract the world's big capital. This is the famous **race to the bottom**, which causes worldwide competition among countries to achieve lower taxation, secrecy for business and security for capital. Furthermore, its influence is not restricted to the smaller, more marginal territories on the world stage. Countries such as the UK, with the strong financial interests of its powerful City, the Netherlands, Cyprus and Ireland are still gambling heavily on this race to lay down the red carpet for the world's great fortunes.[71]

Let's take a look at the impact this has. If the average corporate income tax rate for the countries considered to be the richest in the world (OECD member states) was 50% in 1950, by 2011 it had shrunk to half this figure: 25%.[72] If after the Second World War the marginal tax rates applied to the highest income bracket topped 90%, the average for this same bracket today stands at around 20%. What has happened? Part of this income has shifted from the channel of individual remuneration (income tax) to that of capital gains (capital gains tax).[73] Firms have been set up to handle part of this income at a lower tax rate, and fiscal engineering has paved the way for capital flight to tax havens and offshore zones. Once again, here we need to recall the turn that the world economy took in the 1970s: the scrapping of Keynesianism as

information that may be revealing is that according to the Swiss consulting firm Helvea, in 2009, 31% of German assets in Swiss bank accounts were declared to the authorities of their country, as opposed to 1% of Italian and Greek assets and 3% of Spanish assets. Robinson A. (2013). Op. cit., p. 178.

71   Where do the Europeans keep their money? This was the question asked by a Boston Consulting Group report in 2013. The results showed that, of the €2.5 trillion quantified, €981 billion were in Luxembourg, €775 billion in Switzerland, and €533 billion in the UK. Behind these came the Caribbean and Panama with €106 billion, the USA with €88 billion, and Hong Kong and Singapore with €73 billion. Heredia S. (2013). "Suïssa, darrere el nom perdut". *La Vanguardia Diners*. 13 October 2013.

72   Robinson A. (2013). Op. cit., p. 159.

73   In the USA in 1992, the 400 richest Americans declared 26% of their income as salary and 36% as capital gains. Now they declare 6% and 66% respectively. Robinson A. (2013). Op. cit., p. 175.

the economic orthodoxy and the erosion of the legitimacy of the role of the state in the economy.

Robinson explains how the fiscal erosion of a multinational such as Burger King, belonging to two private equity funds, works in a territory such as Spain. The multinational's core idea is to externalize the costs of their products and increase the net margin as much as possible. According to the prevailing tax rate, the multinational should pay 25% of its profits as tax. On its operating margin, the subsidiary in Zug charges 5% of the turnover as a fee for the use of intellectual property rights and another 5% for advertising. It pays practically no tax. The outcome is that its products are cheaper than those of a Madrid tapas bar, which is unable to make use of the profit shifting (transfer pricing) techniques employed by this major multinational. Using identical techniques, after ten years operating in the UK, the multinational Starbucks has achieved the record of making no profits and therefore paying no tax. Apple makes no money in Spain, despite the fact that its star product, the iPhone, has an enviable sales margin of 50%.[74]

Tax havens and offshore territories therefore have a very important impact. They push the tax burden down, weaken the financial structure of the welfare state, give shelter to capital of dubious or illicit origin and encourage the deregulation of the financial system. In a country with a serious fiscal crisis such as Spain, in the immediate postcrisis period, while revenue from tax was plummeting, 80% of stock exchange listed companies acknowledge that they had a direct presence in tax havens through stakes in investee companies.[75] This lack of solidarity of large corporations penalizes small and medium-sized enterprises and wage earners, who not only are unable to escape the tax burden but furthermore find that the tax burden they have to bear increases to compensate the drain on resources resulting from tax avoidance.[76] This strangles consumption (60% of the GDP in developed countries), increases the public deficit, raises the financial costs

---

74   Robinson A. (2013). Op. cit. Chapter 7.

75   In Spain, revenue from corporate tax plummeted by 55% between 2007 and 2009, although the business profits of large corporations in the same period had fallen by only 14%. Moreover, whereas the nominal rate of corporate tax is 30% for big business, exemptions and deductions mean that in practice the effective rate on average is no higher than 10% on profits. See "El 80% de las empresas del Ibex está presente en paraísos fiscales." *El País.* 11 February 2011.

76   It is ironic that the government of the Swiss Confederation has forced the canton of Zug to contribute to interregional solidarity because of its unfair competition with the rest of the Swiss cantons, which also suffer the onslaught of Zug's fiscal and deregulatory aggressiveness. Would Switzerland be willing to pay the

of debt payment and weakens growth. From the business perspective, in order to maintain their profits, the large multinationals intensify their profit shifting systems, thus offsetting the lack of consumption. These are the same corporations that, in forums such as Davos, sing the praises of having a balanced public budget.

To sum up, the range of agents we have seen above (hedge funds, sovereign wealth funds, rating agencies and tax havens) have contributed decisively to the radical transformation of the economic system and have conditioned society's approach to globalization. We will close this chapter with a summary of their effects:

- Strengthening of the financial economy, to the detriment of the real economy.

- Increase in financial speculation and operations that seek income without contributing in any way to the generation of global wealth.

- Increase in global financial opacity and systemic risk as a result of deregulation, giving rise to the deepening of global financial crises.

- Increase in the vulnerability of public budgets due to the growth in public debt, with the consequent weakening of social protection systems.

- Increase in the procyclical tendency of countries' economies, which are flooded with capital in boom periods and kept apart from the financial system in bust periods.

- Diminishing of the capacity of the state to control the economy and the funding of its debt.

- Rising inequality, a fundamental characteristic of financialization,[77] and weakening of global demand, paving the way for future crises due to lack of growth.

We cannot finish this chapter without mentioning the negative image of the financial sector as a whole. This loss of reputation is attributable above

---

same solidarity toll to the rest of the world's countries? It seems unlikely. See Robinson A. (2013). Op. cit., p. 174.

77 None other than egalitarian Calvinist Switzerland, a clear beneficiary of tax avoidance movements, has evolved from an income pyramid of 30:1 between the richest and the poorest to one of 916:1 in only ten years. Robinson A. (2013). Op. cit., p. 185.

all to the growing doubts that have arisen around the true contribution that financial activities make to society, a contribution that is becoming more and more difficult to justify. If the financial sector is supposed to manage risk, allocate capital, run the payments mechanism, and all at a low cost,[78] the inordinate rise in purely speculative activities and its direct facilitation of capital flight cast doubt on the above-mentioned patterns of behaviour. This amounts to a reversal of the expectations that society has traditionally had of the activities of the financial sector, and gives rise to all-time records in mistrust towards the sector's institutions as a whole.[79]

78   Stiglitz J. (2010). "The non-existent hand." *London Review of Books*, 32 (8). 22 April 2010, pp. 17-18.

79   The financial sector is given the lowest level of trust of any sector, worldwide. See Edelman (2013). Trust Barometer. www.edelman.com/insights/intellectual-property/trust-2013/trust-across-sectors/trust-in-financial-services/.

5
Contemporary corporate culture

The array of socioeconomic changes we have described up to now cannot be disengaged from other equally profound changes that have altered the way companies—here we are talking above all about large corporations—see themselves and explain their function in the framework of globalization. These changes affect the more practical side of business management, but also its ideology and theoretical foundations, as expounded in universities and business schools. As we will see below, these elements are closely linked to the reproduction and development of the neoliberal tide we discussed earlier, which has made inroads as the majority current within globalization, despite the ideological and circumstantial hurdles—among them the present crisis—that stand in its way.

In this chapter, we will attempt to grasp the systemic impact—i.e., the impact on the world about us—of today's corporate culture. We will strive to comprehend the social and economic consequences of business management *as it reaches us*, and as it is reproduced by the media and academia. We will end by proposing to advance towards an understanding of the alternatives that management science itself has generated in recent years in order to incorporate social expectations into the way companies are run through the corporate social responsibility (CSR) movement, and we will explore its shortcomings.

5.1 The rise of functionalism in management science

One of the inevitable consequences of processes of opening up and liberalization of markets has undoubtedly been to reinforce the role of the major corporations in the global economy. The opening up of new markets, the regulatory "race to the bottom" that states have engaged in to attract capital and enterprises, and above all the rise of offshore territories—deregulated territories that compete as such in the economic specialization of each part of the world and in the attraction of the great flows of world capital—have propitiated what J.K. Galbraith called **corporate gigantism**:[1] the deployment of corporate giants under the imperative of perpetual growth.

An image will help us to visualize this trend. By comparing the GDP of states with the revenue of large corporations we can gain a graphic insight into the loss of power of the former to the benefit of the latter. Thus, taking only US large corporations, and using data for 2010, we find the following: Nike, with revenue of $19.6 billion, concentrates more wealth than Paraguay. The revenue of Amazon, with $34.2 billion, is bigger than the GDP of Kenya. Apple, with $65.23 billion, is bigger than Ecuador. Bank of America, with $103.57, is bigger than Vietnam. And at the top of the list sits the giant Walmart, which with revenue of $414.46 billion beats the GDP of Norway, the owner of one of the largest sovereign wealth funds in the world.[2]

If we now look at this process of concentration of wealth in a handful of oversized decision-making units from the perspective of the actual ability to choose the products we consume, we find that the much praised maximization of effective consumer choice—one of the cornerstones of liberal thought and the consumerism upheld, for example, by neoliberalism—is more fiction that fact. Despite the apparent plurality of products we can find in a supermarket in the US, the bulk of what we consume is reduced to products owned by very few brands, mainly Unilever, Coca-Cola, PepsiCo, Nestlé, Kraft and Johnson & Johnson.

What in department stores is seen as variety (Lipton, Toblerone, Pizza Hut, Nesquik, Tampax, Ralph Lauren, Lacoste, Nespresso, Perrier, Tang, etc.) in the accounting ledgers all boils down to ten huge multiproduct

---

[1]   Galbraith J.K. (2004). *The Economics of Innocent Fraud: Truth for Our Time*, Houghton Mifflin. Chapter 6: "The Corporate Power".

[2]   The comparison we have made here is not devoid of academic discussion. Are GDP and revenue really comparable, or should we use the variable *profits* instead? For the purposes that concern us here, namely to observe the increase in size—and therefore power—of the large corporations, we take the comparison as valid. The figures we quote are taken from the Fortune 500 ranking and the International Monetary Fund. See: Trivett V. (2011). "25 US mega corporations: where they rank if they were countries", *Business Insider*, 27 June 2011. www.businessinsider.com/25-corporations-bigger-tan-countries-2011-6?op=1.

conglomerates.[3] We are surrounded by an apparent plurality that in the reality of financial reports is far poorer than meets the eye. However, what we are interested in here is to understand this new and pre-eminent role of the large corporations not in the realm of market dynamics but specifically in that of the changes that have occurred in the world of management in recent decades and that have come to justify the upsetting of the status quo to the benefit of big business. We contextualized these changes in the previous chapter, when discussing the financialization of the economy and management. Thus, it is important to bear this phenomenon in mind.

Over the last century, the landscape of large corporations has been altered by a fundamental transformation: the appearance of the professional executive. This new figure, increasingly removed from the figure of the owner or shareholder, has led to the formation of theories on his function, the construction of a set of tools for the deployment of the tasks that this executive will be required to perform and, above all, the establishment of an evaluative framework—i.e., a pattern of behaviour—making it possible to anticipate his actions, to render them foreseeable and especially to link them closely to the needs of the market: shareholders, governments, financial institutions and others.

We are talking about the birth of the *ideology* of management science. It is an ideology in the full sense of the word,[4] and with the passing of time it has come to hinge around:

- An academic doctrine, which emanates principally from business schools, especially American ones

- Market pressures, the demand coming from the corporations themselves

- The indispensable role played by the media and consultancy firms, always on the lookout for the *latest* management recipe to

---

3   For the complete list, see Lutz A. (2012). "These 10 corporations control almost everything you buy", *Business Insider*, 25 April 2012. www.businessinsider.com/these-10-corporations-control-almost-everything-you-buy-2012-4.

4   As we saw earlier, these ideas and beliefs are widely shared and accepted as true by significant groups of people in a society. They are *functional* beliefs, offering a pattern to explain the world, helping to organize the information that reaches us and converting the complexity of the environment into patterns or constellations of facts that are easy to interpret. They are also *proselytizing* beliefs, insofar as they seek acolytes, followers, and attempt to impregnate society with their norms and values. See the first chapter again.

help companies reduce their anxiety, or at least their feeling of uncertainty[5]

The omnipresence of large corporations on a day-to-day basis and their awesome financial muscle have caused these management principles to spread to other spheres hitherto removed from private enterprise, such as public education, healthcare and administration. The core idea behind the extension of this model of good organizational governance into areas far removed from business management in the strict sense is to sell a management model that is *successful* and recognized as such. The starting point would be: what has worked for big business—a set of models, tools and patterns of behaviour—can and *must* work for other types of organization. No matter that many of them are not intended to make a profit, or to maximize utility. We are witnessing an increasingly successful attempt to rationalize decision-making and to generate a vocabulary to transfer values of management science—i.e., the values of business and the globalized economy—to other managerial spheres. Thus, the 20th century could be read as the century of the deployment of this *professional* management model towards areas other than those of private enterprise, the original source of management science as a discipline.

As we observe this shift towards *professional* management, we need to highlight an element that is linked to the functionality of this discipline: management must serve the interests of capital, of the shareholder. In the social acceptance of this pattern of management that we call *professional*, we have generated, on the one hand, a code of conduct and a theoretical corpus to justify the social pre-eminence of this new ruling class. On the other hand, however, as a group we have failed miserably to construct a code of ethics linking this new profession—that of the professional manager—to an ideal of good practice, inspiring the admiration and respect of society, and linking his behaviour to the contribution his job makes to society.[6] We have generated, then, a manager who is unconcerned about the social impact of his actions and cares only about the needs and wishes of the shareholders.

---

5   See Abrahamson E. (1991). "Managerial fads and fashions: The diffusion and rejection of innovations", *Academy of Management Review*, 16: 586-612.

6   This would be the idea set out in Khurana R. (2007). *From Higher Aims to Hired Hands: The Social Transformation of American Business Schools and the Unfulfilled Promise of Management as a Profession.* Princeton, NJ: Princeton University Press.

The numerous corporate scandals—from increasingly unequal pay within companies to the existence of exploitation practices in supply chains, tax avoidance and monopolistic practices—show that the spirit of this *good* management, to quote Khurana, is increasingly removed from the ideal of a profession *at the service of society* that we are used to applying to teachers and doctors. The Hippocratic Oath obliges healthcare professionals to put the patient first; teachers, to value the education of their pupils above all else. Can we apply this disinterested social mission to senior management? Behind this question lies the following conundrum: if this new ruling class does not serve society, or at least it does not serve it as society expects, whom does it serve? The short answer, as we said earlier, is the shareholders, at least in theory. Nevertheless, as many management thinkers hold, and the constant scandals linked to the financial sector demonstrate, in more than one case we could say that they simply serve themselves.

We have to acknowledge, though, that to attribute the actions of these executives to an academic discipline is undoubtedly a risky exercise. However, when we come down from the level of theory to the specific practices advocated by management science, we find conduct that clearly reveals huge mismatches between the manager's function and the expectations society has of his function. If we want to observe the development of management science as a discipline from its origins in the USA at the end of the 19th century—a time of massive inflow of European capital, with the expansion of the railway and the need to find loyal and capable administrators for the new corporations—we have to observe the development of its theoretical corpus to ascertain how it has become transformed into the discipline we know today.

Over past decades we witnessed the transformation of management science into a discipline that was increasingly linked to practice; an activity that above all had to be attentive to the needs of the market and in particular to the dictates of the main users and requesters of its theories: once again, big business. This management science was indeed linked to a professional activity, but at a scientific level it had yet to justify and legitimize its weak academic status. The questions that concerned the academics of this branch of knowledge were along the lines of: is this a serious discipline? A scientific one? Progressively implanted into universities, in the shape of faculties and schools with growing acceptance in the economic world, it was forced to compete in the sphere of public recognition with other disciplines considered *scientific*—and therefore with predictive capabilities—such as physics, mathematics and medicine, as well as other humanistic and social disciplines. What was the place, the academic status, of this new discipline linked to business management?

In the autonomous and relatively isolated world of the university, the thirst for academic knowledge took the form of a struggle for social status among management-linked academics and professionals. Bestowing prestige on the discipline meant bestowing prestige on those who worked within it: academics and professionals. In the academic sphere, the main strategy of this struggle for recognition, with the impetus of a powerful and ever larger market of new management professionals, was to mimic another up-and-coming social discipline, economics, in an attempt to get some of its level of acceptance and recognition to rub off. Thus it incorporated from economics the preference for the abstraction of its underlying assumptions—the functioning of the market and the individual—and the use of mathematics as a method for calculation and abstraction. But also, fatally, its lack of modesty in the face of somewhat scanty predictive capabilities of the discipline in question.[7]

From economics, and especially from the neoclassical economics developed as of the 1970s (as seen in previous chapters), management science inherited substantial theoretical components and a particular social perception, which we will analyse presently. In short, management science was to merge with the dominant ideology in order to respond *functionally* to what was expected of it: to provide management tools, guidelines and codes of conduct that would not clash or strike a discordant note with the requirements of the market. Amid this theoretical legacy, with a considerable social spin attached, we find elements that are closely associated with the habitual behaviour of the large corporations referred to above and the neoliberal ideology we discussed at the beginning of these pages. Among these elements, we can highlight the following:

- Smith's notion of **the invisible hand of the market**, whereby supply and demand, wisely guided by selfishness, are unconsciously

---

7   The interminable dispute about the scientific status of economics forms part of this debate. Is economics a science? What sort of science is it if its predictive capabilities are so limited? The debate can thus be extended to management science. For the case of economics, see the position taken by one of the latest Nobel economics prize-winners: Shiller R. (2013). "Is economics a science?" *The Guardian*, 6 November 2013, www.theguardian.com/business/economics-blog/2013/nov/06/is-economics-a-science-robert-shiller.

designed to serve the utilitarian ideal of generating "the maximum good for the maximum number of people."[8]

- The perception of the individual—in marketing, finance and economics—as belonging to the species *Homo economicus*, according to which our actions in society are determined by a supposed set of behavioural characteristics, namely materialism, individualism, perfect rationality, access (in theory) to all available information, the maximization of our personal preferences through the market, and the general confusion of the variables *value* and *price* of a good.[9]

- The **shareholder value theory**, according to which the main objective of a manager should be to maximize the value of the stock in the market.

- The **efficient market theory**, according to which markets—consisting of a supply and a demand—always stand at an equilibrium price at

8   An economic notion that, surprisingly, originated in cultural and religious elements that can be traced considerably further back: the Protestant Reformation of the 16th century. "By privatizing, deregulating, and decentralizing religion, Luther prepared the way for what would eventually become the modern notion of the market. Educated in the Calvinist atmosphere of Scotland, Adam Smith translates Calvin's notion of divine providence and the fortunate fall into the notion of the invisible hand and machinations of the market through which pursuit of personal ends serve the good of the whole." Taylor M. (2013). "Madness of choice", *Capitalism and Society*, 8(2), article 3. Furthermore, there has been a neoliberal appropriation of Adam Smith himself, a thesis I have defended in Murillo D. (2007). "Rescatar la ética económica de Adam Smith". A: Alcoberro, R. (co-ord.): Ética, economía y empresa. Barcelona: Gedisa, 2007: 29-44.

9   In opposition to this narrow vision of individuals' behaviour, a whole field has developed and is currently on the rise within economics: behavioural economics, the above-mentioned Shiller being one of its clearest exponents. Seminal works in this field include those of social scientists Shiller, Tversky, Kahneman, Thaler and Sunstein. In any event, this de-substantivization of the individual, reduced to a set of primary behavioural attributes thanks to the Chicago school of economics, with Milton Friedman and Gary Becker at the helm, clashes with the enlightened vision that other economists have had, not only of the individual as an economic player but also of the economy as a whole. An example of this is Keynes's definition of his discipline, when he stated that "no part of man's nature or his institutions must lie entirely outside his regard." Keynes J.M. [1933] (1972). *Collected Works*, vol. X: *Essays in Biography*, pp. 173-4.

which the market empties, i.e., supply matches demand. Its corollary for financial markets holds that the free movement of capitals world-wide would optimize the placement of surplus savings efficiently.[10]

- **Agency theory**, according to which the selfish nature of economic players (see above) forces us to treat managers (also known as *agents*) and shareholders (also known as *principals*) as separate parts of an organization. These two parties have opposing interests (each seeks to get rich at the expense of the other) and therefore it will be necessary to establish a model for the relationship, an explicit *contract*, linking the interests of one party (to maximize the value of the stock) to those of the other (to maximize their compensation). This is achieved by means of a system of incentives (performance-based bonuses, stock options, etc.) and controls (establishment of a mechanism for supervising their functions, diversity in the com-position of the board of directors, etc.).

- The last contribution of economic utilitarianism to business man-agement was to establish a de facto code of ethics for managers whereby their only social responsibility is to help to **maximize shareholder value**.[11]

Thus, the weight of the ideological, economic and social context that came with globalization also made an imprint on the world of business management. The influence of the Chicago school, which as of the 1970s left a clearly visible mark on the economic sphere, was also to make its pres-ence felt in the way companies are managed. This new ideology of man-agement, made in the image of neoliberalism, was developed in opposition to other alternative ideologies, which we have defined above. If neolib-eralism takes the primacy of the market as its source of social order, and management science basically follows in its wake, the alter-globalization movement holds precisely the opposite and places the emphasis of its pro-posal on correcting the perverse mechanisms associated with globalization. This correction is based on the alleged power of the state to act in order to control the economy. Thus, from the alter-globalization perspective, the

---

10   A statement that, in view of the previous chapter, we would do well to put into quarantine.

11   Maximization *within* the law. See Friedman M. (1970). "The Social Responsi-bility of Business Is to Increase Its Profits". In: Hoffman W.M., Frederick R.E. & Schwartz M.S. (ed.) (2001). *Business Ethics—Readings and Cases in Corporate Morality*. McGraw-Hill, pp. 156-60.

state should become an impediment and a lightning rod against corporate wrongdoings.[12]

As of the 1970s we find big business increasingly locked within itself, its objectives and its interests, alongside a state progressively weakened in its regulatory and corrective capacity. This spelt a transformation in the management sphere that Mintzberg[13] describes as the rise of lean (tending towards the outsourcing of superfluous services) and mean (socially autistic) organizations: large corporations that are increasingly identified as huge bureaucratic networks that seek rents and profits and externalize the costs.

Nevertheless, management science today is undoubtedly a great deal more than the set of theories and approaches we have set out above. Marketing contains elements of social psychology; corporate finance has developed a growing tendency to borrow theories and models from the behavioural sciences and sociology; business economics also draws on heterodox readings of economic theory, the influence of neo-Keynesian and institutionalist currents. However, we cannot help but notice the undercurrent: the *functional*, submissive contribution made by management science to the balance of forces and power that exists in our societies. It is a management science that does not aspire to transform its environment or encourage a profound debate on its social meaning, its contribution to the common good.[14]

5.2 The management function and big business

What social impact does business management have *as it stands*? Inevitably, it leads to the devaluation of the social contract established between society and big business. The notion of the social contract, imagined by

---

12   However, this approach rests on a doubt: can states and institutions really regulate the economy? On the basis of Galbraith J.K. (2004), op. cit., the answer would be yes. As we will see presently, especially in the light of the recent crises, the answer would be no.

13   Mintzberg H., Simons R. & Basu K. (2002). Beyond Selfishness, *MIT Sloan Management Review*, 44 (1): 66-74.

14   As Bourdieu put it, the most successful ideological effects are those which have no need of words, and ask no more than complicitous silence. Bourdieu P. (1977). *Outline of a Theory of Practice*. Cambridge: Cambridge University Press, p. 188.

Rousseau in the 18th century, involves the establishment of an implicit agreement between society and agent whereby the legitimacy of the agents' actions guarantees their right to operate. Neoliberal globalization is starting to fracture this social agreement. There is nothing outlandish in the claim that there is a crisis of management models at the beginning of the 21st century. It is simply the outcome of adding up tax erosion, disregard for the social and environmental impact of business activity, and the lack of solidarity shown by large corporations towards the communities in which they operate. They pay less tax, they accumulate sanctions for malpractice, they outsource activities to regions with low regulatory pressure, they intensify the insecurity of jobs considered replaceable, and they step up lobbying and regulator-capturing activities. We observe this breaking of the social contract in a particularly graphic way in the widening gap between the salaries of senior management and those of the rest of the workforce.[15]

At this point we should stress that this is a disease that basically affects big business. Let's take a look at how economic power is distributed among companies in terms of their size, using data provided by the Statistical Office of the European Union. Large-sized enterprises account for only 0.2% of all enterprises in the EU. They concentrate a third of the employed population (according to data for 2008 for the nonfinancial sector) and 41.4% of overall added value. With data from the report published in 2003, we see that 41.9% of income is concentrated in these large enterprises. Turning our attention to their slice of the profit cake, this figure can easily exceed 75% of all private-sector profits.[16] By way of example, in South Korea the 20 largest business groups amass assets equivalent to 85.2% of the country's GDP, and the assets of the top five groups equal 55.7% of the South Korean GDP.[17] It seems fairly clear, then, that when we talk of economic power we are basically talking about large corporations.

---

15   Are they really justified? What do they reflect? Merit, productivity differentials, strategic importance for the company, or the ability to impose them within the organization? For further reading on this debate see Robinson A. Op. cit., p. 87.

16   EU (2011). *Key Figures on European Business with a Special Feature on SMEs.* Luxembourg: Eurostat Pocket Books. See http://epp.eurostat.ec.europa.eu/cache/ITY_OFFPUB/KS-ET-11-001/EN/KS-ET-11-001-EN.PDF.

17   Data taken from the statistical office of the South Korean government, published by Murillo D. & Sung Y. (2013). *Understanding Korean Capitalism: Chaebols and their Corporate Governance.* ESADEgeo Position Paper, No. 33. http://itemsweb.esade.edu/research/esadegeo/201309Chaebols_Murillo_Sung_EN.pdf.

But let's get back to their executives. As we were saying, management science today has inherited the illnesses we observed earlier. It has inherited instrumental rationality and the construction of a management model based on a series of theories, axioms and premises unrelated to the social and collective impact of their actions. It has also inherited a self-perception as a *scientific*, hard, *amoral* (i.e., morally neutral) discipline: it presents itself as innocuous from the perspective of values. It is a management science affected by an amnesia that prevents it from seeing the twists and turns of its own theories over more than a century of operation: the changing patterns and models as regards how an organization should be managed and the recipes to apply to it. Thus we have moved on from management for engineers (the Ford Model T production line) to management for humanists (the motivation theories of the 1950s and 1960s), *applied* management, and management oriented towards solving specific problems. It is a *scientific* management, progressively linked to the use of complicated risk management formulas, the cult of financial innovation that arrived with financialization, and the use of a lavish mathematical paraphernalia that nevertheless has done nothing to prevent colossal financial debacles and if anything has actually brought them on.

The rise of functionalism in business management has tended to generate social autism, lack of concern about the noneconomic impact of management, and also the sort of executive who is simplistic and simplifying, obsessed with reducing the complexity of management by applying predetermined management recipes and models. This is an uncritical, robotized, instrumental, utilitarian, pragmatic and positivistic executive. Management science, insofar as it has been financialized through the ascent of financial profiles to senior management positions, has been contaminated by economism: it is dazzled by the beauty of mathematical models (aesthetically perfect, in the ideal context of spreadsheets) and distanced from the real world and its origins as a humble social science, with excessively limited predictive capabilities.

This is a management science that rigs management models on the basis of often weak empirical evidence (is the firm with the highest market value really the most solid?), founded on absurd theories of rationality and the behaviour of individuals. Executives are not necessarily any wiser, have no better judgement and no more common sense than the rest of humanity. Their attributes are too intertwined with their personal skills, and as such are difficult to pass on, to the extent that they could prove an obstacle to the achievement of the objective of maximizing corporate profit. Over the years, these attributes have been replaced by the cold mechanical repetition of the models currently in vogue. Is this the way forward for the discipline? Many management thinkers say no.

And, of course, inasmuch as management science is an instrumental discipline, created *at the service* of the market, the failures of the system (market failures: negative externalities, financial crises and so on) inevitably also become failures of management science. In other words, the crisis of global capitalism is also its own crisis, just as the successes of the system and the company (in terms of revenue, profit or market position) also become successes for executives and management science.

Soon, however, a problem pops up that we have talked about before: that of the *performativity of social sciences*. In a social context, the world we preach is the world we make. Therefore, if management science can be seen as a normative discipline—a discipline that offers guidelines for good and bad management—and moreover we know about its performative effects on the world around it, Ghoshal's question becomes extremely relevant: what sort of world does management science *as it now stands* help to build?[18]

Ghoshal himself answers his question: a world tailored to the selfish and socially autistic individuals who the discipline describes in the *Homo economicus* model. An executive reduced to the stereotype of Gordon Gekko, in Oliver Stone's film *Wall Street*, who was guided by a single moral maxim: "Greed is good." Of course, there is no mention of who exactly it is good for. Certainly not for society, and very probably in many cases—recall Enron, or the whole financial sector that collapsed at the end of 2008—not for the firms themselves either.

The forgetfulness of management science is most improper for an academic discipline that likes to see itself as scientific. The fall from grace of those who were once considered management models—Enron in the late 1990s and Lehman Brothers until the 2008 crisis broke out—does not cause the discipline to make any full-blown challenge of the theoretical models behind the choice of these examples. Still less to question the model of success we defend under the heading "good managers".

18   Ghoshal S. (2005). "Bad management theories are destroying good management practices", *Academy of Management Learning & Education*, 4(1): 75-91. Ghoshal quotes Keynes to highlight the enormous influence of ideas and ideologies in the real world: "The ideas of economists and political philosophers, both when they are right and when they are wrong, are more powerful than is commonly understood: Indeed the world is run by little else." Keynes J.M. (1936). *The General Theory of Employment, Interest and Money*. London: Macmillan, p. 383.

The demise of firms and executives merely involves their replacement with other examples of good management, which in turn will receive the favour and attention of the discipline only as long as they are capable of continuing to dazzle us with their performance. The profit and loss account, market value, the slice of the pie obtained, and the applause or rejection generated in the business community at any given moment are all determining factors in the choice and potential replacement of management *models*,[19] which are suitably examined in the classroom with the educational label of *case studies*. The instrumental nature of management science must be understood in the limited time-frame of what is considered as the rise and fall of an executive or a firm. That which is seen as a model—"after all, the results confirm it"—will cease to be so when it stops coming up with the goods.

Let's take an example of this. In 2006, Richard Fuld, CEO of Lehman Brothers, was named top chief executive in the "Brokers and Asset Managers" category by the magazine *Institutional Investor*. In 2007 he received a $22 million bonus. On 15 September 2008, one of the most dramatic days in world financial history, Lehman Brothers filed for bankruptcy and headed for liquidation on finding no buyer. In management school classrooms, a firm and an executive until then regarded as exemplary became what society had already taken the lead in reclassifying: symbols of the excess and malpractice that led to the current crisis.

So now we discuss the suitability of Lehman Brothers's risk management systems, the harmful effects of excessive leverage, the abusive use of the complex algorithms concealed behind the new financial derivatives, and the implications for business conduct of the type of contract between the executive and the firm. We also talk about regulatory failures. However, the theoretical models that have proved to be inaccurate or even counterproductive remain in force. In the mid- and long term, the only change we can see is the replacement of Lehman Brothers with another new benchmark company, for a new case study and a new model of good management. The theory is patched up and tweaked, misuses and misunderstandings are pinpointed, but it is not replaced. Instrumental management science is in debt to the market, the consumers of models, and they continue to claim the same as they used to, but with updated models.

---

19   Definition of *model*: "A standard or example for imitation or comparison." Webster's Encyclopedic Unabridged Dictionary of the English Language.

Khurana talks of the fall of "managerialism", the end of the unfulfilled dream of turning management into a profession. He holds that the traditional management function has been replaced with the ideology of shareholder primacy, and this has brought the erosion of managers' authority, converting them into mere mechanisms to achieve that end. Parallel to this, the growing popularity of quantitative methods to measure managers' performance has deprived them of their ability to bring into play their subjectivity, their values, and to contribute to the common good, aside from corporate objectives. According to Khurana, the most obvious symptom of the deterioration of the executive's reputation is the increase in external signs of success—pay, bonuses, expense accounts, private jets—as a measure of the quality of the executive in question. This goes hand in hand with contempt and belittlement of other intangible forms of reward—free time, social recognition, scope for personal fulfilment, greater freedom in the performance of one's duties, etc.—and the inability to encourage, within the company, alternative theories of the management function that are not based on the selfishness and unfettered materialism of its executives.[20]

The depersonalization of the management function, the reduction of the manager's job to overseeing a limited list of KPI indicators[21] and the gradual restriction of his freedom of action, in a bureaucratized and proceduralized working environment, have helped to delegitimize his function and promote one single way of understanding how large corporations should operate in these globalization times. In short, we are witnessing the homogenization of management science, which in turn has brought about the homogenization of executive profiles.[22]

---

20   One alternative would be stewardship theory, whereby wise recruitment for senior management posts and an appropriate system of remuneration, without excesses, in keeping with the individual's expectations and real motivations, can lead the executive to behave, in the performance of his or her functions, as a *responsible custodian* of the stockholder's assets. See Block P. (2013). *Stewardship: Choosing Service over Self-Interest*. Berrett-Koehler Publishers.

21   Key performance indicators. Depending on the model concerned, the number would range from 40 to 80.

22   This trend has been exacerbated—and it should be recognized—by the establishment of regulatory frameworks, often fostered by stock market supervisory bodies such as the American SEC and the Spanish CNMV, which restrict managerial action to a particular pigeonhole of conducts and functions to be performed. Paradoxically, the law and monitoring mechanisms have greatly reduced the scope for differentiation in managers' behaviour.

The dystopia presented by Bakan in his book *The Corporation*[23] becomes a considerably more pervasive reality than we would like. The economic system that is developed with globalization entails the growth of corporations with a well-defined pathology. They are corporations unconcerned with other people's feelings, with a severe incapacity to maintain lasting relationships and a dangerous indifference to the safety of others. They do not hesitate to use falsehood for their own benefit, they are incapable of experiencing guilt, and they fail when it comes to living up to social standards or respecting the law. Bakan concludes that too many large global corporations display behaviour that points towards what the World Health Organization (WHO) would call a psychopathic personality. What responsibility does management science have in the reproduction of this model? If we observe its instrumental nature we will see that it must have at least some.

In order to get back to the path of the responsible global corporation and the professional corporate management to which Khurana refers, it will therefore be necessary to recover the *social* sense of the business and management function; social expectations, which point towards a different management model. This raises many questions about management science as a discipline. What management model does it encourage? What business model does it help to create? What idea does it put forward for the individual and the educated manager? What social model does it advocate? What model of excellence and professional success does it reinforce? In short: what use is management science *in its present form* for society and business?[24]

5.3 Towards a new corporate culture

5.3.1 Here comes trouble

The process undergone by large corporations of opening up to globalization has inevitably served to highlight many of the shortcomings of today's

---

23 Bakan J. (2004). *The Corporation: The Pathological Pursuit of Power*. New York: The Free Press.
24 I have borrowed this set of questions from the research conducted by Josep Maria Lozano (2012), presented internally in the Department of Social Sciences at ESADE. The section that follows is based on the work of other professors of the department, notably including that of Daniel Arenas, Josep Miralles, Pep Mària and Marc Vilanova.

instrumental and acritical management science and pinpoint its limitations. Let's take a look at some examples.

In the 1970s the Swiss firm Nestlé, the largest multinational in the agri-
food sector, decided to extend the distribution of powdered milk to developing countries. A *functionally* correct action—the extension of products
to markets where they have little presence—was not accompanied by a
minimum of understanding of the real situation in many of these countries, where drinking water is a scarce commodity yet breast milk is a safe
and healthy food for babies, with the result that Nestlé became one of the
most boycotted companies in the world from 1977 on. Its expansion not
only caused suffering and unnecessary deaths; it also became a milestone
of the shortcomings of bad management and the moral limits of aggressive
marketing.[25]

In 1984 it was the turn of the US multinational Union Carbide. A leak at
a chemical pesticides plant the company owned in Bhopal, India, caused
500,000 people to be exposed to toxic gas. The official death count immediately after the disaster exceeded 2,000, although other sources, including
the Government of Madhya Pradesh, doubled this figure. The company's
CEO fled to the US. Compensation to the families and victims had hardly
reached $100 million by the time the company was purchased by Dow
Chemical in 2001. New issues were raised within management science
regarding efficient risk management and the implications of industrial
activity for public health and the environment. The very notion of limited
liability became a problem that was manifested in all its starkness in the
victims of the disaster.[26]

In 1993 a new case concerning public health in the US reached the media:
the court ruling against the firm Brown & Williamson for price fixing in the
tobacco industry. A year later, the state of Minnesota submitted a lawsuit
against the tobacco industry. In the trial it was revealed that for decades the

---

25   To understand the issue and the consequences of the boycott, see Save the
     Children (2007). "A generation on: Baby milk marketing still putting chil-
     dren's lives at risk": www.savethechildren.org.uk/resources/online-library/a-
     generation-on-baby-milk-marketing-still-putting-childrens-lives-at-risk; The
     Guardian (2005). "Branded": http://blogs.theguardian.com/businessinsight/
     archives/2005/09/01/branded.html.

26   See Labunska I. *et al.* (1999). *The Bhopal Legacy. Toxic contaminants at the for-
     mer Union Carbide factory site, Bhopal, India: 15 years after the Bhopal acci-
     dent.* Greenpeace: https://webdrive.service.emory.edu/users/vdhara/www.
     BhopalPublications/Environmental%20Health/Greenpeace%20Bhopal%20
     Report.pdf.

producers had manipulated the percentage of nicotine in the tobacco, fully aware of the addictive nature of this drug.[27] Once again, everything came second place to fulfilling the corporate goals. And public health and respect for fair competition practices guaranteed by the law were no exception.

Let's move on to 1996. The sports multinational Nike was investigated for corporate malpractice in its South-East Asian assembly line, including the use of child labour and working conditions that put the health of its workers at risk. All in all, exploitation practices that in other countries would have been considered inhumane. The company's first reaction was to deny the facts, and subsequently it accused the subcontractors of imposing these conditions on their workers. The turn the case took with public opinion and the boycotting of the brand brought to the fore the different understanding that Nike and society at large had of the ultimate responsibility for the issue. Since then, internal audits and supply chain codes of conduct have succeeded in completely eliminating such practices.[28]

A complete list of business scandals in recent years arising out of the unbridled use of functionalism in the management of the companies involved would be impossibly huge to compile. Functionalism and damage to society, although not always linked to each other, have nevertheless served to expose the limitations of instrumental management science. Thus, the collapse in 2001 of the multinational Enron, one of the most promising, innovative and fast-growing enterprises of the *new* American economy, shed light on a series of extraordinary malfunctions concerning the relationship

---

27   See BBC (2003). "Cigarettes 'engineered' for addiction": http://news.bbc. co.uk/2/hi/393075.stm.

28   How can this be done when these practices fit neatly into the competitive logic of strategy guru Michael Porter, according to which it is essential to limit the negotiating power of customers and suppliers? See Porter M.E. (1980). *Competitive Strategy*. New York: The Free Press. For the Nike case, see the piece by Greenhouse S. (1997). "Nike shoe plant in Vietnam is called unsafe for workers", *The New York Times*, 8 November 1997: www.nytimes.com/1997/11/08/business/nike-shoe-plant-in-vietnam-is-called-unsafe-for-workers.html?pagewanted=all&src=pm. Other similar scandals derived from the working conditions of subcontracting companies in the same part of the world have recently come to involve Apple, with the affair of the mass suicides at Foxconn in China, www.theguardian.com/technology/2012/mar/29/apple-foxconn-audit-labour-violations, and the conglomerate of textile companies, among them Inditex, supplied by the illegal factory in Bangladesh that collapsed causing over 1,000 deaths: http://business-humanrights.org/Documents/Bangladeshbuildingcollapse.

between corporations and auditors, accounting malpractice, market dominance and regulator dominance.[29] Monsanto, the multinational famed for its use of genetically modified seeds and the so-called "transgenics war", has highlighted the dangers of spreading these seeds, the threat that products of this sort represent for the food sovereignty of many countries, and this has been especially important in restoring the old notion of the principle of the responsibility that the present inhabitants of the planet have towards future generations.[30]

Environmental disasters involving Shell and BP, accusations of human rights violations by Google in China, lawsuits against Microsoft for market dominance in the European Union, and so on. The image of these large corporations is eroded and this affects their value. An increase in company revenue, when it is accompanied by violations of social expectations, may entail the deterioration of the value of the brand, the opposition of a large number of consumers and the ineffectiveness of a large part of the resources dedicated to advertising, which will be met with the scepticism that the brand awakens in its public.[31] All this, together with the problems we detected earlier on, is the product of neoliberal globalization: the contagion of financial crises, the rise of tax havens, the spreading of inequality, the erosion of the tax base and therefore also of the welfare state. Much of the hostility to globalization is due to the phenomena set out above.

5.3.2 Enterprise and the rediscovery of social expectations

However, management science itself has generated a new field of management which has made it possible to start to address this whole series of changes in the collective perception of the role of big business in our globalized world. The process of technological globalization and market expansion, the dissemination of brands and designs and their omnipresence in the media have also exposed the enterprise to new dangers and threats that come from the social front.

29 See the Santa Clara University website: www.scu.edu/ethics/publications/ ethicalperspectives/enronlessons.html.
30 On Monsanto, see Robin M. (2010). *The World According to Monsanto*, New York: The New Press. On the principle of responsibility, once again: Jonas H. & Herr D. (1984). *The Imperative of Responsibility: In Search of Ethics for the Technological Age*, University of Chicago Press.
31 At the very least, loss of social trust makes it more difficult to convince the potential consumer of the virtues of the product or company in question. See the Edelman Trust Barometer (2013). Op. cit.

The spread of information and communication technologies has not only served to strengthen economic globalization and contribute to business growth; it has also made corporations more vulnerable. We are talking about the disclosure of trade secrets, earmarked business practices and sensitive information up to now kept well away from the gaze of citizens and consumers.[32] Social networks, the Internet, blogs and microblogs and initiatives such as WikiLeaks have thrown corporate cultures into confusion and threaten to reveal information until recently considered available only to a handful of well-informed brains. Nowadays we can find information on a particular issue with a speed and in a depth that were unknown only 20 years ago. Of course, having access to more information is not necessarily the same as being better informed. It can also mean the opposite: to be victims of lies or distortion. For the citizen it can also mean the inability to tell between what is true, what is likely, what is rumour and what is propaganda.

In the case of corporations, the trend is towards more transparent, more vulnerable companies with greater exposure to the public eye, in which intangible assets such as brand value, trust, corporate culture and even the workers' sense of belonging to the company can be toppled by an anonymously published item of information. Obviously, the large corporations strive to uphold their own version of the facts. They have three channels to achieve this influence: to advertise in the media; to fund the media by lending them money; or to acquire a shareholding in what they consider to be influential media.[33]

---

32   One extraordinary example of this exposure to public scrutiny is provided by the leaking of lists of alleged tax evaders to the media. See Minder R. (2011). "Top Spanish banker faces inquiry on tax charges", *The New York Times*, 17 June 2011: www.nytimes.com/2011/06/17/business/global/17santander.html.

33   Here we refer to the financialization of the media, which is just another episode of a broader phenomenon that affects the economic system as a whole. As an example of the advertising investment that is necessary to convey the image that the large corporation has of itself, see the budget of Telefónica, the largest company in the communications sector in Spain. It is estimated that, counting both direct and indirect advertising (the latter through investee companies), in 2011 the multinational spent €294 million to this end, considerably more than the €197 million the three largest Spanish newspapers together earned from advertising that same year. Other systems for swaying public opinion that we have already looked at and are used in addition to control of the media are the funding of political parties (whether legally, quasi-legally or illegally), lobbying legislators, and recruiting politicians and senior civil servants as consultants. All these phenomena have already been discussed above. See Reality

This greater transparency entails the need to establish more mechanisms to attract and retain talent, especially in high value-added companies. It also means greater exposure to boycotting, precisely at a time when corporations are increasingly becoming focal points of information, data and other intangible elements. It means asking ourselves what contribution each enterprise makes to the common good and how it is perceived by public and published opinion.

Let's see how Interbrand defines brand value. According to this consultancy, the strength of a brand is due to internal and external factors.[34] Among the internal ones we find variables as hard to pin down, from an accounting point of view, as clarity, commitment, responsiveness and protection. As far as external factors are concerned, the elements are relevance, authenticity, differentiation, consistency, presence and understanding. Quite an array! We can add some figures to this information: in 2013, the brand value of Apple stood at \$98.3 billion. The brand Google had a value of \$93.3 billion. Coca-Cola was worth \$79.2 billion, and the brand alone amounted to 80% of the value of the company.[35]

Impact on the brand can disrupt—for good or for ill—a company's reputation, and therefore also its profit and loss account. This trend towards the world of intangibles—a trend that is to be seen in the light of Castells's thesis of the information society and the financialization of the economy in recent decades—has led enterprises to rethink what elements affect their competitive strategy with a view to incorporating social elements.

For years, business competitiveness[36] has traditionally been defined as the strength of an organization in comparison with that of its competitors.[37]

News (2013). *Papel mojado. La crisis de la prensa y el fracaso de los periódicos en España*. Barcelona: Debate, p. 116.

34   See their corporate website: www.interbrand.com/en/best-global-brands/2013/best-global-brands-methodology.aspx.

35   See www.smh.com.au/it-pro/business-it/apple-overtakes-cocacola-as-most-valuable-brand-study-20130930-hv1uw.html and www.observatoire-immateriel.com/index.php?option=com_content&view=article&id=1284&Itemid=49&lang=en.

36   The following paragraphs are based on the work of my colleagues Vilanova M., Lozano J.M. & Arenas D. (2009). "Exploring the nature of the relationship between CSR and competitiveness", *Journal of Business Ethics*, 87 (supplement 1): 57-69.

37   Murtha T.P. & Lenway S.A. (1998). "Country capabilities and the strategic state: How national political institutions affect MNC strategies", *Strategic Management Journal*, 15(5): 113-19.

Michael Porter, in his influential essay *Competitive Strategy*,[38] interpreted the competitiveness of an organization as its capacity to generate higher profitability than its sector. And this profitability could be achieved in two ways: by increasing the differentiation, and therefore the uniqueness of the product, or by reducing overall costs. Porter's recipe consisted in confronting, in an appropriate way for each organization, the **five forces** that, according to him, explain the competitive intensity of a given sector. These five forces are:

- The existence of barriers to the entry of new competitors
- The capacity to generate non-substitutable products
- The bargaining power of consumers
- The bargaining power of suppliers
- The intensity of the rivalry among competing enterprises

Thus, the competitiveness of an organization would boil down to its ability to manage these five forces.

However, this model of the parameterization and reductionism of the variables at play has gradually been pushed out in the face of the complexity and intangibility of the competitive context in which we live. Not everything is transformable into figures, or easily measurable. Nor do Porter's five forces offer any clear road to competitiveness, insofar as, to mention only one counterexample, reducing the bargaining power of suppliers to an extreme might force them to close and therefore might jeopardize one's own company.[39] In this way, modern business management has progressively incorporated other approaches to competitiveness. In the early 1990s, D'Cruz and Rugman[40] defined competitiveness as the capacity of an organization to design, produce and/or market products and services that are superior to those offered by its competitors, taking into account price and

---

38   Porter M.E. (1980). Op. cit.
39   This is an element that Porter himself addressed in a more recent essay, which signalled a veritable reinvention of the author towards more sophisticated positions regarding business competitiveness. See Porter M. & Kramer M. (2011). "Creating shared value", *Harvard Business Review*, Jan.–Feb. 2011, 89: 1-11.
40   D'Cruz J. & Rugman A. (1992). *New Concepts for Canadian Competitiveness*, Canada: Kodak. In the same paragraph, there are references to: Barney J. (1991). "Firm resources and sustained competitive advantage", *Journal of Management*, 17(1): 99-120; Cameron K.S. & Quinn R.E. (1999). *Diagnosing and Changing Organizational Culture*, Reading: Addison-Wesley; and Kay J. (1993). *Foundations of Corporate Success*, Oxford: Oxford University Press.

other qualities apart from price. In turn, Barney introduced elements such as the flexibility of an organization, its adaptability to the context, the quality of its products and its reputation. Cameron and Quinn talked directly of the relevance of corporate culture for the success of an organization. Kay focused on its capacity for innovation, its skill in managing key internal and external relations; once again, its reputation.

What has happened in the world of management science in recent decades is the rediscovery of the importance of social expectations, managers' values and *responsible* leadership. In 1971, Andrews,[41] one of the fathers of corporate strategy, explained the process of elaborating a company's strategy as the result of setting forth *what* needs to be done to achieve a certain outcome. The drafting process included the identification of the risks and opportunities of the environment, the determination of the company's competitive resources, and two elements that have been largely overlooked by management science ever since: the analysis of the senior executives' personal values and aspirations, and the recognition of the noneconomic responsibilities of the company. These last two factors have been hidden away for years from the world of management, waiting to be rediscovered.

In 1980 none other than the Porter of the five forces discussed above—a disciple of Andrews—spelt out the context in which the strategy of an organization was to be elaborated: a context that incorporated the values of the key executors of the strategy, and also social expectations. The Edelman Trust Barometer[42] reminds us that this relational component is the cornerstone of corporate reputation. In order to win the trust of society, it is necessary to listen to the consumer, treat the employees well, put the consumer *before* profits, communicate frequently and honestly, have ethical corporate practices, take responsibility when a crisis or problem arises, and so on. What we have observed in recent decades is, then, the rediscovery of the importance of social expectations in management; social expectations that in some cases had even been forgotten by those who theorized about them 30 years ago.

There are ample manifestations of the changes introduced, new trends in both consumer and corporate behaviour; trends in responsible consumption that, for example, make the purchase of organic or local produce into a new pattern of consumption.[43] We find movements in the field of self-regulation, for instance, in the automotive, cement and energy industries,

41   Andrews K.R. (1971). *The Concept of Corporate Strategy*, Homewood: Irwin.
42   Edelman (2013). Op. cit.
43   www.sustainable.org/living/responsible-buying-a-consumption.

especially with regard to greenhouse gas mitigation.[44] In the financial sector, we have seen the proliferation of responsible investment indices,[45] which enable ethical, social or environmental criteria to be introduced into the management of an investment portfolio. In the public sphere too, we have witnessed the introduction of a series of legal guidelines, on either a voluntary or a compulsory basis, that have forced companies to reconsider the expectations society has of them.

One of the milestones in the popularization of this trend was in 2002, when the European Commission decided to provide a definition of definitions in order to fix what is considers to be the meaning of corporate social responsibility (CSR): "Most definitions of corporate social responsibility describe it as a concept whereby companies integrate social and environmental concerns in their business operations and in their interaction with their stakeholders on a voluntary basis."[46] The underlying idea, at least in the European framework, was to offer a regulatory umbrella for promoting the integration of the triple axis of social, environmental and economic factors within organizations, both in their business operations and in their relations with third parties.

Over recent decades we have seen the proliferation of similar terms to integrate this set of social expectations into business management. The list includes concepts such as **social marketing**, **corporate citizenship**, **responsible competitiveness**, **philanthropy**, **triple bottom line**, **value-based management**, **impact investing**, **base-of-the-pyramid initiatives**, **socially responsible investment**, **responsible leadership**, **social innovation**, **shared value** … It is a long list that evinces the irruption of social concerns into management.

A survey conducted for the liberal news magazine *The Economist* in 2007[47] centred the corporate responsibility debate no longer on whether

44   See   www.wbcsd.org/Pages/EDocument/EDocumentDetails.aspx?ID=69& NoSearchContextKey=true, http://csiprogress2012.org/ and www.wbcsd.org/ pages/edocument/edocumentdetails.aspx?id=125&nosearchcontextkey=true.

45   See www.sustainability-indices.com/.

46   European Commission (2002). *Communication from the Commission Concerning Corporate Social Responsibility*, COM(2002) 347 final, Brussels, 2.7.2002: www.csr-in-commerce.eu/data/files/resources/717/com_2001_0366_en.pdf. For the latest initiatives developed by the Commission, see *A Business Contribution to Sustainable Development*: http://ec.europa.eu/enterprise/policies/ sustainable-business/index_en.htm.

47   *The Economist* (2007). Global Business Barometer: www.economist.com/ media/pdf/20080116CSRResults.pdf.

companies should incorporate this movement or not, but rather how they should do so, and noted the growing importance that corporate responsibility would have in the immediate future. Over 50% of respondents answered that CSR is a necessary cost of doing business. An almost identical percentage understood CSR as a differentiating factor from the competition. And only 3% felt that it was a waste of resources. Among the benefits of incorporating CSR into management, respondents cited a better reputation, the introduction of sustainability and a long-term perspective into the management of the business, the ability to attract and retain key personnel, and the response it provides to customers' ethical standards. The nitty-gritty, for *The Economist*, was the existence of a business case, a corporate interest, for this sort of initiative. Here we should stop and think. Note that we haven't moved an inch from the instrumental logic: investing in this field, *The Economist* tells us, is worthwhile.

All this CSR has become a driving force for academic research, consulting business and in some cases a source of disappointment in the face of its poor performance as a factor for transformation.[48] We can only place this measure in the context of the expectations it generated in its incipient and radical beginnings back in the late 1960s and early 1970s. In the opposite direction, Sandra Waddock,[49] a professor at Boston College, positively emphasizes what she calls the *corporate responsibility infrastructure* that we have generated in recent years: the Principles for Responsible Investment, the United Nations Global Compact, the Principles for Responsible Management Education, and also a corporate responsibility auditing system (SAI or ISO 26000); a format of accountability on social, environmental and governance issues; sectoral initiatives, corporate sustainability promotion networks, rankings, certificates, and so on. They are all institutional commitments, tools and advancements that, even if merely voluntary, according to Waddock are here to stay.

This Boston College professor claims that however evil corporations might be, they can also be an efficient substitute for the state. One example

---

48 It is interesting to see the position taken by one of the first entrepreneurs to adopt corporate social responsibility as a driving force and foundation of her company: The Body Shop. See Roddick A. (2011). "Questioning the Ethics of Corporate Social Responsibility", *Big Picture Videos*: http://on.aol.com/video/questioning-the-ethics-of-corporate-social-responsibility-516923273.

49 Waddock S. (2008). "Building a new institutional infrastructure for corporate responsibility", *Academy of Management Perspectives*, August 2008, 22 (3): 87-108.

would be their reaction to disasters such as that of Hurricane Katrina, which devastated the city of New Orleans in 2005: the much berated Walmart, which in 2013 promoted a Christmas campaign in solidarity with its poorer employees (*sic*),[50] in 2005 contributed its logistics know-how and infrastructure to get humanitarian aid to where the army and public means were unable.

However, social pressure requires transparency, demands authenticity and scrutinizes corporations in search of incoherencies. Once again, we need to overcome the old division of roles between an increasingly powerful market and an increasingly debilitated state. It is becoming more and more obvious that neither can companies function on their own in the absence of a social commitment, nor can the state on its own guarantee the correct functioning of the markets. So we need to rehabilitate corporate managers to make them aware that they can make the difference;[51] that society needs them.

Beneath this corporate response to the social expectations raised by the CSR movement we find a threefold root:

- The rise of management models that integrate the relational and normative elements of business activity and have come to determine how companies should *behave* ethically[52]

- The need for large corporations to respond to the social legitimacy problems derived from their increased power, as they are perceived by a large part of the population as organizations that cannibalize the benefits of the market economy[53]

---

50   Lutz A. (2013). "Wal-Mart asks workers to donate food to its needy employees", *Business Insider*, 8 November 2013: www.businessinsider.com/walmart-asks-customers-to-donate-food-2013-11#ixzz2lf4QQ7zg.

51   Again, it is enlightening to read Goodpaster K.E. & Matthews J.B. (1982). "Can a corporation have a conscience?", *Harvard Business Review*, Jan.-Feb.: 132-41.

52   Among them we would find the stakeholder management model by: Freeman R.E. (1984). *Strategic Management: A Stakeholder Approach*, Boston: Pitman. Another is set out in: World Business Council for Sustainable Development (2000). *Corporate Social Responsibility: Making Good Business Sense*, Geneva: WBCSD. And another: United Nations (1999). *Global Compact Initiative*: www.unglobalcompact.org.

53   Among the classic texts that discuss corporations' so-called *licence to operate*, we find: Davis K. (1960). "Can business afford to ignore corporate social responsibility?", *California Management Review*, 2: 70-6; Donaldson T. (1982). *Corporations and Morality*, New Jersey: Prentice-Hall; and Preston L.E. & Post

- A gradual institutionalization of management tools, models and indicators, which have been imitated, duplicated and reproduced to the extent that they have become veritable systems for the *professional* management of social expectations[54]

Continuing with the core idea of the article in *The Economist* mentioned above, in this progression from *whether or not* to manage CSR to *how* to do it, we still detect corporate attitudes that hinge on the managerial instrumentalism we referred to earlier on. Thus, we can classify companies according to the different levels of response they have to these social expectations. We can identify three types:

- A minimalist approach focused on compliance with the law that only tends towards standpoints close to CSR when they become legal requirements

- A reactive approach to CSR, an approach based on risk analysis and willingness to respond or adapt to these pressures, in terms of a strict cost–benefit analysis

- A proactive approach, in which we find companies that have made CSR into an opportunity to preempt social changes, transform organizational culture towards sustainability and differentiate themselves from the competition[55]

On taking stock of this trend towards sustainability and CSR, one wonders whether the bottle is half full or half empty. Between Roddick's pessimistic position and Waddock's optimistic one there is a broad middle ground

---

J.E. (1981). "Private management and public policy", *California Management Review*, 23(3): 56-63.

54   These processes of institutionalization of CSR within companies can be found in texts as long ago as Ackerman R.W. (1973). "How companies respond to social demands", *Harvard Business Review*, 51(4): 88-98. See also Jones T.M. (1980). "Corporate social responsibility revisited, redefined", *California Management Review*, 22(2): 59-67.

55   For years, the Body Shop and Interface have been examples of companies that are radically committed to a sustainable way of doing business and have incorporated into their management a clearly proactive strategy towards CSR. The sustainability and CSR rankings that appear in the media yield more questionable results and usually reproduce the budgets that these large corporations can dedicate to this end. See Liodice B. (2010). "10 companies with social responsibility at the core", *Ad Age/CMO Strategy*, 19 April 2010: http://adage.com/article/cmo-strategy/10-companies-social-responsibility-core/143323/.

with many shades of grey, populated by a mixture of pioneers, opportunists and firms that are just interested in investing in image through the channel of sustainability. The obvious danger of this trend—some would say fashion—of sustainability is that of making a merely superficial and instrumental reading of CSR: an instrumental use of the corporate reaction to social expectations, which can affect how the company is perceived yet fail to alter the way its business is actually done.

According to Scherer and Palazzo,[56] this instrumental CSR feeds off three premises:

- There is a clear separation between the business sphere and the political sphere

- Companies must maximize their profits and their executives have fiduciary responsibilities to the shareholders

- Corporate social responsibility can only be assumed if it increases the value of the firm in the long run

This is what Michael Jensen has called "enlightened value maximization."[57]

In fact, this vision is not very far removed from the one subsequently popularized by Porter and Kramer with the shared value paradigm,[58] the central idea of which would be to equate CSR with philanthropy and expense—and as such, something to be overcome—and *shared value* with the symbiotic creation of social and corporate value at the same time. The principal idea, however, would be to contribute to social, environmental or altruistic causes *if and only if* they have a positive repercussion on the company. Once again, we see the limits of instrumentality. From this perspective, if a company can solve a serious social problem, it will only do so if it stands to gain something.

So we are dealing with a pretty meagre step forward from Milton Friedman's old maxim of 1970, whereby the only moral imperative of the corporation was to maximize its shareholders' profits by legal means.[59] It is

---

56 Scherer A.G. & Palazzo G. (2011). "The new political role of business in a globalized world: A review of a new perspective on CSR and its implications for the firm, governance, and democracy", *Journal of Management Studies*, 48(4): 899-931.

57 Jensen M.C. (2001). "Value maximization, stakeholder theory, and the corporate objective function", *European Financial Management Review*, 7(3): 297-317.

58 Porter M. & Kramer M. (2011). Op. cit.

59 Friedman M. (1970). Op. cit.

interesting to note here that despite the undeniably Anglo-Saxon inspiration of this Nobel Prize winner, the intellectual father of the neoliberal current, today only 43% of the British and 56% of Americans accept this maxim as a moral foundation for good business practice. Paradoxically, to find Friedman's most unconditional defenders we have to look in countries that would appear to be clear beneficiaries of the latest wave of globalization, namely India, Indonesia, Mexico, Singapore and South Korea. At the top of the list we find the United Arab Emirates, in which 84% of the respondents agreed with the thesis of the Nobel laureate. Germany, Italy and Spain are at the bottom of the ranking.[60]

In short, the social diseases that we can associate with corporate gigantism—disregard for social and environmental impact, undermining of the regulating role of the state, etc.—have generated changes in the field of corporate management that have led to the integration of social expectations into management. The problem and the paradox is that this approach continues to be heir to the application of instrumentalism to management, and in many cases it has given rise to cosmetic and reactive incorporations of these social expectations. The question we have to ask ourselves is that posed by Sandra Waddock in one of her latest essays:[61] Does present-day management science encourage wisdom, judgement and moral imagination among executives? Or are we faced instead with the diagnosis Khurana made in 2007 when he spoke of the demise of the enlightened executive before the primacy of the instrumental and profit-maximizing executive?

Regardless of the answer to the above question, we now need to understand these changes in management science also as a social and entrepreneurial reaction to the power vacuum left by states in our globalized world.

60   *The Economist* (2011). "Milton Friedman goes on tour. A survey of attitudes to business turns up some intriguing national differences", 27 January 2011: www.economist.com/node/18010553.

61   Waddock S. (2010). "Finding wisdom within—The role of seeing and reflective practice in developing moral imagination, aesthetic sensibility, and systems understanding", *Journal of Business Ethics Education*, 7: 177-96.

6
State sovereignty and world governance

In order to understand the uneasiness and anxiety caused by globalization, we have to analyse the impact that technological and economic globalization has had in diminishing the role of the state. In what has been regarded up to now both *home* and *foreign* affairs, this reduction has meant having to rethink the boundaries between these two concepts, which used to be so clear-cut but have now ceased to be self-evident and require prior precision and definition. Is the Greek crisis a domestic affair of that country? Is the possible paralysis of the US administration due to the disputes between Republicans and Democrats a foreign affair, alien to the interests of EU countries?

Moreover, as we will see presently, this loss of state power is inseparable from the ascent of other agents that have come to question the homogenous role of states in international relations. This factor has introduced further complexity into the already overwhelmingly complex attempt by various international organizations and supra-state institutions to establish a new conflict-solving model of a global nature. Let's start, then, by trying to grasp what lies behind this erosion of the role of states.

6.1 Erosion of state sovereignty

The present model of international relations rests on the legacy of the Peace of Westphalia, which put an end to the Thirty Years' War. In 1648 the pre-eminence of states was established in the international sphere and their sovereignty was circumscribed by the framework of their borders. The concept of sovereignty was thus associated with exclusivity in the use of power and a specific territory. Until well into the 20th century, in the wake of the Second World War, the international system was to be understood as the result of an order that hinged on states, with very few international institutions that were often no more than the outcome of dynamics of unequal influence among the various diplomatic powers of the time.

For centuries, then, we have had to take international relations as the sum of the interactions occurring around the interests of a fairly small number of Western great powers (UK, France, USA, Russia), together with other more minor powers (most of Asia and Africa and practically all of Latin America) with different degrees of dependence on the larger countries. Alongside states, there was a gradual development of organizations of a civic nature, such as the Red Cross (1863); others with an ideological slant, such as the Communist International (1919); others in which states were present, such as the International Labour Organization (ILO) (1919); and still others formed exclusively by these nation-states, such as the League of Nations (1920), the forerunner of today's United Nations (UN).

In the context of globalization, it is important to understand the idea that in their origins these organizations were overlaid on the central role of states, which still retain, at least formally, most of their governmental responsibilities over their respective territories. Parallel to globalization, we have seen the gradual addition of a wide range of players: civil society coming together to form non-governmental organizations, multinational corporations, trade, political or military associations (Asia-Pacific Economic Cooperation or APEC, Free Trade Area of the Americas or FTAA, European Union or EU, North Atlantic Treaty Organization or NATO, Association of Southeast Asian Nations or ASEAN, and Shanghai Cooperation Organization or SCO), together with others already discussed elsewhere, such as the World Trade Organization (WTO), International Monetary Fund (IMF), United Nations (UN) and the International Criminal Court (ICC). They are organizations of a diverse nature, purpose and composition that have gained power precisely by taking on the role once played by states, in the handling of affairs considered both supra-national (creation of international accounting standards) and domestic (collective bargaining).

Several authors help us to make sense of the transformations in state sovereignty that have led to the current situation. The main geopolitical trends of the 20th century are the result of the following changes:

- Loss of prominence of the state in international affairs. The end of the exclusive conception of sovereignty can be observed in such varied issues as human rights, the environment or economic regulation. Furthermore, we note an increase in transnational relations—relations between non-state players that act across state borders—as opposed to strictly *international* relations, i.e., relations between states.

- What is known as Doyle's law, named after its author, Michael W. Doyle, according to which liberal democracies do not go to war with one another and are a source of peace in the international sphere.[1]

- The extension of shared legal principles in the international arena, with common courts (ICC) and the creation and extension of international institutions of a co-operative nature, which implies the creation of an incipient code of shared values on the conduct of the various players that operate in the international sphere. Thus, we are dealing with a shared global architecture that is under construction, with its operating procedures, its language and its values.

- The current expansion phase of international institutions, with milestones such as the EU (the most institutionalized international organization in the history of humanity, with 55,000 civil servants working in its various institutions and agencies),[2] NATO (the strongest and longest lasting security alliance in history), the WTO (the most important global institution in the regulation and control of large-scale commercial transactions), the IMF and the World Bank (WB), powerful economic bureaucracies with a great capacity to mobilize resources and impose policies on states.

The big issue in international relations today is this: what is state sovereignty? In international relations, it is clear that the above changes have meant the end of the notion of state sovereignty as it was wrought by the Peace of Westphalia in 1648. Globalization and the series of new international agreements that constantly fill the pages of the newspapers—from the signing of a free trade agreement to an accord for the dismantling of the Iranian nuclear programme—imply, at state scale, new transfers of

---

1   Doyle M.W. (1983). "Kant, liberal legacies and foreign affairs", *Philosophy and Public Affairs*, I and II (12): 205-35, 323-53.
2   See http://ec.europa.eu/commission_2010-2014/sefcovic/administration/eu_civil_service/the_eu_civil_service_en.htm.

sovereignty, on top of those already made towards the major international organizations such as the WTO, the ICC and the EU. This surrender of sovereignty means, for example, new models of trade relations or the use or withdrawal of diplomatic sanctions.

We are dealing with a much less obvious concept of state sovereignty, the flip side of which is the increase of the influence of states in the international sphere. In other words, classical (exclusive) sovereignty is relinquished in exchange for the capacity to influence global affairs through channels that are often indirect and collective, i.e., together with other states, which also cede sovereignty. There is no such thing as an international agreement that does not involve some degree of surrender of sovereignty. When a country enters the WTO it accepts its rules and regulations, and its capacity to settle trade disputes by overruling the legislations of states.[3] We are moving from a stage of individual decision-making by states to one of collective and co-operative decision-making. In a globalized context like ours, the difficulty now is to determine which areas of decision-making are exclusively domestic.

If we distinguish three areas of political decision-making—local (or sub-state), state and supra-state—we can see the depth of the transformations that have occurred in recent decades by examining the development of these three areas of decision-making in the economic and social sphere. Thus, we find the deployment of relations between the economic, social and political levels for regions such as Baden-Württemberg, Bavaria and Catalonia, where local governments interact with employers' associations, enterprises and third sector organizations. In the same way, at supra-state level, a similar phenomenon happens in Brussels between large corporations and NGOs in the setting of the European Parliament and Commission.

What we are seeing, then, is the intensification of horizontal and vertical relations between the various levels of power and government; a process of legislative and fiscal harmonization, and the devaluation of state sovereignty, with paradigmatic cases such as the replacement of the Greek and Italian governments in 2011 with technical governments—led by Papademos and Monti respectively—in which the popular sovereignty of the citizens of these countries was overruled by international organizations—ECB, EC and IMF—in order to impose technocratic governments that could respond "better" to the pressures of the market and supra-state government levels. The consequences of this action, in terms of both the redefinition of

3　Solana J. (2012). "Whose Sovereignty?", *Project Syndicate*, 12 March. www.project-syndicate.org/commentary/whose-sovereignty-.

state sovereignty and the meaning of participatory democracy in the 21st century, are still to be seen.

6.2 Crisis of the nation-state

However, there are also elements that are intrinsic to the domestic field of action of states and have propitiated the current crisis of the nation-state. As early as 1987, sociologist Daniel Bell envisaged the following for the world of 2013: "The nation-state is becoming too small for the big problems of life, and too big for the small problems of life."[4] Some of the questions that affect us are: is there a need for a Ministry of Culture in a multicultural decentralized state? Or a Ministry of Defence, when the security umbrella of many states is provided by an international organization such as NATO? If, according to a principle of administrative efficiency, each level of government has its appropriate area of decision-making, what area corresponds to the state in our globalized world?

Philip Bobbitt lays out how we have arrived at this crisis of the nation-state by establishing five main reasons or forces[5] that have brought us here:

- The internal rules of states are losing primacy to other standards

- Any modern nation-states are already ineffective at defending their own borders[6]

- New transnational threats—climate change, international terrorism, the proliferation of weapons of mass destruction, speculative capital flows—highlight the ineffectiveness of the state in its traditional area of activity

- The advance of global capitalism reduces the capacity of states to manage their economies nationally

---

4   Bell D. (1987). "The World and the United States in 2013", *Daedalus*, 116(3): 1-31.
5   Bobbitt P. (2002). *The Shield of Achilles: War, Peace, and the Course of History*. New York: Random House.
6   For the Spanish case, there are precedents for the current debate, such as that of the former army officer and historian Amadeo Martínez Inglés, who as early as the late 1980s testified to the incapacity of the Spanish army to defend the state's borders in the event of a hypothetical external attack. See Martínez Inglés A. (1989). *España indefensa*. Ediciones B.

- Global communication networks render cultures and customs permeable, and erode internal cohesion and citizens' identification with the state

Above all, this is a time of particular erosion of what we could call the centripetal forces of state cohesion:[7]

- In the supra-state sphere, as we mentioned earlier, the freedom of action of states over their own borders derived from the Peace of Westphalia (1648) is disappearing.

- Furthermore, globalization weakens the channels that once served the state to articulate a sense of citizenship and an identity:

  - The non-mercenary conscript army, created by Napoleon after the French Revolution (18th century), is either disappearing or being professionalized.

  - Identity cohesion, born of wars with external enemies, becomes residual or vanishes in peacetime.

  - Compulsory schooling (19th century) is breaking up and its content is diversifying, and at the same time competes with other narratives on collective identity originating from our multicultural environment or other information sources—the media, Internet, etc.

  - Political control over the public narrative created by the media is weakened due to the proliferation of the media and the privatization and internationalization of its capital.

- Lastly, as historian Tony Judt[8] points out, the crisis of the welfare state involves the breaking of the notion of community, the social covenant that bound the state to its individuals. Political liberalism and economic neoliberalism fracture citizens' sense of belonging to the community, as a result of growing individualism and social segmentation and the lower capacity of the public sector to provide services.

7　Fontana J. (2005). "La construcció històrica de la identitat", in *La construcció de la identitat. Reflexions sobre el passat i sobre el present.* Editorial Base, Chapter 1.

8　Judt T. (2010). "The World We Have Lost", in *Ill Fares the Land.* New York: Penguin Press. Chapter 2.

The days of compulsory military service have come to an end. The threats that justified the conscript army have either disappeared or become incommensurable for a traditional army. The notion of the nation-state, the monopoly of the narrative on the common origin, is cracking up. Immigration, technology, the Internet and mass tourism fracture the perception citizens have of their own state. School has to compete with more agile and recreational instruments, and transforms the process of enculturation whereby the future citizen gives shape to his or her culture and identity on the basis of the narrative that the adults in the group convey to him or her.

Let's take a look at two moments of crisis of the nation-state that exemplify what we have just said:

The first happened between 11 and 13 March 2004. At seven o'clock in the morning of the 11th, a terrorist attack wreaked havoc at Atocha railway station in Madrid. The Spanish government immediately blamed the Basque organization ETA for the massacre, which caused nearly 200 dead in total. The next day the front page of the leading Spanish newspaper, *El País*, reflected the official interpretation. That same day, the international press started to link the perpetration of the massacre to Al-Qaeda and the support given by President Aznar's government to the war in Iraq. The President of the Government contacted the media personally by telephone to confirm the official version of the attack, a version that was becoming increasingly questioned by all and sundry. The Internet and mobile telephones spread suspicion among the population.

On the 13th there were demonstrations in protest against what was seen as an attempt to manipulate public opinion. That evening the government was forced to admit the possibility that the attack had been the work of Islamic terrorists. Too late. In the elections the next day, 14 March, the ruling party was toppled, against all odds. The identity of those responsible for the killings in Gernika, in 1937, during the Spanish Civil War, and in Katyń, perpetrated by Soviet forces in 1940, were concealed from public opinion for more than 30 years. In the case of the Atocha killing, the official version lasted 48 hours and led to the ousting from government of the party that until then had been favourite in the opinion polls.

Social networks, the Internet and mobile telephones have been central to the social uprisings of 2011 known as the Arab Spring, the accusations of corruption against the Chinese government, the WikiLeaks and Snowden cases, and the erosion of banking secrecy in several tax havens by whistle-blowing former bank employees. The quasi-monopoly on the official interpretation that states have enjoyed for decades, indeed centuries, has been definitively broken and has made censorship a much more sophisticated mechanism.[9]

The second example lies in the framework of the current crisis, and serves us to redefine how far economic sovereignty is possible. We shall focus on the same country, Spain, but from the perspective of a German saver. Let us suppose that this saver deposited his savings in a German bank from 2000 to 2007. The bank in question, observing the demand for credit in Spain, transferred this savings surplus to a bank in that country, thus converting the loan received by the Spanish bank into loans granted to citizens and businesses in Spain. A Spanish citizen can now buy a car and a house thanks to the abundant credit coming into Spain.

This consumption serves to boost the country's GDP, feed economic activity and increase the state's tax base. At the moment this credit chain is broken—when the German bank decides it has become too risky to lend to the Spanish bank—the cycle of economic dependence on external sources will manifest itself as less credit, less economic activity, less employment, less consumption, less tax revenue, a smaller GDP and a bigger budget deficit. This will force the Spanish government—from the orthodox economic perspective that we have labelled as neoliberal—to put up taxation, cut back spending and increase external borrowing through channels other than those used up until then: the ECB from 2010 to 2012. What economic sovereignty is possible in this context? At most, a severely reduced sovereignty.[10] If, for the eurozone countries, monetary policy disappeared with the single monetary authority, it is now fiscal policy, the second leg of a state's economic policy, that is seriously affected.

Now let's take a look at our immediate surroundings. The relationship between patriotism and the names of our cities' streets is becoming more

9   For all that, it has not ceased to exist, as we know well enough. The most prominent case would be that of China, which has succeeded in replacing Western social networks—Facebook, Twitter, WhatsApp—with more easily controllable home-grown ones, and forcing search engines such as Google to remove certain web pages that contradict the government's official version—references to the Tiananmen massacre of 1989, dissident and 2010 Nobel Peace Prize laureate Liu Xiaobo, or the ChinaLeaks scandal of January 2014 concerning the networks of patronage generated around the country's top political leaders. The last resort, of course, is always to prohibit access to these pages on Chinese territory.

10   The macroeconomic explanation for this phenomenon of cycles of indebtedness based on the different current account balances of states is given at the beginning of the chapter on financial globalization.

and more anachronistic for a large number of citizens, who cease to make the connection between their cities' street names and the battles, heads of government, poets or generals they are named after. Once again, the capacity to create collective identity is weakened, as are the official histories of states, based on imposed historical interpretations, self-taught myths that strike an increasingly false note with more informed and sceptical citizens. Historian Josep Fontana talks of the repercussions of competition with historical narratives within the nation-state, the appearance of alternative interpretations of our common past. All this adds up to the eclipse of historical narratives, built on a mythological past, and the corresponding rise of histories based on the common resolve to exist and expressed in the will of the people, the desire to be a community.[11]

Through contemporary eyes, the "*Gott mit uns*" ("God with us") on a German soldier's buckle in the Second World War, the "God bless America" of the American patriotic song, or the "*Caudillo de España por la gracia de Dios*" ("Leader of Spain by the grace of God") on coins from the Franco period, are increasingly seen by citizens as reminiscences of a mythical historic past, recreated in times of homogeneous one-way narratives that guaranteed divine support for the patriotic cause of each country.

Fontana stresses the difficulty of defending traditional visions of the nation-state. The nation is a community with a shared culture, created out of a particular cultural reality, with linguistic and identity-related foundations that are considered common. The nation-state, on the other hand, is no more than the historically determined and modern response to the governance needs of the *res publica*. This nation-state has traditionally been built on the dissemination of shared myths, an official education understood as a "factory of subjects", an "official" history, a national anthem, administrative structures, commemorations and monuments.[12]

---

11   Fontana J. (2005). Op. cit., p. 139.
12   Two quotes are fitting here to round off this paragraph. Both refer to the political dimension of the historical narrative. The first: "History is a struggle between conflicting narratives in which the winner is the one with most power to impose itself. Once this has happened, the other versions cease to be repeated and reproduced, and become implausible because they are unfamiliar to us." Miguel-Anxo Murado, *La invención del pasado*. Debate. 2013. The second: "History—An account mostly false, of events unimportant, which are brought about by rulers mostly knaves, and soldiers mostly fools." Bierce A. (1911). *The Devil's Dictionary*. Neale Publishing Co.

The nation-state is, then, a human construction with an as yet undetermined historical duration that in its genesis usually mixes:

- Elements mentioned above such as pressure against external enemies, the case of North Korea today being paradigmatic in this respect

- Indoctrination

- Either the shielding of differences—in cases such as Finland, Denmark or Canada—or, more commonly, their elimination[13]

Is the state in crisis? Judging by the changes related above, we will have to conclude that indeed it is. Nevertheless, a glance at the political map of the world shows us a more complex reality. In 1914, Europe had 22 states; at the end of the First World War, 31; by 2010 there were 50, including the recently independent Republic of Kosovo. In 2014, other European countries aspire to become states, notably Scotland, Catalonia and Flanders. It seems that, no matter how much the state as an institution may be in crisis, no historical community wants to forgo the instruments of power associated with having its own state.

In a developed country such as the one we live in, the state inevitably continues to perform necessary functions for the governance of community life. It meets the need to regulate global markets, which Rodrik considered necessary institutions for economic development. It continues to provide enterprise with a safe environment so that it can flourish. It takes responsibility for internal law and order, the protection of property rights and the struggle against the threat of global terrorism. Furthermore, it guarantees the development of road, rail and communication infrastructures. It takes care of supplying a skilled workforce, and guarantees education and

---

13 Some examples of this homogenization in the nation-state are France after the introduction of the republican departmental administrative reform in the 19th century, which eliminated the historical nations; the Spain of the expulsion of Jews and converted Moors in the modern period; the America of the annihilation of the native communities in the 18th and 19th centuries; and present-day China, with the elimination of diversity in provinces where historically the majority ethnic group, the Han, were either absent or in a minority, such as Xinjiang, Tibet and Inner Mongolia. This last case encompasses all these practices aimed at eliminating differences. See Murillo D. (2011). *Understanding China through a cultural rather than economic perspective.* ESADEgeo Position Paper 21. ESADE. October 2011.

training for citizens.[14] And if necessary, it even supplies the financial system with liquidity, buys "toxic" stock or nationalizes financial institutions in order to prevent the collapse of the financial system. No mean feat.

6.3 The state face to face with the globalization trilemma

So is there some specific role that corresponds to the state in the present context of globalization, beyond continuing to lose power to other organizations and bodies? Apparently there is. Although the tendency to cede power even affects states as strong as Germany and the US, formidable defensive walls are also raised in an attempt to stem this tide towards homogenizing and reducing the traditional function of states.

On the one hand, we are witnessing the rise of what at the beginning we called the authoritarian model of globalization: states such as China and Russia have reinforced their positions in the last decade and have sought to put up walls against the model that weakens the nation-state by associating a neoliberal approach with minimum-state capitalism.

On the other hand, in Europe we are witnessing the rise of protest, populist and far-right movements, which earlier on we pigeonholed into the category of anti-globalization movements. They are reactive movements, reminiscent of those of the 1930s; with rare exceptions, they base their political proposal on the return to the model of the traditional nation-state, and support a certain degree of isolationism in foreign affairs. Nevertheless, as we have already seen, this proposal is unlikely to provide an answer to many of the demands and threats that today's globalized context has in store for us. By the same token, states such as Spain have embarked on a process of retrieval of powers previously transferred to lower administrative levels, at the same time reinforcing their message of a common identity. If on one side we find trends at work that weaken the nation-state, on the other there are attempts to reaffirm it against other administrative levels, be they higher (EU, IMF, WB, etc.) or lower (autonomous communities, in the case of Spain).

---

14   The above defence of the state is taken from Manuel Villoria, Chair in Political and Administration Sciences, in Villoria M. (2009). "Crisi econòmica, globalització i corrupció", *Revista VIA*, No. 10, pp. 83-95. Centre d'Estudis Jordi Pujol.

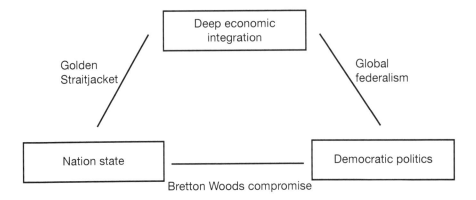

FIGURE 6.1 The political trilemma of the world economy

Source: Reproduced by kind permission of D. Rodrik

So, what state sovereignty is possible? And what global governance is necessary and feasible, if we have to think of a new planetary and global level of collective government, over and above the framework of the nation-state? To answer these questions, we need to return to Rodrik and the theses he expounds in *The Globalization Paradox*.[15] However, first we have to understand exactly what we mean when we talk of governance. According to the World Bank, we can define governance as "the process by which authority is conferred on rulers, by which they make the rules, and by which those rules are enforced and modified".[16] In a broader context, we could say that governance is the system of institutional structures and formal and informal rules and mechanisms that determine the exercise of power, the way decisions of public interest are taken and the scope of citizen engagement.[17]

We can now get back to Rodrik. In the so-called "globalization trilemma", in the face of the challenges of the new hyper-globalized economy, Rodrik

---

15   Here I will follow primarily Rodrik D. (2011): *The Globalization Paradox. Democracy and the Future of World Economy*. New York: W.W. Norton & Co. Chapter 9: "The Political Trilemma of the World Economy", pp. 184-206.

16   World Bank (2013b). "What is Governance?" http://go.worldbank.org/G2CHLXX0Q0 (last accessed: 5 December 2013).

17   "Governance can be described as 'the processes and institutions, both formal and informal, that guide and restrain the collective activities of a group'." See Keohane R.O.; Nye J.S. (2002). "Governance in a Globalizing World", in Keohane R.O. (ed.): *Power and Governance in a Partially Globalized World*. London: Routledge, p. 202.

asks us to choose the components that will determine the governance model we want. In other words, the way we respond to the challenges of globalization will depend on how we solve the decision-making equation. And Rodrik will say that we have to choose two of the following three elements: a robust nation-state, a representative and functional democracy, or a high degree of integration in the global economy. It is impossible to have all three (Figure 6.1).

Option 1: The budget girdle

In the first case that Rodrik sets forth, states can choose to retain their role as strong countries and embrace hyper-globalization in exchange for forgoing representative democracy. This would mean social, economic and labour policies in line with international standards. Rodrik borrows the concept from the journalist who has applauded this hyper-globalization most, Thomas Friedman.[18] According to Friedman, we are dealing with a golden straitjacket, in which states have to cede part of their economic sovereignty to global institutions such as capital markets and multinationals. The consequences of this, according to Rodrik, are as follows:

- Isolation of economic policies from public debate

- Disappearance or privatization of social security

- Downward pressure on taxation

- Erosion of the social compact between employers and workers

- Replacement of the objectives of economic development with the objectives of the market

In short, if we followed this trend—which we can identify as that which has been put into practice by many of the countries that have succumbed to the current crisis[19]—we would be whittling away the space for democratic

---

18   Friedman T. (1999). *The Lexus and the Olive Tree: Understanding Globalization.* New York: Farrar, Straus and Giroux, LLC.

19   A non-exhaustive list would include countries such as Ireland, Greece, Portugal, Italy, Spain and the UK. The description would not serve for the case of the US, where the Federal Reserve (the American equivalent of the ECB) has implemented expansive credit policies to make up for the collapse of capital markets as of 2008. This is because the aim of the Federal Reserve is not only to control prices but also to keep the unemployment rate low. If we go further back in time, we find that the treatment is not so different from that of the countries that

deliberation within nation-states and the observed differences in those states' social and economic policies. The policies applied in the European periphery as of 2009 would corroborate the primacy of the trend of the budget girdle. Here we should once again emphasize the breaking of popular sovereignty inherent in the technocratic governments of Papademos and Monti—which were not publicly authorized through the ballot box—and the modification of Article 135 of the Spanish Constitution, one day in August 2011, to establish the concept of budgetary stability and introduce the absolute priority of paying the public debt and its interest, if necessary overriding the payment of old age pensions and education and health expenses. This reform was not submitted to vote.[20]

Rodrik presents his objections to this option. Can you really save an economy by lashing it to the mast of this ship called globalization? Are democracy and hyper-globalization incompatible? Do foreign creditors matter more than the rights of local citizens? And what sort of popular support could be mustered for the above measures? For Rodrik, the confluence of free capital markets, free trade, free enterprise and a minimal state is incompatible with democracy. It requires reducing democracy to a strictly formal process, devoid of decision-making, and keeping the technocrats isolated from popular demands. According to Rodrik, this route is neither desirable nor possible.

Option 2: Global federalism

The second option is what Rodrik calls the **road to global governance** and identifies primarily with a large part of the alter-globalization movement referred to earlier. The main idea arises out of the evident incapacity of international organizations (as opposed to states) to solve most of the challenges generated by globalization: financial and environmental imbalances, terrorism, etc. The nation-state is to be dropped, and a determined commitment is to be made to the democratization of global institutions, in what would amount to a sort of global federalism.

experienced similar financial crises in and after the 1980s and were subjected to what in 1990 was called the *Washington Consensus*. Of all the characteristics expounded by Rodrik in his book in 2011, the only one that has not actually happened is the tax cut. This can be explained by the need to satisfy a new demand imposed by the markets: to give priority to balancing public budgets.

20   See Gutiérrez V.; Muñoz R. (2011). "Reforma exprés y sin referéndum", *El País*, 23 August 2011. http://politica.elpais.com/politica/2011/08/23/actualidad/1314128715_080054.html.

Of course, this involves creating strong world institutions with clear-cut regulations, a new wave of transfer of powers to these bodies, enabling standards to be fixed for global governance, and lastly, the elaboration of new mechanisms of accountability concerning the task of government by these institutions. Without these mechanisms, they would lack the necessary legitimacy, which would be essential to ensure popular support for its functioning.

The option of shifting the bulk of political deliberation to the global, supra-state level makes it possible to benefit from the many positive attributes of globalization: exchange of goods and services, the creation of a platform for solving global problems such as terrorism, the proliferation of nuclear weapons, climate change, and so on. However, as Rodrik points out, its main handicap is the difficulty of putting it into practice. Rodrik gives two powerful reasons for this: first, it is unfeasible and difficult to implement, and would generate an avalanche of practical and organizational difficulties; and second, experience shows us that a globalization of politics such as is sought here, consensual or at least broadly multi-party, would be a minimal globalization, with weak and ineffective rules, which would give rise to weak world governance.

The talks on the fight against climate change, with the precedent of the Kyoto Protocol and the difficulties involved in renewing it, the halt in the expansion of trade liberalization as a result of the disagreements that arose in the Doha Round, and the long, complex discussions on the reforms of the United Nations Security Council and the governing bodies of the IMF and the WB, are the litmus test that according to Rodrik introduces realism into the discussion. This road is neither easy nor fast, and the results are hardly encouraging.

Option 3: The choice of limited globalization

The third option is the one defended by Rodrik as the most feasible and beneficial, and consists of a return to the Bretton Woods consensus. Different routes should be allowed towards development and integration into the global economy. In the end, we have to choose between democracy in the context of states and hyper-globalization as it stands today. This requires deciding who should set the economic objectives of societies: states through their governments or markets? According to Rodrik, hyper-globalization comes up against four insurmountable difficulties:

- Public opinion is opposed to open markets

- The marginal economic benefit of the opening up of new markets is decreasing[21]

- A minimum space for state policies must be guaranteed

- Voluntary clauses of exclusion from international trade agreements must be guaranteed

In the present context of nation-states and hyper-globalization, this is not possible.

Whereas, in the face of the current financial crisis, the Irish solution to the failure of its financial system as a result of the rapid deterioration of its balance sheets entailed the nationalization of private debt and therefore the shifting of the cost from the private to the public sector (i.e., Option 1, namely, the laws of the market are my laws), according to Rodrik the route to follow should perhaps have been different: maybe the Icelandic option, where in an identical situation a referendum was held to measure the willingness to nationalize the financial sector debt. The result was negative, and the depositors who had lost their money—many of them British and Dutch citizens—were left uncompensated. This would appear to be Rodrik's option: state sovereignty and democracy.[22]

What global governance is possible, then? Can democracy really be extended to a supra-state level? According to Rodrik, we need a global political community with bodies representing the will of the people and accountability mechanisms, exactly like the parliaments of liberal democracies. But who authorizes and legitimizes the actors of global politics today? With the very notable (yet still partial) exception of the EU through its parliament, few international organizations have a system of government with direct participation by means of popular vote. And of course the main difficulty is that there is no global governability without global citizenship. For Rodrik the conclusion is clear: we need to recover the role of the state.

---

21 In other words, each new advance in the liberalization of a new area of world trade generates less social and economic benefit than the one before. Or to say the same thing differently, hyper-globalization has already liberalized all those areas that yield a visible, immediate and unquestionable benefit. The next advance in trade liberalization will produce very little or no benefit.

22 This second option involves more risks than might appear at first glance. Diplomatic risks for Iceland in its relations with other countries; financial risks, insofar as it undermines the trust of foreign operators and depositors; and economic risks, if we bear in mind that non-compensation is not irrevocable and creditor pressure is felt for a long time, forcing a partial or full solution of some sort.

Global governance would not solve our problems, as it would devalue global standards and rules. The *race to the bottom* in the global tax system—where states compete with each other to attract foreign capital by reducing tax burdens—is an example of what we could expect from this globalization of standards. The same would happen if we tried to get an agreement out of such different countries as the US, North Korea, Saudi Arabia and China to reach a single definition of what we mean by human rights. According to Rodrik it is preferable to have different regulatory frameworks, especially in areas such as labour rights or security.

On the other hand, the first option, to let the markets determine what policies should be implemented, linked to neoliberalism, is not a realistic option either. The long list of market failures provided by the economic literature serves us as a lesson. Could we trust market solutions, then, to come up with these global standards? It seems not. The certificates and accreditations of all sorts that are generated by the market, and the outrageous example of the rating agencies, show that they too fail. So there are limits to global governance. The world is too diverse and complex and the market is too inefficient for us to place all our trust in the first or second options.

And Rodrik makes an interesting digression in terms of cultural analysis. This heterogeneous and diverse world creates specific difficulties for global governance: identity-related difficulties. More interconnection between cultures and new improvements in information and communication technologies do not mean more global awareness. Furthermore, they enable British citizens to convert to radical Islam, and Chinese citizens in New York to maintain their identity more easily, by Skype, satellite dishes and email, in isolated cohabitation with the rest of the country's population. Technological globalization thus hinders the integration, enculturation and assimilation of communities that until recently were obliged to share many more aspects of social life in the community.[23] At the same time it allows greater participation in one's own culture and less awareness of world citizenship. In a statement that reminds us of Sklair's in Chapter 1, according to Rodrik, in the end global citizens tend to be wealthy and highly educated. In short, they are a prominent minority.[24]

---

23 Here we will not enter into the debate as to whether this is desirable or acceptable, because it would take us too far from the purpose we have set in this section.

24 Along the same lines, Robinson A. (2013), op. cit., says that the only real citizens *of the world* are those that sit in the meetings in Davos, headquarters of the World Economic Forum: the elite who govern the world, or at least try to.

To sum up, the limits to global governance are grounded on three findings:

- Political identities are built around the nation-state
- Political communities are based on states
- There are few truly global standards.

Thus, it would be advisable to think of globalizing only that which can be regulated and supervised: "the scope of application of feasible global regulation limits the extent of desirable globalization."

Having presented Rodrik's trilemma, we cannot conceal the difficulties that face the option chosen by Rodrik, namely that of defending the return to the nation-state. Let us examine some of them:[25]

- Historically, the return to the state has meant protectionism, trade wars and conflict. Rodrik himself, when reviewing the various stages of globalization, is well aware of the events of the 1930s and their dramatic outcome. It does not seem clear that his option would avoid a similar fate.

- The nation-state option does not solve the problem of the global commons. We still need broad global agreements, common structures and supra-state regulations enabling us to face global risks.

- The complexity of what he proposes is not minor, as he claims. One of the main benefits of the present system—particularly within the WTO—is that it is advancing towards symmetry: the same laws for all. It is not clear that Rodrik's proposal would not turn into the law of the jungle, in which each looks after his own interests and hinders, once again, the creation of clear and universal standards for everyone.

- Rodrik also brings us back to unilateralism, bilateral relations between states that belong to the past but should be regarded as a period overcome by events, particularly in view of the multilateral platforms for dialogue aimed at conflict resolution within the major international organizations.

- The option of recovering the state, insofar as it is conceived as a flexible option, open to choice, also opens the door to the confiscation

---

25 I follow part of the arguments explored in Zedillo E. (2011), "Book Review of *The Globalization Paradox* by Dani Rodrik", *Journal of Economic Literature*, 49(4): 41-3.

of assets, nationalizations, and for whole continents—think of Latin America—a return to the 1980s, a decade characterized by corruption, inefficiency and supply shortages.[26]

- Lastly, we need to bear in mind that there is no such thing as perfect frictionless globalization. Opting out of global governance holds its own distinctive difficulties, as does the option of returning to the state.

6.4 Global governance: rethinking power at the beginning of the 21st century

What has happened with the globalization of politics over the last century? One phenomenon stands out: we have witnessed a radical transformation of the notion of power, in turn accompanied by a transformation of the main agents that sustain this power in the international sphere. A thorough analysis of the concept of power requires an understanding of the military, economic and cultural variables that comprise it and the transformation of its importance with the passing of time. However, we can start to pin down this notion of power by describing the period 1945–89 as a period marked by a bipolar relationship between the Western capitalist bloc, led by the US, and the socialist USSR and its allies. It was a bipolarity of a military, economic and cultural nature, and only came to an end with the sudden collapse of the Soviet bloc.

The long and for many people imperceptible decline of the USSR can be seen as the result of the erosion of its power. In the political field, the crises in Hungary (1956) and Czechoslovakia (1968) sowed the seeds of the breaking of the ideological cohesion of international communism and the

26   This is the context of the expropriations of YPF, owned by Repsol, in Argentina in 2012. And that of the subsidiary of the Spanish firms Abertis and AENA that managed Bolivian airports, in 2013. Without entering into the specific cases concerned and the debate about the breaches of contract that supposedly gave rise to the nationalizations, this does not appear to set a very good precedent for the legal certainty of firms operating in these countries. Nor for those countries that are forced to look on as these affairs are brought before arbitration bodies, such as those used by the World Bank to make its presence felt in the region. Finally, it remains to be seen whether the population will obtain much benefit from the management of the services that have now been nationalized.

strengthening of the Soviet bloc around a political conservatism that was enforced *manu militari* by the USSR throughout the countries of the eastern bloc. In the technological field, the miracle of the "Sputnik moment", which in the 1950s nurtured the belief that Soviet technology would overtake its American counterpart, turned out to be a mirage. In the closing stage of the Cold War, the USSR had to spend more than 14% of its public budget on sustaining its army, which placed the superpower's finances close to the limit.[27]

The Soviet empire that had to respond to America's last military propaganda attack—the Strategic Defence Initiative, promoted by President Reagan—was practically exhausted, and not only in the economic sphere. The last attempts by Gorbachev (1985–91) to introduce regeneration mechanisms into the system were a failure. There was also a patent cultural gulf between the government and a population with expectations of change that the institutions were incapable of offering. With the fall of the Berlin Wall (November 1989), the system slid towards disintegration. The USSR was dissolved in 1991, shortly after its bloc of satellite countries was. Thus began a period of unipolarity with a single superpower: the United States.

Are we still in this historical period, characterized by unipolarity under the leadership of the US? It seems not. The period from 1990 to 2013 is marked by the decadence of this great power, but we can distinguish three stages.

The first decade, from 1990 to 2001, was one of apparent stable equilibrium for the global status quo. America consolidated its position as the number one power not only militarily but also economically, with the disappearance of the Soviet opponent and the relative economic backwardness of the rest of the world.

The second stage would extend from 2001 to 2008. US leadership took its first blow with the attack on the Twin Towers (11 September 2001), which upset the world political balance, but furthermore the reaction to it—the so-called War on Terror waged by Bush Jr.'s administration—proved to be particularly destructive for the finances and the reputation of the US.

---

27 Although there is considerable controversy over how to interpret the data, it is estimated that in the US the percentage of the GDP allocated to the military budget gradually decreased: 9.3% in 1960, 8.1% in 1970, 4.9% in 1980 and 5.2% in 1990. In contrast, in the USSR the curve was a rising one: from 11.1% of the GDP (1960) to 12.0% (1970), 12.8% (1980) and 14.3% (1990). Sources: United States Government (2010), "Historical Tables", Office of Management and Budget, www.whitehouse.gov, and RAND National Defense Research Institute (1989), "Long-Term Economic and Military Trends 1950–2010", The RAND Corporation, Santa Monica, April 1989.

Finally, the third period began with the financial crisis, which started in the US and brought with it the appearance of the following phenomena: the onset of a period of weak domestic growth, accompanied by high public debt; weakening of the international community's trust in the minimum-state model of Anglo-Saxon capitalism, and the questioning of the privileged role of the Western powers, particularly the US, in dominant positions in the main international organizations. US leadership thus continues to be questioned, yet no rival power to speak of is taking its place in the political sphere.

The first change of tack in recent history, with major repercussions for global political order, came as a result of the reaction by George W. Bush's administration to the 9/11 attacks of 2001. It was a period of entrenchment of the conservative thought of the Republican administration, with an expansive attempt to consolidate its power in the world. And this military expansion entailed economic expansion. The so-called "Bush Doctrine" aimed, first, to pursue global terrorism, second, to confront the Axis of Evil (the group of countries that were perceived as promoters of terrorism), and lastly, to fight against the proliferation of weapons of mass destruction. The most important point was how all this was to be achieved. The Bush administration's reaction was based on guaranteeing military superiority and carrying out preventive attacks to combat sources of instability wherever they might appear.[28]

In order to achieve these objectives, they resorted not to international legality but to an alliance with other powers or countries that shared their goals. The first major military campaign had the support of the United Nations, and its military objective was to remove the Taliban of Afghanistan from power (Operation Enduring Freedom, 7 October 2001). The second campaign involved unilateral action by the US and its allies, without having achieved a favourable resolution from the United Nations Security Council

---

28   Putting together a brief and accurate summary of neo-conservative thought is no simple task. However, we could reduce it to a handful of key ideas: the idea of the end of history (see Fukuyama, 1989, op. cit.); the formulation of an aggressive foreign policy (see Barnett, 2003: "The Pentagon's New Map", in O'Tuathail, Dalby & Routledge, ed., *The Geopolitics Reader*, New York: Routledge Press, pp. 151-4); the defence of unilateralism and contempt for multilateral organizations (see, for example, Perle, 2003: "Thank God for the death of the UN", *The Guardian*, 21 March), and the primacy of ideology and history over the economy in political decision-making (see Kristol, 2003: "The neoconservative persuasion", *The Weekly Standard*, 25 August, 8, p. 47).

(20 March 2003), and the beginning of a unilateral stage of identification and resolution of challenges to world order caused by global terrorism, consisting of preventive attacks against what are considered to be sources of global instability (military doctrine of rapid dominance or "shock and awe", which favours the massive use of military resources to paralyse the enemy's defensive efforts).

The consequences of the failure of this type of intervention were several. Let us highlight some of them:

- It revealed the inefficiency of military responses to conflicts with much deeper roots (religious, cultural, economic and others).

- It showed the arbitrariness of the reasons that led the Bush administration to consider a country to be an enemy or a source of instability.[29]

- It evinced the damage done by the US to the cause of international legality and its own reputation.

- It testified to the bottomless pit of instability to which these two actions have led, more than a decade later. In particular, this is the case with regard to the strengthening of Islamic fundamentalist positions worldwide, especially in the Middle East.

However, we should stress that the consequences were to affect first and foremost the US, in terms of the legitimacy of its actions—and therefore of doubt about the authority of its leadership—and of trust in and the credibility of its actions and institutions alike. The end of George W. Bush's second mandate and the beginning of the B. Obama era (2009–) brought a gradual return to a multipolar model of governance and the realization that the West has ceased to be the centre of world power.

So how should we define *power* in view of our most recent past? It can be defined as the ability to get the results one wants, and also to get others to change their behaviour in order for this to happen. But if one wants

29   It is both surprising and disturbing to read how David Frum, the US president's speechwriter, coined the concept of the Axis of Evil in the same way as a barman might improvise a cocktail, with the acquiescence and support of Condoleezza Rice, who months later was to become US Secretary of State. See the eye-opening account by González E. (2003), "Cómo se fabricó el 'eje del mal'", *El País*, 9 January 2003, and Frum's self-atonement ten years later in Frum D. (2013), "The speechwriter: Inside the Bush Administration during the Iraq War", *Newsweek*, 19 March 2013.

to exercise power in the international context, according to Nye it is not enough to make use of traditional power to achieve one's goals.[30] One needs to combine this old *hard* power with indirect *soft* power, built on winning support and good will rather than exerting force. For Nye, hard power is the power of command, a power that can either be coercive, based on the use of force and the threat of using it; or compensatory, based on the ability to make use of economic incentives to succeed in getting its way.

In the context of the time—and Nye wrote his reflection after the second Iraq War, in 2004, at the height of American neoconservatism—it is important to pay attention to this second type of power. Soft power is the power to sway, the ability to prompt other agents to share one's own point of view. It is an indirect form, but depending on the context, according to Nye it can be as effective or more so as the other sort at generating conviction and obtaining compliance. Soft power includes diplomatic power, the ability to put certain topics on the discussion table and keeping others off it. As such, it is power to negotiate and plan. On a different note, there is another branch of this soft power that is based on the ability to project values to the world, to foster a world-view, a lifestyle, and trust in its institutions. This is cultural power, the power to persuade and attract.

If we analyse power in the first decade of the 21st century, the image we get is more complex than that of the decade before. From a military perspective there is no room for doubt that the world is unipolar (not for nothing is the military budget of the US practically equal to that of the rest of the world put together), yet when it comes to economic power the diagnosis is much more complex than it was at the beginning of the 1990s. The US is still the world's number one power in GDP terms, but the extraordinary rise of China in the ranking in the wake of Deng Xiaoping's reforms in the 1970s has led to the questioning of this pre-eminence today. The same could be said of the EU if we considered it as a single economic power. So at the beginning of the 21st century we are dealing with a multipolar, divided economic power with the upsurge of what for decades have been considered emerging powers. In addition to China, they comprise Brazil, Russia and India (the BRIC economies). We should probably also include other countries that are moving from emerging to emerged status, such as South Africa and Turkey.

How is soft power gained, Nye wonders? While American culture, its values and institutions, arouse admiration and respect (and here we should stress

---

30   Nye J. (2004). *Soft Power: The Means to Success in World Politics*. New York: Public Affairs.

the importance of its popular culture, with brands such as McDonald's, Hollywood, Facebook or Twitter), a great deal of soft power is also derived from the appeal of its style of government, which is appreciated, according to Nye, for its freedoms and the opportunities it affords for immigrants.[31] And how is soft power lost? In the case of the US, through initiatives such as the Helms-Burton Act in 1996,[32] the refusal to sign multilateral agreements such as the Kyoto Protocol and to form part of the International Court of Justice, and the *War on Terror*, with infamous prisons such as Guantanamo Bay and Abu Ghraib in Iraq.[33]

Today the prestige of America has to cope with issues such as that of the spy network targeting allies and enemy countries indistinctly that came to light with the National Security Agency scandal, or the selective killing of terrorist *suspects* outside US territory using drones—which moreover cause civilian casualties. And on the home front, partisanship and political sectarianism characterize the relationship between Republicans and Democrats in US institutions, a relationship that is hard to understand from outside and translates as the malfunctioning and blocking of the country's legislative machinery.

31   Obviously, the US is not the only country to accumulate and use soft power. China, with its worldwide network of Confucian institutions, spreads Chinese culture and language and strives to compete in this race to capitalize on appeal and cultural influence. In the same way, Korean pop and TV series and *Hallyu* (the Korean wave) spread its cultural influence all over the world, not just among its Asian neighbours (proof of this is the boom in Korean language classes demanded by young audiences with a cultural consumption of Korean TV series and pop). India does the same with its Bollywood cinema. And we could extend this list indefinitely.

32   Enabling sanctions to be applied to non-US firms violating the US trade embargo against Cuba (for example, foreign hoteliers collaborating with the Cuban government).

33   The list of legal and moral aberrations committed by the US in its *War on Terror* is far from minor. Among them we find the *Torture Memos* (2002), a series of reports prepared by university professors that put down in print the *justifiable* degree of torture in the new type of diffuse, imprecise, unconventional warfare the country was required to engage in. And also the illegitimate, illegal war with Iraq. And the category of "unlawful enemy combatants", which has made it possible to apply special treatment, different from the traditional treatment given to soldiers in wartime, to jihadist combatants and anyone unjustly accused of being so.

6.5 Europe as the embryo of global governance

If at this present historical moment, marked by multipolarity, global conflicts can no longer be resolved unilaterally by a single agent, what is there
left? Clearly, the need to recover a plural and necessarily more complex, and
therefore multilateral, approach to the resolution of these conflicts. In the
light of the rapid demise of the unipolar American period, the European
model of governance—a model built around European institutions with
the EU at the epicentre—might perhaps provide a role model. However, the
doubts and uncertainties that surround the Union at present seem to question its viability as a model. Thus we need to examine to what extent Europe
is the embryo of a future model of world governance.

Let's start by considering a central factor that the phenomenon of globalization has done nothing but accelerate: the governance deficit. This concept refers to the growing distance between the development of the world
economy and the human capacity to govern it. If we analyse the evolution
of this economy over the last centuries and compare it with population
growth[34] and the development of man-made institutions of government,
we see that this deficit is increasing: the challenges are now greater and
more complex (Figure 6.2).

And it is in this context of deficit of global governance that we can understand the nature of the governance proposal made by the European Union,
in comparison with that of the US discussed above. The governance model
defended by Europe is built on the following basic premises:

- To apply the principle of legality: compliance with international
  legislation for the resolution of international conflicts
- To defend a multilateral approach in the identification and resolution of these conflicts
- To establish a dialogue that does not merely revolve around the diplomatic positioning of states but also incorporates the rest of the
  supra-state institutions and international organizations
- To focus the dialogue on the will to reach consensuses, attract interests and aspire to co-operation among those involved, by integrating the different viewpoints—thus making use of the soft power
  referred to by Nye

34 In June 2013, world population stood at 7.2 billion people. The United Nations
    projections for 2025 and 2050 are 8.1 and 9.6 billion respectively. http://esa.
    un.org/unpd/wpp/Documentation/pdf/WPP2012_Press_Release.pdf.

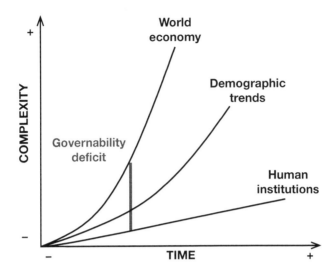

FIGURE 6.2 The governability deficit

Source: A. Castiñeira. Class notes. 2010

- To seek a governance model for the world that is based on a transparent decision-making process, which will inevitably become
  slow and bureaucratic

If we now analyse the components of the model of global governance that
emerge from the action of the United States in the first decade of the new
century we see that: a) the prevailing principle is that of rapid and *efficient*
resolution of conflicts in which b) the establishment of consensuses to take
the resolution of these conflicts forward does not seek to include all the parties involved or gain the support of the whole international community but
only that of those who make similar readings and diagnoses of the conflicts
that c) have been previously identified as such by the superpower itself and
d) tend to be resolved using force and economic and military muscle (Nye's
hard power) in a process that e) as efficiency and speed are paramount in
conflict resolution, seeking ad hoc alliances of interests, inevitably makes
for more flexible and agile decision-making. However, these advantages are
inseparable from the opacity with which these decisions are made, under
the leadership and according to the designs of the superpower itself.

Having set out these two main models of world governance, let us underline what we already know: that at this stage in the game this governance
proposal involves not only states, such as the US, and groups of states, such
as the EU. It involves a whole cluster of agents in addition to nation-states,

European Union	United States
Principle of legality	Principle of effectiveness
Principle of inclusion	Principle of the coalition of the willing
Multilateral approach to conflict resolution	Unilateral approach to conflict resolution
Soft power	Hard power
Transparent, slow, bureaucratic process	Opaque, flexible, agile process

TABLE 6.1 Two proposals for global governance: European Union vs. United States

made up of the major international bodies, set up for the most part at the end of the Second World War, and various sorts of organization arising out of civil society (NGOs, trade unions, pressure groups and so on) or the business world (large corporations, the World Economic Forum and lobbies working in defence of specific interests). It also involves regional groups of countries[35] and substate bodies. At present nearly 67,000 organizations are registered that fit into the category of IOs,[36] both non-governmental, if they arise out of civil society, and governmental, when states participate in them as such.

All these agents form part of the present architecture of global governance, which hinges around three main structures, located one level below the United Nations:

- The International Monetary Fund, presented as the principal defender of neoliberal thought in the international organizations, its mission being to guarantee and supervise the stability of the international financial system and fight inflation and public deficit, and its objectives being to foster world prosperity, prevent crises, promote the balanced growth of world trade, provide exchange rate stability, prevent competitive devaluations between states, and correct balance of payment problems in an orderly fashion

- The World Bank, the mission of which is to fight poverty and act as international borrower by facilitating low-interest loans and providing economic support

35 From a global perspective, "regional" refers to associations, mostly economic, such as those mentioned above (ASEAN, FTAs, EU), but could also include others that would go beyond this category, such as OPEC, NATO, SCO, G8 and G20.

36 See a complete list at: www.uia.org/ybio/.

- The WTO, the mission of which is to defend free trade and solve trade disputes

In 2005, Europeanist Mark Leonard published a book that made an ardent defence of European integration and its validity as a benchmark for global governance. In *Why Europe Will Run the 21st Century*,[37] Leonard held that this new century, which he calls "the European century", contrasts with the 20th or "American century", particularly in some of its values: the unilateralism, violation of international law and preventive warfare that characterized the decline of the G.W. Bush administration. The values that Europe proposes for the world are the defence of international law, the promotion of democratic values, a multilateral vision of the world, and co-operation and humanitarian interventions. Its approach is that, beyond cultural differences, ultimately we all aspire to a peaceful, democratic and prosperous world.

And it would appear that, from a historical perspective, despite the consequences the crisis has had on structures and Europeans' trust in its model of common government, Europe is indeed a valid example of what a future world government should be: an example of free transfer of power, without coercion, based on the ability to seduce—the soft power described by Nye—of its institutions and its values, and a successful example of how to resolve a long history of armed conflicts through a collective series of institutions, a government and a purpose.

Rodrik[38] falls short of Leonard's fervent defence of the European model and grants the European experiment only partial validity. Rodrik acknowledges that the European Union has indeed been a success in terms of the creation of supra-state governing bodies. The European Court of Justice, the European Central Bank and the European Parliament itself are examples of this upward transfer of sovereignty. The Treaty of Lisbon, which came into force in 2009, granted more powers to the European Parliament, established new voting rules that reduced member states' power of veto and created the post of President of the European Council. However, we see that real power does not reside in the EU bodies but rather in the Council of Ministers, a body in which each state is represented equally by one of its ministers. Furthermore, there is a clear democratic deficit in the functioning of the EU,

---

37   Leonard M. (2005). *Why Europe Will Run the 21st Century*. London: Fourth Estate.

38   Rodrik D. (2011). Op. cit. Chapter 10: "Is Global Governance Feasible? Is It Desirable?", pp. 207-32.

with minimum government capacity in the hands of the representatives elected directly by the citizens.

In the same way, adds Rodrik, when we try to make the EU into a model for global governance, although we must recognize its merits, we observe that this model only works thanks to a common geography, culture, religion and history. Europe is a half-built house; an example of success, but also of its limitations. Rodrik makes a *possibilist* reading of world governance and its prospects of success, and questions the idea of a European-style governance model. The limits to global governance are the limits of the ability to *pull upwards*, i.e., to transfer democracy to a supra-state level of government. Is it feasible, then, to think of a model of democracy that surpasses the level of states?

According to Rodrik, in order to reach this level we will need several elements:

- A **political community** that identifies with this new supra-state body, and therefore shares its successes, failures and hopes, in the same way as nation-states do today

- A broader set of **common operating rules** than exist at present

- **Mechanisms of accountability**, control, responsibility and responsibilization of leaders in relation to the community they serve

All told, elements that are still too far removed from the reality that surrounds us. Rodrik's conclusion, made visible in his scepticism about the model he calls **global federalism**, points to the only possibilist way forward: we can only hope to globalize what we can aspire to regulate efficiently. Therefore, the hope of a European-style global governance model must inevitably be scant.

Is Rodrik fair in his judgement of the European Union? We have to admit that he is realistic, and hence pessimistic. If we look at the facts, the European Union has certainly being through a rough patch for the last few years. Citizens' level of trust in the European institutions is low. Euroscepticism is a crucial element in many countries. Furthermore, there is a certain amount of fatigue after the various waves of expansion that have put the total number of member states at 28, with the incorporation of Croatia in July 2013. The hopes that the EU inspired in many citizens, for whom the Union was not just a framework for economic relations but also a factor for the consolidation of social and democratic rights, have also been brought into question. The Europeans' identification with Europe as one of the core elements of their national identity is waning in many countries. This factor has been aggravated in many countries, by the end of 2013 divided between those who support policies of austerity as a way out of the crisis—led by Germany—and those who question the wisdom of such measures—with Greece at the fore.

However, from a historical perspective, it is impossible to ignore what the EU has meant for the continent. It has been and continues to be a factor for cohesion, an initiative that has brought peace to a continent devastated by wars and that had come to extend its most recent armed conflicts to a worldwide scale. Moreover, even recognizing the shortcomings of the European project, we have to admit the progress that has been made overall. The European institutions have been a moderating factor for state rivalries, authoritarian temptations and human rights violations, and they still are today.

In short, Rodrik has a point, but he belittles the transforming impact that the Union has had on the continent. The soothing effect exerted on the world as a whole by its soft diplomacy, to use Nye's words, is no mean feat: from Georgia to Turkey, Ukraine and Iran, to take a few examples. Furthermore, Rodrik neglects the extraordinary versatility of a Union that is capable of tackling such serious crises as that of the single currency from 2010 to 2012, and make them a factor for change and regeneration.

And so we bring this chapter to a close. In the period 1994–98, the recently deceased South African leader Nelson Mandela succeeded in turning leadership, hope and self-confidence into factors for social, political and institutional transformation, making it possible to turn the South Africa of apartheid inside out and transform it into a free and prosperous country where the various different ethnic minorities could live together in harmony. This capacity to look forward into the future and overcome adversity through resilience, with all its shortcomings, has been part of the EU since its beginnings. There can be little doubt that when it comes to emulating, on an institutional level, government platforms that go beyond the framework of states and make it possible to advance towards a model of global governance, there are few examples more pertinent than the EU. For this fact alone, it is worth giving credit to Mark Leonard's Europeanist dream.

7
Values and challenges of global governance: Europeanizing the world

7.1 The new distribution of power in the world of today

In the summer of 2008 several events took place that were transcendental enough to demonstrate a shift in the tectonic plates of world power and diplomacy. On 15 September Lehman Brothers nosedived on the stock exchange, heralding a financial storm centred on the US that was to affect the entire planet, especially Western countries as a whole. A month earlier, on 8 August, the XXIX Olympic Games were declared open in Beijing in a ceremony intended to show to the world the return of China to the front line of the world geopolitical chessboard. The splendour and magnitude of the event was taken as proof of this return. Just one day before that, at the crossroads of Asia and Europe, another important geopolitical phenomenon occurred. On 7 August war broke out in South Ossetia, in the southern Caucasus, with the small pro-Western state of Georgia fighting against its own Russophile provinces, which received support from the Asian giant. After a brief and unequal conflict, these provinces became de facto independent states. Thus Russia, with a show of force, likewise expressed its desire to return to the forefront of the international political scene, after the post-Soviet hiatus. An action which, incidentally, put a stop to any attempt by the Western powers to continue to expand their area of influence across central Asia.

In a matter of weeks, the American colossus, bled by the long drawn out wars in Afghanistan and Iraq, revealed the internal weakness of its economy at the same time as two giants, Russia and China, staged before the world their return to the front row of the global powers. In next to no time at all, we witnessed what the historians of the future will call a turning point. However, as is usually the case, at the precise time this was happening we were barely aware of the impact, both symbolic and real, of this chain of events.

After a few months had passed, the diagnosis began to emerge. The gradual economic deterioration of the West, accompanied by the resulting loss of military influence and the commercial rise of the Chinese giant, enabled us to start weighing up the magnitude of the shift in power and its possible consequences on a global scale. Over the last few years, a whole range of interpretations have yielded quite a wide variety of interpretative essays. In this way, bookshops started to stock the theses of those who defended the idea of the decline of the US and the West: from *Zero-Sum World*, by *Financial Times* journalist Gideon Rachman, to *The Post-American World*, by Fareed Zakaria, including the more sensationalist *After America* by Mark Stein, and *Becoming China's Bitch*, by Peter D. Kiernan. Other authors, such as Niall Ferguson in *Civilization: The West and the Rest* or Arvind Subramanian in *Eclipse*, admitted the decline but relativized it or put it into context. Lastly, a few, a small minority, rejected the premise: both the neoconservative Robert Kagan, in *The World America Made*, and Joseph Nye himself, in *The Future of Power*, considered that America was undergoing no such thing as a decline in power.

So, can we talk of a global trend reversal, a new redistribution of power, or even the beginning of a turnaround in global governance, now following non-Western cultural patterns? What are the consequences of this transfer of power in the process of permanent interconnection and this worldwide extension of the economy that we have called "globalization"? And, of course, what does all this tell us about the way our societies are governed and the role of citizens in this redefinition of the political sphere? Are we heading towards a more liberal world, as Fukuyama and Barber announced, or rather towards its antithesis, contained within the model we have called "authoritarian globalism"?

7.1.1 The post-2008 scenario: So what is power?

Many thinkers have attempted to understand what has happened to the notion of *power* in the post-2008 world, with large and powerful multinational companies, weakened states, new emerging countries, and structures of world government still at an incipient stage. And they have tried to do so in the complex context of today, still under the impact of the crisis that began in that year, in full intellectual disorientation due to the demise of the mantra of perfect markets and hyper-globalization to everyone's benefit.

In 2011, Zygmunt Bauman reinforced the notion of discontentment with globalization that Joseph Stiglitz had coined a decade earlier, and he did so in the tempestuous months of the European Union's sovereign debt and single currency crisis. According to the Polish sociologist, we are witnessing a divorce between *power*, or the ability to do things, and *politics*, or the ability to decide what needs to be done.[1] Back in the days when states were strong, they used to have both power and politics. There might be differences of opinion, but once the decision was reached, no one questioned the state's right to implement whatever policies it deemed appropriate. Nowadays, holds Bauman, politics decides but then has to wait for the reaction of the markets. The very notion of democracy, the sociologist tells us, has deteriorated parallel to the weakening of states' capacity when it comes to dictating the policies they see fit. The alliances made by governments are sporadic, he sustains. No organization believes in long-term agreements; governments' approach to crisis management is always one of brinkmanship. Moreover, no organization exists that is capable of doing things ethically and efficiently.[2]

In a context such as this, we can understand the social movements that sprang up that same year: *Occupy Wall Street* in New York, the *Indignados* in Madrid and Barcelona and similar social outbreaks that spread through London, Athens and other European cities were to be taken as the discontented response of a large part of the population, mainly young people, to the dissolution of citizens' ability to manifest their social concerns through

---

1   Capdevila C. (2011). "La meritocràcia està greument ferida. Entrevista amb Zygmunt Bauman", *Ara*, 25 December.

2   We should bear in mind the context in which Bauman expresses these ideas: the fall of the governments of Papandreu in Greece and Berlusconi in Italy, elected by universal suffrage, at the end of 2011, and their replacement by the technocratic governments (not publicly elected) of Papademos and Monti under the pressure of the constellation formed by the Troika (European Commission, International Monetary Fund and European Central Bank), likewise chosen undemocratically, the alliance of pro-austerity countries led by Germany, and the whim of the "world markets", as measured by the indicator of the risk premium.

politics.[3] Today the political power of states can do little to withstand the unstoppable force of the markets.

Mark Leonard circumscribes this political crisis to the Western world, in which the effects of globalization, exacerbated by the impact of the crisis, have led to the erosion of state sovereignty.[4] In emerging countries, however, this is not so. Indeed, quite the opposite: there has been an accumulation of power and *sovereignty*—understood as the capacity to act both inside and outside a country's own borders—on a previously unknown scale. According to the director of the European Council on Foreign Relations, we are witnessing an unprecedented challenge to the liberal global order established after the Second World War and reaffirmed after the collapse of the Soviet Union. This challenge is made tangible in the weakening of what Leonard considers to be the four dimensions of power:[5]

- **Coercive power**, measured in military and economic resources (Nye called this **hard power**). The Great Recession, the Wall Street mentality of the Western economy, low rates of economic growth in the West, the increase in foreign exchange reserves in emerging countries (especially China), and the increase in military spending by these countries—in contrast with that of the countries in the NATO orbit—are rapidly reducing the power of the West in relation to the rest.

- **Institutional power**, linked to the ability of states to design the frameworks of supra-state governance. The emergence of the G-20, the loss of influence of Europe in international organizations

---

3   It would be unwise to lump these together with the citizen revolt movements, mainly among young people, known as the Arab Spring, which flared up at the end of 2010 in Tunisia. Or with the Taksim Square protest, in Turkey, of 2013. The origin of these, although it has points of contact with the issues we present in this chapter, is considerably more complex and linked to the sociopolitical reality of these countries. In contrast, the reasons for the revolts in Western countries include the erosion of citizens' ability to influence political power, the protest against the pre-eminent role of the markets, and society's powerlessness in the face of the crisis.

4   Leonard M. (2011). "Europa i el desafiament a l'ordre liberal d'Occident", *VIA. Revista del Centre d'Estudis Jordi Pujol*, No. 16: 50-61.

5   In the previous chapter we followed the definition of power set out by Nye in *Soft Power: The Means to Success in World Politics*, based on the distinction between hard and soft power. Leonard redefines the components through references to other authors such as Waltz, Keohane, Wallerstein and Foucault.

(World Bank and International Monetary Fund), the development of an explicitly non-Western order of supra-state co-operation (Shanghai Cooperation Organization[6] and the BRICS permanent forum)[7] and the new Chinese diplomacy of active participation in global institutions (particularly the United Nations Security Council) all weaken the West.

- **Structural power**, linked to the role of the state's dependence and/or influence on the global economy. The ability to invest and so condition states' domestic policies has been turned on its head. The West is losing its ability to influence emerging countries economically, and looks on as emerging countries invest more and more in Western countries. These new investor states, far from practising the free market economy as the neoliberal creed proclaimed, are in favour of various forms of state capitalism or authoritarian globalism, focused on strict competition rather than co-operation.[8]

- **Productive power**, defined as the ability of a state to influence the identity of the citizens of the planet (roughly what Nye called **soft power**). Unlike Nye, Leonard considers that we are witnessing a second decolonization in which the younger generations of emerging countries are freeing themselves of Western cultural patterns, particularly in Arab countries.[9] This would translate as less ability for the West to influence the world culturally.

---

6   See www.sectsco.org/EN123/.

7   See www.bricsforum.org/.

8   Here we are talking of the clash between a liberal economic model, focused on the idea (following the core theses of neoliberal ideology) of a win–win scenario for the parties involved, and a reading of the economy as a zero-sum game (for me to win, somebody has to lose), which emphasizes competition, understood as a race with one single winner. One example of this notion of the international economy as a zero-sum game is to be seen in China's aggressive dual commercial practices, taking advantage of the opening up of foreign markets and at the same time blocking the access of companies from abroad to its own market by means of trade barriers and bans. Nevertheless, we must admit to a certain geographical and ideological interpretational bias in the reading we have just made, which is not universally acknowledged. In China itself, for example, *guanxi*, i.e., the traditionally accepted notion that both sides who sit down at any negotiating table must stand to gain something, is still widely practised.

9   See Nye J. (2010): "The future of American power: Dominance and decline in perspective", *Foreign Affairs*, November 2010. As regards the thesis of globalization as an element of de-Westernization, it should be stressed that it is seriously

Beyond Leonard's diagnosis, which we can share wholly or in part, what we are particularly interested in here is to discuss one of the key consequences of this shift of power from West to East. According to Leonard, today we are living through a change of model. We would be moving away from the **Washington Consensus**, the single neoliberal recipe for how our societies should hinge around a common economic and growth pattern, towards the **Beijing consensus**, a consensus made in China, in which the best indicator of hope and social stability for a country is the growth of its economy, measured in GDP terms. This would be the will of the citizens: to guarantee growth, even if this growth is achieved with neglect to democratic values, a basic notion of the equality of citizens before the law, or any model of ecological and sustainable development. All these elements are secondary to the initial goal: to guarantee the *what*—growth—as opposed to the *how*—the model of government.

This sort of consensus is alien to the notion of liberal democracy and is therefore a model that collides head-on with the Western tradition of social and political rights. We would be dealing, then, with a clash, not of civilizations as Huntington would have it, but rather of world-views, of values. In short, a clash of models of global governance and globalization between different cultural perspectives. If the erosion of states in the globalized world in which we live weakened the participation of citizens in the shaping of the model of society those citizens wanted, according to Leonard the non-Western alternative is no improvement in this respect; in fact quite the opposite, insofar as it reinforces authoritarian patterns of government.

Moisés Naím[10] provides a different vision of changes in power in the wake of the crisis. The principal phenomenon to watch is not the shift of power from West to East, but rather the transformation of the notion of *power* itself. Power is *dissolving*; it is becoming blurred. All the geopolitical players mentioned up to now, from large corporations to states—including important states such as Russia, China and Venezuela—are *losing* power. According to Naím, power is becoming easier to obtain, more difficult to use, and easier to lose. Thus the erosion of power is not exclusive to the nation-state, or to Western nation-states; it is a global phenomenon. Three key elements sustain Naím's thesis and serve to illustrate this dissolution of power:

questioned. There are many authors in favour of it, but also many against it, as we have discussed at length above. For example, Nye's paper cited here argues in the opposite direction.

10 Naím M. (2013). *The End of Power: From Boardrooms to Battlefields and Churches to States, Why Being In Charge Isn't What It Used to Be*. Basic Books.

- **Bigger is not always better**: in disaccord with the views of Machiavelli and Hobbes, two of the fathers of classical political realism, the size of the player is in itself no longer an advantage. The power of seduction (Nye's soft power) and the agility of small organizations lay bare the old notion of power linked to size. Power and dimension are no longer associated.

- **Constant change** makes it difficult to generate captive audiences, to hold on to customers or voters, or to definitively subjugate one's subjects. New companies are set up; new terrorist groups threaten states; new leaks of secrets on the Internet call states' official stories into question. In a context marked by division, political consensus is increasingly difficult to reach. Parliamentary politics is fragmenting and populations are more difficult to control. We live in unstable times and possession of power is temporary.

- **Changing mentalities** erode power in democracies and authoritarian countries alike. When those in power make mistakes, the price they have to pay is higher than it used to be. Conflicts, both large and small, become deeper. In the business world, the turnover of executives and corporations at the head of rankings such as Fortune 500 is faster than it once was. Staying at the top is becoming more and more difficult.

Sociologist Saskia Sassen pinpoints and delimits the magnitude of the changes described by Naím. According to her, it is not the notion of power—the ability to get somebody to do what *you* want—that is in crisis, but that of *authority*—the ability to get those who are subjected to this power to accept it.[11] Power continues to exist; what is weakened is its legitimacy. This is the case in the institutional sphere, for example, with the increase in the power of independent state agencies and international organizations created on the sidelines of elections and control by citizens. Thus, Ministries of Economic Affairs and Finance, arm in arm with the central banks of their states, have to negotiate responsibilities and policy responses with the European Central Bank, the World Bank and the International Monetary Fund. The citizen has very little to say in the matter. In a context of politico-economic

---

11   This is the classical distinction between *potestas* and *auctoritas*: a teacher can have the *power* to expel a pupil from the classroom, but he will only have *authority* when this power is considered legitimate, and as such, is accepted by his pupils.

crisis, the urgent responses referred to by Bauman translate, according to Sassen, as a growing independence of the *executive* power, increasingly reinforced and empowered to cope with the crisis (or globalization), from the *legislative* power, which loses the capacity to audit and supervise it.[12]

7.1.2 The dimensions of power today

In spite of the above discussion on the notion of power, a discussion that we find as far back as classical Greece and in Machiavelli, we will have to arm ourselves with a minimal argumentational apparatus to see to what extent this decline of the West is real. We can reuse frameworks that we already presented earlier to analyse this power in three areas: *hard* economic and political power, institutional power, and power related to the dimension of values. Let's see what has happened so far.

7.1.2.1 The dimension of hard power

Following Leonard,[13] the financial crisis has accelerated the perception of the transfer of power from West to East, which has some very clear indicators. First, if we compare the annual GDP growth rates of the US and the EU with those of China, we can draw some conclusions. According to World Bank and International Monetary Fund data, in the period 2009–12, while annual growth stood at –2.8%, 2.5%, 1.8% and 2.8% in America and –4.5%, 2.1%, 1.6% and –0.4% in the European Union, in China it was 9.2%, 10.4%, 9.3% and 7.8%. So, moderate growth and stagnation in the Western world, while China registered huge growth which, although it slowed slightly, remained at spectacular levels. If the usual perception—of the markets, the media, citizens—is to establish a direct relationship between an increase in economic power and an increase in political power, the lesson seems clear. This is a pattern of thought that follows what Anne-Marie Slaughter called "the Wall Street mentality": global attention is turning towards countries with higher growth rates.

---

12   Here it is not difficult to draw a historic parallel between the present moment and the transformation of the Republic into the Roman Empire, where the growing military, political and economic complexity of managing the territories conquered by Rome led to the demise of the system of balanced powers between the Senate and the Government. This institutional imbalance brought the dissolution of Roman census-based democracy, the concentration of power in the hands of Augustus, and ultimately the weakening of the political and social legitimacy of the figure of the emperor.

13   See Leonard (2011). Op. cit.

Then, as we have already mentioned, there has been an increase in the foreign exchange reserves of the Chinese superpower and a rapid weakening of the West's capacity to condition the world through foreign investment, which is reduced, and through the action of major international organizations of a Western persuasion, which are forced to compete with new non-Western platforms of power. This place is gradually, although not exclusively, being occupied by China, which has become the big spender in a huge belt that extends from Africa, the Middle East and Latin America to Europe and the US. Today's global scenario tells us that the bulk of the world's economic growth occurs in the BRICS, followed at some distance by the bloc consisting of the rest of the emerging countries and those considered rich.[14] It is important to stress that this trend already existed before the crisis, but was reinforced as of 2008.

Militarily, despite the extraordinary standing of the US on the world scene as a result of the long technological and rearmament legacy of the Cold War era, the main observation to be made is that, notwithstanding the still huge gap between the military budget of the US and that of the rest of the world, this gap is gradually narrowing. Thus, if total world military expenditure was $1,750 billion in 2012,[15] the US military budget shrank by 6% to $682 billion, whereas China's increased by 7.8% to $166 billion, and Russia's did so by 16%, reaching $90.7 billion. In the case of the European Union, in a context of crisis and policies of austerity, the military budgets of its member states actually stood, with few exceptions, below the minimum contribution to military spending in NATO, which is set at 2% of the GDP. Thus, for example, the world's fourth largest military power in budgetary terms, the UK, reduced its military budget by 1%, with expenditure totalling $60.8 billion for 2012. France and Italy did the same.

The indebted Western countries show low or stagnating economic growth rates, and the forecast is that the gap separating them from the pack, in both the economic and the military field, will continue to close. The exercise—a highly speculative one, incidentally—of making linear projections on the basis of the present situation enables us to anticipate the emergence of China in first place in the world economy in the course of the next decade and number one in the ranking of absolute military expenditure within 30

14 www.economist.com/news/economic-and-financial-indicators/21586611-world-gdp.
15 See SIPRI data: www.sipri.org/research/armaments/milex/milex_database.

years. Using the same criterion, we could predict that no European country will figure separately in the privileged group of the G7 in 2050.[16]

What's the problem with predictions of this sort? For a start, it's not one problem but several. First of all, they are based on the use of the implicit *ceteris paribus* clause, which we could formulate as follows: "If everything else stays the way it is …, such and such will happen." The trouble is that *everything else* never stays the way it is. Nassim N. Taleb explains this in *The Black Swan: The Impact of the Highly Improbable*: "History does not crawl, it jumps." Political and economic powers such as the USSR disappear, in a wiping of the historical slate. Seemingly unlikely events—such as the discovery of black swans in Oceania at the end of the 18th century—nevertheless happen. The psychological need of humans to cling on to certainties, to foresee the future, drives us to indulge in these juggling tricks with trends, but they are not unquestionable prophecies. And the problem with uncertainties, as Keynes pointed out, is their immeasurability, linked to such a complex psychological mechanism as the need for the human being to anticipate the future.[17]

Moreover, as we have already seen, there are many other dimensions to life in a social environment—identity, ideologies, ecology, natural resources, technological progress—that have a great impact on our present and will continue to have a bearing on our future. Social revolutions happen; technological advances help us in the face of collective misfortunes and hitherto incurable diseases … but they can also cause others. And lastly, identity clashes trigger imbalances and conflicts that we cannot always anticipate. In short, foreseeing the future is as impossible as it is humanly understandable.

7.1.2.2 The institutional dimension

Let's now go on to analyse another dimension of power, the institutional dimension. What does this trend tell us about the decline of the Western world? First of all, we note the decline of the West's influence within its own home-grown international organizations. The extension of the United Nations Security Council to other non-Western states, and the resulting erosion of the ability of America, Britain and France to influence the world

---

16   See the PwC reports and *Foreign Policy* magazine's Decline Watch: https://www.pwc.tw/en_TW/tw/publications/events-and-trends/assets/e248.pdf and http://blog.foreignpolicy.com/category/topic/decline_watch.

17   Skidelsky R. (2009). *Keynes: The Return of the Master*. New York: Public Affairs, pp. 83ff.

scene, is on the table. A similar phenomenon is to be seen in the two other major organizations that were set up as part of the Bretton Woods agreements: the World Bank and the International Monetary Fund. The days when Europe and the US took turns at the steering wheels of these two vehicles of economic globalization seem to be numbered.

A glance at the names and nationalities of recent presidents of the World Bank affords something of a surprise in such a rapidly changing world. Robert B. Zoellick (2007–12), Paul Wolfowitz (2005–2007) and James D. Wolfensohn (1995–2005) were all US citizens, as were their predecessors in the post.[18] The sign that times are changing has come in the form of the last president to be chosen for the institution, Jim Yong Kim, likewise American but South Korean by birth. Things are starting to change, but for the time being only on the surface.

In the case of the International Monetary Fund, this exercise yields similar results. Christine Lagarde, a French citizen, has been managing director since 2011; Dominique Strauss-Kahn, also French, held the post from 2007 to 2011. Before him, we find Rodrigo de Rato (Spain, 2004–2007); Horst Köhler (Germany, 2000–2004) and Michel Camdessus (France, 1987–2000).[19] If we go even further back, the nationalities we find are Dutch, Swedish and Belgian, in addition to French (again). Quite a record for a continent that at present is losing economic strength at a rate of knots and represents only 7% of the world population.[20] This exercise reinforces the central idea that our supra-state institutions are fashioned in the image of a world that no longer exists, a world in which Western countries shared out among themselves the main spheres of world power and influence. Inevitably, the European Union and the United States will soon have to share power in these international organizations.

We do not have to stray very far from the story above to see the parallel decadence of the group of leading Western economies, the G7, and the rise of a new and until recently unknown platform: the G20. This marks a shift from a cluster of markedly Western countries to a plural and complex one. Let's stop here for a moment and take a look at what this change represents. The G7 was a forum created in the mid-1970s by Henry Kissinger, then US Secretary of State,[21] to establish an informal mechanism for

18   www.worldbank.org/en/about/archives/history/past-president.
19   https://www.imf.org/external/np/exr/chron/mds.asp.
20   Calculated on the basis of EU-27 data: www.census.gov/popclock/.
21   Saul J.R. (2009). *The Collapse of Globalism*. London: Atlantic Books. Chapter 10: "The gathering force".

co-ordinating Western economic policies and confronting jointly the world economic crisis that was then raging. It is important to stress that this initiative grew up aside from the major organizations of economic globalization that had been extant since the end of the Second World War and are discussed earlier in this section. Still in the Cold War framework, the incipient G4 (US, UK, France and Germany) were joined, for both ideological and economic reasons, by Italy (threatened by communism), Canada (rich in natural resources) and the Japanese ally. The reason for the annual meetings of the finance ministers of these countries was to seek growth models focusing on international trade, from a perspective that was increasingly in line with the ideological trend of the day: neoliberalism. This was the beginning of the wave of hyper-globalization, the prelude to today's disorientation.

As we have seen, the collapse of the USSR and the economic upturn in the 1990s—with the notable exception of Japan—were to attest the neoliberal turnaround and consolidate the economistic profile of these summit meetings. The summits were managed through their own administrative infrastructures, guidelines and protocols, and as of 1997 incorporated Russia, thus giving rise to the G7+1 and so eventually the G8. Over the following years, the world was to change at an almost imperceptible rate. A gap gradually grew between the co-ordination capacity of the economic policies of the G7 member countries and their actual impact on the world, which began to wane. The crisis of 2008 evinced this shift of power. A minor platform, arising in the wake of the Asian crisis (1999), was to grab the attention of the world media. The world started to talk about the G20.

The G20 summit held in Washington in November 2008, still under the presidency of the neo-conservative George W. Bush, highlighted the powerlessness of the West to find answers to the umpteenth world crisis and above all to do so without taking into account the so-called emerging economies. Hopes of co-ordination were suddenly pinned on this mixed group of countries, from all the continents, that now really did represent the bulk of the world economy—corporations aside. Eleven new countries (Argentina, Australia, Brazil, China, India, Indonesia, South Korea, Mexico, Saudi Arabia, South Africa and Turkey), plus the European Union as a unit, were added to the G8, in an attempt to provide a concerted response to the causes of the crisis, prevent new ones, and do all this in co-ordination with the rest of the international organizations.[22]

22   https://www.g20.org/about_G20.

As yet it is too early to certify the definitive shift of power or influence from the G7 to the G20; we can see a number of elements that warn against getting too far ahead of events. At present, the G20 might seem to have become the main platform for states to make decisions about the reforms the world economy needs. In this respect, the growing importance that the international community attaches to the meetings of this forum, particularly since 2008, does indeed point to the economic weakness of the Western powers. However, the lack of concrete results of the various annual meetings of the G20 underlines the intrinsic difficulties of this numerous but diverse group.

Thus, there is a clear lack of effective co-ordination within the G20, in which we see the disparity of its members' proposals, interests and objectives. All this amid the difficulty of overcoming cultural and geostrategic differences that have to do with how the governance of the global economy is effectuated.[23] The rise of the G20 certainly serves to visualize, quite clearly, the global transfer of power, but it also reveals, as Rodrik pointed out, the intrinsic malfunctions of supra-state platforms that are not built on a clear, shared set of common values. For the moment, all these problems are important enough to question the functionality of this institution. It is still too soon to say whether the G20 will push out the G7. In the meantime, we are confronted with a still unsolvable tension: the tension between representativeness and efficiency. In comparison with the G7, what we gain in representativeness with the G20 we lose in efficiency. The future, then, is still wide open.

This point—not a minor one—of the shift of power eastward obliges us to address China's role in the world. At the end of the 1970s, Deng Xiaoping initiated a 180° turn in China, known as "Socialism with Chinese Characteristics". This country/civilization, still immersed in the aftermath of Mao's terrible Cultural Revolution, embarked on a curious and complex journey, in which political communism was mixed with economic reforms inspired by the neoliberalism that was taking shape at that time in the Western world. China was going about the Americanization of its economy.[24]

This was the beginning of China's *peaceful rise*, which on the diplomatic front initially took the form of a low profile—low commitment, low conflict—on the international scene, in which the Asian giant sought, for the

---

23   To mention just one of the difficulties referred to here: how to move from a neo-liberal world, governed by a Washington pseudo-consensus and the utopia of the win–win economy, to one that brandishes development at any price and without democracy, is a difficult leap to imagine, especially for Western citizens.

24   See Leonard M. (2008). *What Does China Think?* London: The Fourth Estate, pp. 16ff.

time being, to go unnoticed. China would not pose a problem for the rest of the international community and in return expected to be left undisturbed to choose its own road to development. China presented itself to the world as what it was and is: a country that is increasingly rich (at the time of writing, 2012, with a GDP of $8,200 billion; half that of the US, with $16,200 billion), but also a poor and emerging country, with $6,071 per capita (2012), as opposed to the $51,703 of the average American.[25]

Is this period of China's *peaceful rise* now over? It seems to be. China's undeniably spectacular growth has inevitably gone hand in hand with increasing self-confidence among its leaders.[26] This is a power that is more and more sure of itself, one that has and will have an important impact on international relations. China's diplomatic role, until now minor and almost contemplative, has gradually become assertive, affirmative, in defence of its diplomatic, territorial, energy and other interests, both in the main international organizations and in its diplomatic relations with neighbouring countries. Following Leonard, the *new* China is attempting to change the world order discreetly, and fortunately stands at the antipodes of the aggressive militaristic policy of the Bush era (2000–2008), at least for the time being.

China presents itself as a peaceful, multilateral power, willing to sit down and talk to other countries in the world to solve common problems, a defender of non-interference by the international community in each country's domestic affairs. Furthermore, China's increasingly active role in international bodies—WTO, IMF and especially the United Nations Security Council—forms part of a strategy to offset the power of the West, particularly the US, in these organizations. Thus, China participates in these major international bodies, but not to give support to the programmatic and foundational goals of these organizations, which it considers to be *of Western origin*, but rather to defend its own interests. This diplomacy of participation in international organizations is compatible with the generation

---

25   Data (at current prices) taken from the IMF website (2013). *World Economic Outlook Database*, October 2013.

26   In order to grasp the magnitude of the growth, consider that both total and per capita GDP increased sevenfold from 2000 to 2012. Data from IMF (2013), op. cit. This unprecedented figure continues the trend that started, as mentioned earlier, with the about-face initiated by Deng Xiaoping in the late 1970s. As regards the concept of the *peaceful rise*, it should be noted that it refers primarily to a political culture, a way of doing things, that began to be formulated as such in the mid-1990s and was put to use by the country's leaders in the following decade. See Leonard M. (2008), op. cit., pp. 88-93.

and promotion of specifically and deliberately non-Western platforms of power, including the BRICS summits, the Shanghai Cooperation Organization and ASEAN.[27] These structures can be seen as *minilateral* organizations: multilateral, but always within the sphere and the profile of certain countries, in which not all states are welcome.

In this respect, if the Western world has been accused, not without reason, of double standards when it has outwardly defended a set of values that it has not always been able—or even wanted—to apply either internally, within its own countries, or externally, in its relations with the rest of the world's countries (the fight against corruption, the defence of human rights, etc.),[28] today China is perceived as a global free-rider in the economic sphere. It makes use of the economic advantages of the free market and international free trade, at the same time protecting part of its internal markets from access by foreign business.[29] Such is the influence exerted by each side on the major institutions of world governance.

7.1.2.3 The dimension of values

Is it relevant to think what a world made in China's likeness would—or will—be like? Does this exercise make any sense? Well, it undoubtedly does, but to a limited extent. Inevitably, a world with even more power in China's hands will leave an even more perceptible imprint on globalization. However, this statement demands a cautious reading, insofar as, if the demographic forecasts are correct, the world could be more African, with Brazilian or

27   See www.brics5.co.za, www.sectsco.org and www.asean.org.

28   Proclamations that have been no impediment to doing business with corrupt regimes (Nigeria) or tyrants and dictators who subjugate their peoples (Libya), or to steadfastly opposing the oppression and persecution of minorities (Tibetans, Uyghurs and Christians in China), and that have not been seen as contradictory with the creation of a network of espionage and violation of citizens' and politicians' privacy worldwide, including in allied countries (see "The NSA Files", www.theguardian.com/world/the-nsa-files).

29   Incidentally, nothing that has not been done at some time or other in history by countries now considered liberal, such as the UK. As has been shown by development economists such as Rodrik (2011) and economic historians such as Shuman (2009), in order to open up domestic markets to international competition first you have to ensure that the companies of your own country are sturdy enough—in terms of productivity, organization and capacity to generate innovation—to compete internationally. Otherwise the outcome is an entrepreneurial desert, with emblematic cases such as Venezuela or Russia, where today there are practically no globally competitive companies except those engaged in exports of energy resources.

South African traits, if their economies take off. Or more American again, if the US becomes the new energy superpower of the 21st century, as the announcements of the shale gas revolution seem to indicate.[30] If, despite all this, we carry on with our attempt to tell the future on the basis of our more recent economic history, we would do well to contrast the axiological (value-related) proposals of the West with those of China. What do we see in the realm of each side's values—both as expressed and as actually practised?

Although we are aware that we are committing a generalization, the values promoted by countries with a democratic and liberal tradition, headed by North America in particular and to a lesser extent Western Europe, form part of Western values. We find these values in much of this globalization with distinct economic and cultural features that we have observed above, and would serve us to compile the following list:

- The value of transparency: providing information, being open to the scrutiny of the governing bodies of our institutions and political leaders, is seen as something positive.

- Normativity: the idea that there are values that are good, that we can and must defend and that are better than their alternatives.

- The universality of values, which gives rise to their defence over and above cultural differences—the notion of human rights, for example.

- The bureaucratization of political processes, which proceduralizes them, slows them down and submits them to the separation of powers inherent in the modern state and the pace of the electoral system, which conditions a political agenda that is renewed every four or five years.

- Democracy, as a guarantee of political and social stability, and the ultimate source of legitimacy of the political system for the citizenry.

- The cult of change and novelty, which arises out of the self-perception—pre-eminent in the US and much less so in Europe—of being self-made countries, in contrast or opposition to *tradition*, which is seen as a stage to be overcome.[31]

---

30 Stevens P. (2012). *The "Shale Gas Revolution": Developments and Changes.* Chatham House. www.chathamhouse.org/sites/default/files/public/Research/Energy,%20Environment%20and%20Development/bp0812_stevens.pdf.

31 On the subject of America, Steiner says: "Its ideology has been that of the dawn and futurity [...] The memories that are most deeply rooted in American

- The limited role of the state, as a value handed down from the classical liberalism of Anglo-Saxon origin, which limits the capacity of states to act over the individual.

- The notion of progress as an essentially Western element, to the extent that the two words tend to be taken as synonyms.

- Linear thought, inherited from patterns of thought originating in the Graeco-Latin tradition and developed in the modern era, whereby a rational and logical solution, better than its alternatives, must always exist for any problem.

What is the nature of the Chinese world-view? It is a world fundamentally closed in on itself, built on a long cultural tradition, to a large extent traceable to the Confucian social ethics of the 6th century BC—a veritable standard for the conduct and functioning of politicians and institutions—and continuing, with interruptions but no major upheaval, to the present. It is a set of values that shows substantial differences from Western thought and values and may condition the future of global governance over the coming years:

- Opacity: shunning attention and keeping one's thoughts to oneself are considered principles of good behaviour.[32]

- Relativism with regard to the idea that there are principles or values that surpass one's own cultural sphere, indicating the futility of seeking to reach major transcultural collective agreements.

- The primacy of domestic over international affairs, a notion according to which the recognition and purpose of any policy—whether domestic or international—is to serve Chinese citizens.

- Political pragmatism (or instrumentalism), whereby the yardstick and the main source of legitimacy of any public policy are the results achieved, rather than the nature of the process that leads to their achievement.

sensibility and language are those of the promise, of this covenant with broad horizons that have turned westward expansion, and soon planetary travel, into a new Eden." Steiner G. (2004). *The Idea of Europe*. Nexus Institute.

32   Deng Xiaoping defended, in the sphere of international politics, that "China must hide brightness and nourish obscurity … to bide our time and build up our capabilities." However, translations from a language such as Chinese to Western languages are always reductionist, insofar as they lose the shades of meaning that are so abundant in the former.

- Hierarchy in decision-making, the legacy of a long tradition of pyramidal social organization—the mandarinate—in which political or institutional leadership hinges on obedience to the leader.

- Reliance on tradition: the *new* is none the better for being new; first it has to prove its usefulness. The country's institutional and cultural solidity rests on respect for tradition.

- Anti-Westernism, which in the Chinese mind is associated with the colonialism, submission and warmongering that led to the occupation of the country in the mid-19th century, a time that corresponds to the darkest period of its recent past.[33]

- Non-linear thought, understood as adaptability, the ability to understand that problems can have multiple solutions, all of which may be good.[34]

7.2 Where are we heading? Imbalances of a multipolar world[35]

When we look back and try to understand the world in this brief period of time that goes from the fall of the Berlin Wall to the present, we can only take note of the clear disorientation felt by citizens and leaders alike about the times we live in, and the magnitude of the imbalances of all sorts that this hyper-globalized globalization has brought us. The fleeting victory of Fukuyama's thesis on the notion of the end of history, with his forecast of

33 Up to here, we have addressed and developed these features using Murillo D. (2011). *Understanding China through a cultural rather than economic perspective.* ESADEgeo Position Paper, 21. ESADE.

34 The above points should be taken with a certain amount of caution and the shades of meaning we mentioned earlier when talking about the *civilizing* features, the characteristics of the different cultures and the processes, parallel in time, that are generated with globalization: the Americanization or Westernization and the return to identity that are inherent in globalization. Rather than definitive characteristics, they would add up to an *archetypal* Chinese culture which bears a greater or lesser resemblance to reality.

35 Many of the debates presented here arose out of the reflection and research carried out by colleagues at ESADE, including Àngel Castiñeira and Javier Solana. It must be admitted that transcribing and resorting to other people's thinking docs not always improve on the original version; sometimes quite the opposite.

living in an increasingly Westernized, democratic and prosperous world, far from generating consensus today, generates doubts and even outright rejection, particularly in the Western world.

If the world is becoming more Western, it is doing so with considerable additional costs, and often underlining not those values regarded as the most prized our culture has to offer, but rather the most spurious and dehumanizing. The thesis of democratization is also brought into question. In the light of the transformation of the USSR into the oligarchic Russia, the weak and unstable democracy of most of its now independent former republics, the recent invasions of Iraq and Afghanistan, which have brought these countries to the brink of being *failed states*,[36] and the apparent failure of the Arab revolutions, we cannot afford to be as optimistic as we would like.

Furthermore, the health of democracy, in both Europe and the US, is hardly at its best, with growing dysfunctions generated by the crisis, technocratic governments and the rise of populist movements that would all too well fit into what at the beginning of these pages we called the *anti-globalization movement.*

Lastly, even the thesis of prosperity ceases to apply: it depends on which measuring stick we use and who we hold up as a subject of this progress. As the growing inequality shows, the promise of freedom that Fukuyama had visualized in the early 1990s has not lived up to expectations on this level either. Too many countries and too many social groups have seen this growth pass them by, especially in those countries that were already counted as democracies back then.

At this point we would do well to recall the five key statements of globalization of the neoliberal persuasion, which still today prop up, in the manner of an increasingly hollow frame, the ideology of the status quo and the optimism of those who consider—such as the character Pangloss in Voltaire's *Candide*[37]—that the current state of affairs is the best of all possible worlds.

The interpretation whereby globalization should be understood as the global integration and liberalization of markets has been undermined in recent years by a host of other readings that place the emphasis on human factors relating to our co-existence, ecological impacts, the generation of global risks, identity shocks, and political dilemmas linked to our collective

---

36   Weak, dysfunctional states in which central government barely holds practical control over its territory.

37   Voltaire (2003) [1759]. *Candide*. New York: Bantam Classics.

organization in this world that is now definitively interdependent. Increasingly, the economistic interpretation of globalization is becoming just *one* of the possible readings of this phenomenon, alongside the vast spectrum that extends beyond the economic sphere.

In the same way, the vision of globalization as *unavoidable* and separate from political debate has been discredited for its social impact and its sullying of our devalued democracy, impoverished as regards its capacity to question the effects of globalization on our societies. It is surprising today when we hear some say that no one is in charge of globalization, when we see the huge efforts made by the main capital funds and large corporations to influence government performance, to the extent of imposing changes on the political preferences expressed by the citizens through the ballot box.[38] The last two statements of the neoliberal ideology—globalization benefits everyone and promotes the spread of democracy around the world—have already been discussed above.

Thus the Western optimism of the 1990s, with Fukuyama's statements about the end of history and the definitive Westernization and democratization of the whole planet, have given way, 20 years on, to an increasingly complex globalization, with fewer certainties and more insecurities, particularly in the West. The world seems to be turning eastward. The demographic, economic and maybe even cultural weight of non-Western countries is leading us towards a world in which the West is losing its traditional self-confidence and an unknown arises. For the first time in history a non-Western power, China, can play a fundamental role in the reshaping of the world economic and political orders, a fact that generates concern in view of its position regarding such essential values for the Western world as democracy and human rights. This concern is also felt on the economic front, with the perspective of a race to the bottom in which the institutional standards and quality of life of the West will be jeopardized by the rise of the more precarious, less democratic, more ethnocentric and less liberal— in the classical sense of protecting the rights of the individual—counter-model represented by China.

---

38   Including the Troika's coup against the legitimate governments of Greece and Italy at the end of 2011, discussed at length above, and the almost habitual pressure to deregulate applied to states by large corporations, with some paradigmatic examples such as the magnate Adelson's interest in installing his Eurovegas project in Spain, an investment that carried the condition that a large part of the labour, public health and tax regulation would be done away with.

On the one hand, China forges diplomatic alliances and understandings with countries with a low or non-existent democratic profile (Russia, Burma, North Korea, Iran and Syria), and on the other it sets itself up as a counter-model to the types of state and supra-state institution defended and promoted by the West. We stand before a wave of state capitalism, associated with a set of authoritarian practices that clash head-on with the representation of the world that the West has embraced for decades and indeed centuries. If until very recently China yielded to the economic dictates of the major global corporations, most of them Western, which took advantage of the poor working conditions in that country, today it is busy promoting its own public enterprises worldwide. The current state of global governance thus shows this gradual weakening of Western influence with the advancement of the new configuration of power on a global scale.

However, it is difficult to imagine any attempt to respond to the global problems generated by globalization that does not involve establishing global, inclusive and therefore worldwide platforms for co-operation between states. The world needs governance structures aimed at creating spaces for dialogue between countries with different world-views, platforms designed to combat the abuse of power, protect citizens from their rulers and defend global public goods (from threats to the interruption of world trade to the environment).

A world without global government structures runs the risk of becoming a chaotic, competitive race between states *to the bottom*—a scramble to deregulate markets and leave environment and workers unprotected—in the face of the threats proffered by the major capital funds and criminal networks. Another danger that lurks all too close is that of reproducing the protectionist reaction that led us into worldwide conflict in the 1930s. We need to recognize that our world is multipolar, yet that our institutions still fail to reflect this multipolarity. This recognition forces the Western world to take on the twofold and not always straightforward task of relinquishing prominence in the major global international organizations without ceasing to stand up for a set of common principles—democracy, human rights, respect for the environment—for this new global citizenship that is under construction.

Let's recap the changes that have occurred so far. States are losing power and capacity to act in the face of other players (citizens, corporations, markets). Power is becoming blurred and liquid: it spreads out and is becoming imprecise and difficult to keep hold of, while the West is forced to give up its seat to the new global players. But we must also bear in mind another point we have seen above: in the military sphere, the world is still unipolar—the annual military expenditure of the number one superpower still accounts for 45% of the entire global budget in this field (2012). In the economic sphere, there is little room for doubt that the world is now multipolar, with emerging players such as the BRICS, which claim their place in the major international organizations. And lastly, in the sphere of cross-border transactions, the world is now definitively *apolar*: with multiple players who are not always easy to identify. It is a world in which the state has to share power with noncriminal actors with different standards of legitimacy (NGOs, multinationals), and also criminal actors (terrorists, international criminals, mafias) the eradication of which requires concerted action by states.

For the wide range of challenges surrounding issues such as poverty, the proliferation of nuclear weapons and the fight against climate change, we need co-operation between states. The same can be said of the prevention of war over energy resources, food and access to farmland or drinking water. In a world where the population is set to increase by nearly four billion people by the end of this century,[39] with both demographic and economic growth, pressure on the existing resources will rise. And it is very likely that this pressure will be exacerbated by changes in the temperature of the planet.

In short, there are several great debates today that hinge on global governance. First of all, we observe the shift away from the ideological debate, the discussion between neoliberalism and alter-globalization that marked the end of the 1990s and the beginning of the new century, giving way to the clash of world-views between liberal capitalism, of Western origin, and other models of authoritarian globalism of Asian inspiration. Furthermore, the new global composition of power poses questions about the legitimacy and the representativeness of the major international organizations; it forces us to think about how we should share the costs of globalization—in inequality, the environment, working and health conditions—and it obliges us all to engage in a calm and thorough debate on the values of globalization.

What principles should guide global governance? Let's mention some of them, perhaps the most urgent. We need democratic governance that facilitates the participation of citizens in public action and the accountability of its organs of government. We need effective governance, focused on getting results and solving the problems that afflict the public agenda. We want

---

39   The population will rise from 7.1 to 10.8 billion, and this growth will happen mainly in Africa, according to projections made by the United Nations (2012): www.un.org/en/development/desa/population/publications/pdf/trends/ WPP2012_Wallchart.pdf.

good governance, based on values that the citizens identify with and the strengthening of ethical behaviour in all the actors involved in the running of the major international organizations.

Who is the subject who seeks, wants or hopes to solve the issues mentioned above? It ought to be any citizen of this planet, although actually this statement is difficult to verify. However, this is no reason to stop defending this paradox. After all, what can we do with this world? Well, we will have to choose between the "four Cs":

- **Capitulation**: to do nothing

- **Confrontation**: to slip towards conflict and the struggle for scarce resources and possibly war

- **Co-operation and competition**: to advance towards a multilateral model that would allow the solution of global problems and at the same time make it possible to establish a set of common rules on competition between countries and corporations

Given the importance of the task before us as citizens of this planet, we can only hope to avoid making the wrong choice.

7.3 Europeanizing the world

7.3.1 In defence of European values

Let's return to the debate we initiated earlier. What is the best option that we can offer for the governance of this common property known as planet Earth to a citizen of, say, India? If we have to choose from among the existing options, perhaps we should go for that of the European Union, as international analyst Brahma Chellaney holds.[40] It is an institutional model that is debilitated at present, and moreover not at its best economically, but nevertheless it offers the world a viable twofold alternative as regards the politico-institutional organization of states, and as a historically unique

---

40   I reproduce Chellaney's words as quoted in Giné S. (2012), *Asia marca el rumbo* (Barcelona: Dèria Editors), p. 15: "Today the European Union is—much more than the United States—the example that the citizens of emerging countries would like to follow. We Indians want to be like the Europeans in the European Union. So put right whatever needs to be put right, but defend your model, because there is no better one."

and successful attempt to solve supra-state conflicts through the communion of the parties in a set of common interests and values.

McCormick[41] makes a thorough analysis of European values and the proposal that emanates from the European Union for global governance. What does the European Union represent for the world today? No mere trifle, actually. The European Union is a formidable model of a supra-state agreement to overcome war, intimidation and violence. It is a top-level diplomatic power that relies on civil values and its democratic credentials, a power that, unlike its Western neighbour, the US, has given priority to the use of a diplomacy based on *smart power*, meaning the right combination of hard and soft power—for example, traditionally applying economic sanctions rather than the military sort, a historically relevant fact that implies giving a back seat to force when it comes to conflict resolution. Furthermore, it is a power that is capable of absorbing old historic enemies within it (France, Germany, Poland and others).

The European Union is a power that is linked to the political strand of liberal internationalism—at the same time progressive and idealistic—and as such is far removed from the traditional unilateralism of the United States and the political realism of Hobbesian inspiration of other emerging powers. In recent decades this European diplomacy has distinguished itself for supporting global frameworks of security and justice, has become a global power in international humanitarian aid and a leading member in international peace missions, in which it has deployed its armies not to fight but to prevent conflict. Its multilateralism is a product of trial and error, of decades of working together and diplomatic union—relative and precarious on more than one occasion—around a set of core values, such as support for written rules (i.e., international law), co-operation and inclusion. These elements are the foundations for the generation of international legitimacy, without which we would only find, as Hobbes described in *Leviathan*, the imposition of one group over another.

McCormick's markedly optimistic message provides a clear account of the possibilities of using soft power as an element of state transformation. This phenomenon is visible in the very process of enlargement of the Union. Neighbouring states' ideal—because we are talking about an ideal—of joining the European Union is built on the strengthening of democratic values, which inspires institutional change in those countries that want to accede

---

41 Here I follow McCormick J. (2010). "Europe in the World: Towards Perpetual Peace", in: *Europeanism*. New York: Oxford University Press, pp. 191-214.

to the Union insofar as they emulate laws and institutions in accordance with the European model. Is McCormick over-optimistic? The truth is that the world—and Europe is no exception—seems to be getting further and further away from this ideal.

However, getting back to the debate discussed in previous pages between Rodrik and Leonard, one fact is indisputable. As McCormick states, the dynamics of the international system, buffeted by the winds of globalization, "in which interests are defined less by states and territories, and more and more in collective terms, neatly match European perceptions about what means are effective for managing and generating influence."[42] The European model of global governance is the only known system that is, despite its limitations, viable and valid for thinking about the future. The global order that the ordinary citizen of this planet would want, in keeping with Chellaney, would necessarily resemble the European Union more than any of the existing alternatives.

German philosopher Jürgen Habermas, a leading champion of the European Union and European values in the world, makes a stalwart defence of the need to recover European values. And to recover them first and foremost within the Union itself, which he perceives as being increasingly eroded by the harmful influence of markets. We need to recover the centrality of the citizen, in opposition to the technocracy, he tells us. We need to retrieve the power ceded to institutions and posts, within the European Union itself, that have not received the endorsement of the citizens of the Union. Capitalism and democracy need to be reconciled. The progressive dismantling of the role of the citizen in European institutions, developed in recent years with their back turned to democracy, must be reversed.[43]

According to Habermas, European integration is still the mirror for generating the global community of citizens, but it needs to be refurbished. This refurbishment must involve strengthening its legitimacy, re-empowering its citizens, restoring democracy and giving substance to the spirit of the Treaty of Lisbon (in force since 2009), which seeks to make the Union into a more

42   McCormick J. (2010). Op. cit., p. 214.
43   This is attributable to the increasingly important role played by the European Council—the summit of the heads of state or government of the European Union member states—and the demoting of the European Parliament, in which the former acts as a lobby for the strong states (Germany, France) to exert pressure on the rest. This thesis is developed in Habermas J. (2012), *The Crisis of the European Union: A Response* (Polity Press). See also Díez G. (2011), "A philosopher's mission to save the EU", *Der Spiegel*, 25 November.

democratic, more transparent and more efficient bloc of countries, with less weight attached to the member states and more to the democratically elected Parliament. According to the philosopher, these are the only solid foundations on which we can build a true political union within the EU, in the semblance of the nation-state. We have created, he tells us, the embryo of a sort of European federalism that should enable us to transcend the state and all its shortcomings.

The virtue of Habermas's reflection is that it places the emphasis on the fact that this Union, which is more than an international organization but less than a state, is the palpable demonstration of the possibility of generating democratic frameworks that overcome the nation-state; of generating new multiple identities, beyond the individual assignment of individuals to a particular nationality or identity, and concoct new areas of shared citizenship. What contribution, in the sphere of values, does the European experiment make to the world? First, it shows the civilizing power—that is, the power to create areas of civilization, in opposition to areas of barbarity and confrontation—of democratic constitutions in the supra-state sphere. In other words, it demonstrates that democracy, as a process of generation of rules for collective governance, makes us *civilized*. Furthermore, it underscores the possibility of creating a cosmopolitan community. In this respect, the citizens of the European Union are undoubtedly the human community that has gone furthest along the road to becoming citizens of the world.

Delanty defines the European *character* precisely in terms of its distinct cosmopolitanism.[44] Europeanness is above all a tag that we add to our personal identity, an extra level of identification, located above many other levels of identity-based ascription. Being European must be understood as a higher stage than belonging (or not) to the European Union. Thus, it is a feature that is linked to culture, with a set of civil values, an identity bound to the defence of a set of principles of shared law—Habermas's constitutional *patriotism*—beyond the ethnic group. Unlike the distinctive feature of being American, the European condition is an approach to the world that is linked to a cosmopolitan spirit, is characterized by elements such as the defence of a citizenship that is open to the world (unlike Huntington's partisan notion), recognizes the diversity of the world in which we live, and lastly, is distinguished by the need to build bridges of dialogue with the values of *others*. In short, the European condition is a reflective disposition, linked to

---

44   Delanty G. (2005). "What does it mean to be a 'European'?", *Innovation: The European Journal of Social Science Research*, 18(1): 11-22.

the *critical* analysis of our own personal identity in relation to those who are not like us. This characteristic enables us to live with uncertainty, at least from the cultural perspective, a feature that seems to be indispensable for co-existing peaceably in today's complex and unpredictable world.

7.3.2 The European ideal as a firewall in a depersonalized world

"Those who have a 'why' to live, can bear with almost any 'how'," sustained Viktor Frankl in his account on overcoming the Nazi—and therefore European—barbarity in the extermination camps.[45] What role does hope play in this globalized world, with omnipresent financial markets, weakened states, global economic, cultural and territorial tensions and struggles over scarce resources? In fact it plays a fundamental role. The world needs—we citizens need—the hope of a better life, of being able to solve our problems and secure a better future for our children, the environment and the whole planet. And we have no choice but to find this hope in what we are, in the contributions we have made to humanity and in what we want to become.

Today we are witnesses to this vehicle, which is advancing at full speed. A vehicle that some authors call capitalism, others globalization, and others no name at all, in the belief that it is simply the inevitable outcome of the march of history. Is our present really inevitable? Can we imagine the future differently? Do we have any other option, apart from uncritically accepting the world that unravels around us, with its elites, its beneficiaries, its vested interests and its social and environmental repercussions? The answer should be yes. If for no other reason, because a negative answer would mean accepting a return to the world of the cave, where the individual can only aspire to be a victim of the power of the forces of nature and the rule of the strongest.

Our society, our democracy, needs buttresses, it needs critical citizens, aware of the evils that grip the planet and capable of using their power—the power to vote, to choose, to be informed, to stand up to injustice—to help make a better world in which the individual is the centre of things, not an instrument or a means. American philosopher Michael Sandel,[46] who we referred to at length in an earlier chapter, talks of the invisible role of capitalism in the corrosion of people's characters and our way of co-existing in a community. He also shows us the consequences of the subtle invasion of economic thought—of Anglo-Saxon origin, we should note—

45   Frankl V. (2000). *Man's Search for Ultimate Meaning*. Perseus Books Group.
46   Sandel M. (2012). Op. cit.

into our day-to-day activity. This invasion has been abetted by a particular ideology—neoliberalism—and has as its background a set of historical circumstances that, as of the 1970s, made it possible and reinforced it until it became the only accepted way of thinking.

"There is no alternative!" cried its supporters, leaving for posterity an acronym—TINA—that was to become the epicentre of a long battle, at the same time ideological, academic and intellectual. A battle without clear victors, but which has left a long trail of lost and disoriented citizens by the wayside. A large number of Europeans, still reeling from the onslaught of the 2008 crisis, stand at this juncture. In the meantime, we try to assess the damage done to our standard of living, the health of our institutions, the quality of our democracy. And also the origin of the disease and how it might be cured.

Sandel's main lesson, as expressed in his 2012 book, is to remind us that markets are not neutral; they are not mere mechanisms that *must* be accepted without criticism, as if there were no alternative. There is always an alternative. Markets, as we can see well enough if we look closely, reproduce and spread values, displace standards of conduct, erode democracy. We talk of erosion insofar as they break a common notion of good life. As Nussbaum says,[47] the market numbs us; it erodes our ability to feel empathy in the face of other people's pain, to the point of contaminating and impoverishing an educational model that is gradually reduced to being *useful* for the market, even if it becomes paradoxically dysfunctional for a democratic system that also needs critical, sensitive citizens. According to Nussbaum, beyond the obsession with the GDP—a highly culture-bound and technically dubious obsession—citizens, governments and markets need to defend and preserve more plural and complex notions of human development. Democracy needs to be saved from the market. And the European ideal needs to be saved from the market too. But how? In a way that is as obvious as it is simple: by guaranteeing spaces for co-existence, cultural exchange and institutional and organizational management *aside from* the market.

In his brief yet classic work *The Idea of Europe*, Steiner vindicates the civilizing values of Europe as a firewall against the dehumanized globalism we face. While, over the centuries, Europe bled to death in fratricidal struggles that extended well into the 20th century, at the same time it "fostered

---

47   Nussbaum M. (2010). *Not for Profit: Why Democracy Needs the Humanities.* Princeton: Princeton University Press.

civilisation, the notions of tolerance and co-existence, human rights, control over governments, respect for religious, ethnic and sexual minorities, individual sovereignty and economic development,"[48] ideas that nevertheless now form part of the great human ideas, that is, the contribution of European culture to the world. Steiner presents it like this: "To be a European is to attempt to negotiate, morally, intellectually and existentially [...] rival ideals, claims."[49] This is our distinctive feature, in perfect coherence with the interpretation of European values made by Habermas, Delanty and McCormick.

At the time Steiner was writing his essay—remember that 2004 was a year marked by the clash of two world-views, the European and the American, with the war in Iraq as a backdrop—this approach, this way of being part of the world, meant questioning this Anglo-Saxon model of driverless capitalism with increasingly dire social consequences. In the exercise of contrasting European and American values, Steiner cites Max Weber, who as early as the beginning of the 20th century equated Americanization with the impoverishment of our spiritual life and the rise of so-called *managerial bureaucracy*, fully present today in the great depersonalized and automated corporations, aimed exclusively at obtaining ever larger market shares and profits.

"Nothing threatens Europe more radically—'at the roots'—than the detergent, exponential tide of Anglo-American," which uniformizes everything it touches and dissolves difference, holds Steiner,[50] who is French by birth but developed his academic career and has spent most of his life in Anglo-Saxon countries. The role of Europe, he tells us, is to generate a secular humanism, open to everyone, and therefore

> it is vital for Europe to consolidate certain convictions and audacities of the soul that the Americanisation of the planet—with all its benefits and generosities—has darkened. [...] It is not political censorship that kills: it is the despotism of the mass market and the rewards of commercialised stardom.[51]

Europe, beyond its strict economic and institutional reality, continues to be an ideal of civilization, against the globalization of indifference, homogenization and relativism. It is a bastion against barbarity and at the same

48 Vargas Llosa M. (2004). "Una idea de Europa", in: Steiner G. Op. cit., p. 16.
49 Steiner G. (2004). Op. cit., p. 53.
50 Steiner G. (2004). Op. cit., p. 72.
51 Steiner G. (2004). Op. cit., pp. 53, 76-8.

time against the oppression of the weak by the strong and of the citizen by capital. Todorov[52] makes a stand against the depersonalizing postmodern relativism that has become the perfect magma on which our globalized capitalism floats. Citing Bartolomé de las Casas, he reminds us that the barbarians are those who do not recognize the humanity of others, and adds that in order to be civilized we need not only the humanization that makes us equal but also a critical gaze that makes us demanding in the face of injustice and any form of oppression.

The great contribution of Europe is to be found in the ideals that inspired the American Constitution, the human rights declared by the United Nations in 1948 and the European model of the social market economy. According to Todorov, the distinctive feature of the European identity is the way national, cultural and religious differences are handled. Europe has grown out of difference and the cultural permeability of its borders. We are heirs to the tradition of the Enlightenment—Montesquieu, Voltaire and Hume—and the notion that strength is to be derived from division, not homogenization. Isn't this precisely what the world needs today?

Europe is part of the balance between unity and plurality, and sees uniformity—linguistic, ethnic, cultural—as a form of decadence. As Todorov points out, rival ways of seeing and feeling spur intelligence and competition. He goes on to quote the poet Valéry to refer to the threefold legacy of the Europeans. From Rome we have inherited the power of the organized state, law, institutions and the notion of citizenship. From Jerusalem, subjective morality and the notion of universal justice. From Athens, rational argumentation, humanism and the enjoyment of knowledge. Isn't all this worth fighting for? Surely it is. The risk of being deprived of such a vast heritage, perhaps the vastest that the European tradition has bequeathed to the world, is too great. Whether it is in the institutional tradition that the European Union has just initiated or in the world of ideas, it is in this direction that the world should advance. Returning once more to Steiner, we will have to express the so heroic, so Greek and hence so European desideratum that the idea of Europe is an idea that is worth fighting for before it ends up in the great museum of past dreams we call *history*.

52   Todorov T. (2010). "Barbarism and civilization", op. cit., Chapter 1.

Afterword

The reader who has consented to be led as far as these final pages and now looks back could ask a perfectly legitimate question: what contribution do all these ideas, interpretations and theories, with a reading that is not always either easy or obvious, make to my way of seeing the world? To what extent has reading this provided me with something that has enabled me to grow personally and professionally? This twofold question has in turn two answers.

For the romantic reader, imbued with the humanist thought we talked about some pages back, little justification is required: trying to understand the world means opening up to difference; enriching our gaze with nuances and interpretations of which we were unaware, or on which we had found neither the space nor the time to reflect. For this reader a ramble through complexity is worthwhile for its own sake and does not demand much in the way of added explanations.

For the busy reader, with limited time and a sceptical spirit, specific justification is needed. Our journey has sought to contribute to give meaning to a complex and accelerated world, the keys of which often present themselves in a fragmented and partial fashion. This is an important point which should be underlined. In the era of big data, robotization and the automation of processes and functions, our gaze tends to come to rest on the abundant information that exists. Increasingly, our world is made up of snippets; too complex and incomprehensible for the majority, we pit against it the knowledge wielded by scientists and academics, super-specialists with an ever smaller and more fenced-off area of knowledge.

We were given some pointers by the technology entrepreneur Chris Anderson in an article entitled "The End of Theory", published in *Wired* magazine in 2008. Ours is the age of fascination with data, in the same way as the 18th century was the era of faith in reason and the 19th was that of trust in industrialization. But this new era comes with its specific costs: lack of narrativity, of historicity, lack of real understanding of the phenomena that surround us. This signifies taking stock of the incapacity to thread together meaning, to interpret and tie up loose ends. And, of course, a world replete with information but which we are unable to narrate is by definition a world that is impossible to understand.

This is a world that makes us vulnerable, deprives us of critical thinking, weakens our democracies and leaves us at the mercy of the transmitters of information, the experts who interpret it and the powers interested in maintaining the present correlation of forces. The purpose of this book has been to try to fight against all these forces, to row for a few instants against the waves and propose an interpretation of globalization that, being a social one, appeals to our way of seeing the world, politics and the values inherent in it. Nevertheless, although the reminder might be obvious, it is up to each reader to determine in what way these pages have helped him or her to attain these goals.

Sant Cugat del Vallès, 13 December 2014

References

Abrahamson, E. (1991). "Managerial fads and fashions: The diffusion and rejection of innovations", *Academy of Management Review*, 16: 586-612.

Ackerman, R. W. (1973). "How Companies Respond to Social Demands", *Harvard Business Review*, 51(4): 88-98.

Agencias (2011). "El 80 % de las empresas del Ibex está presente en paraísos fiscales". *El País*. 11 February 2011.

Agustina, L. (2010). "El mercado baila al son de banca y '*hedge funds*'". *La Vanguardia*. 14 November 2010.

Albareda, L. (2010). *Consum i valors. La mercantilització dels valors*. Fundació Lluís Carulla-ESADE.

Aldridge, I. (2013). "The Risks of High-Frequency Trading", *The Huffington Post*, 29 March 2013, www.huffingtonpost.com/irene-aldridge/the-risks-of-highfrequenc_b_2966242.html.

Andrews, E. (2008a). "Greenspan Concedes Error on Regulation". *The New York Times*. 23 October 2008.

Andrews, E. (2008b). "Fed's $85 Billion Loan Rescues Insurer". *The New York Times*. 16 September 2008.

Andrews, K. R. (1971). *The Concept of Corporate Strategy*. Homewood: Irwin.

Authers, J. (2009). "Ways to Take Stock of It All". *Financial Times*. 15 October 2009.

Bajoria, J. (2011). "Libya and the Responsibility to Protect", *Council on Foreign Relations*, 24 March 2011, www.cfr.org/libya/libya-responsibility-protect/p24480.

Bakan, J. (2004). *The Corporation: The Pathological Pursuit of Power*. New York: The Free Press.

Barber, B. (1995). *Jihad vs. McWorld*. New York: Crown.

Barnett, T. (2003). "The Pentagon's New Map", In Ó Tuathail, Dalby & Routledge, eds., *The Geopolitics Reader*, New York: Routledge Press, 151-4.

Barney, J. (1991). "Firm Resources and Sustained Competitive Advantage", *Journal of Management*, 17(1): 99-120.

Batalla X. (2010). "Derechos", *La Vanguardia*, 10 October 2010.

Batson, A. (2010). "Not Really 'Made in China'. The iPhone's Complex Supply Chain Highlights Problems with Trade Statistics". *The Wall Street Journal*, 15 December 2010.

Bauman, Z. (1998). *Globalization: The Human Consequences*. New York: Columbia University Press.

Bauman, Z. (2007). *Vida de consumo*. Madrid: Fondo de Cultura Económica.

Baylis, J.; Smith, S., eds. (2001). *The Globalization of World Politics*. Introduction. Oxford University Press.

BBC (2003). "Cigarettes 'engineered' for addiction": http://news.bbc.co.uk/2/hi/393075.stm.

BBC News (2001). *Special Report: The Pinochet File*, 9 July 2001, http://news.bbc.co.uk/2/hi/special_report/1998/10/98/the_pinochet_file/198306.stm.

BBC News (2011): "China to Buy 200 Boeing Aircraft". 19 January 2011. www.bbc.co.uk/news/business-12229585.

Beck, U. (1992). *Risk Society: Towards a New Modernity*. London: Sage.

Beck, U. (1999). *What Is Globalization?* Cambridge: Polity Press.

Beck, U. (2006). "Living in the world risk society". Lecture given on Wednesday 15 February 2006 at the London School of Economics. *Economy and Society*, 35 (3): 329-45.

Beck, U.; Beck-Gernsheim, E. (2002). *Individualization: Institutionalized Individualism and its Social and Political Consequences*. London: Sage.

Becker, G. (1976). *The Economic Approach to Human Behavior*. University of Chicago Press.

Becker, G. (1992). "The Economic Way of Looking at Life": www.nobelprize.org/nobelprizes/economic-sciences/laureates/1992/becker-lecture.pdf.

Bell, D. (1974). *The Coming of Post-Industrial Society*. New York: Harper Colophon Books.

Bell, D. (1976). *The Cultural Contradictions of Capitalism*. London: Heinemann.

Bell, D. (1987). "The World and the United States in 2013", *Daedalus*, 116(3): 1-31.

Berger, P. (1963). *Invitation to Sociology: A Humanistic Perspective*. New York: First Anchor Books.

Bierce, A. (1911). *The Devil's Dictionary*, Neale Publishing Co.

Bin Laden, O. (2002). *Letter to America*, In O'Tuathail, G.; Dalby, S.; Routledge, P. (eds.) (2003), *The Geopolitics Reader*, New York: Routledge Press, 265-9.

Black Capital (2011). "Abu Dhabi Investment Authority". http://black-capital.com/news/2011/03/abu-dhabi-investment-authority/?lang=en.

Block, P. (2013). *Stewardship: Choosing Service over Self-Interest*, Berrett-Koehler Publishers.

Bobbitt, P. (2002). *The Shield of Achilles: War, Peace, and the Course of History*. New York: Random House.

Bourdieu, P. (1977). *Outline of a Theory of Practice*, Cambridge University Press, p.188.

Bourdieu, P. (2005). *The Social Structures of the Economy*. Polity.

Cameron, K. S.; Quinn, R. E. (1999). *Diagnosing and Changing Organizational Culture*, Reading: Addison-Wesley.

Capdevila, C. (2011). "La meritocràcia està greument ferida. Entrevista amb Zygmunt Bauman", *Ara*, 25 December 2011.

Carvajal, D.; Minder, R. (2013). "A Whistle-Blower Who Can Name Names of Swiss Bank Account Holders". *The New York Times*. 6 August 2013.

Castel, R. (1995). *Les métamorphoses de la question social*, París: Fayard.

Castells, M. (1996). *The Rise of the Network Society: The Information Age: Economy, Society, and Culture*. Vol. I. Cambridge, MA; Oxford, UK: Blackwell.

Castells, M. (1997). *The Power of Identity. The Information Age: Economy, Society and Culture*. Vol. II. Cambridge, MA; Oxford, UK: Blackwell.

Chebel, M. (1998). *La formation de l'identité politique*. Paris: Payot.

Collier, P.; Dollar, D. (2002). *Globalization, Growth, and Poverty: Building an Inclusive World Economy*. Oxford: World Bank Policy Research Report.

Cortina, A. (2003). *Por una ética del consumo*. Madrid: Taurus.

D'Cruz, J.; Rugman, A. (1992). *New Concepts for Canadian Competitiveness*, Canada: Kodak.

Davis, B. (2010). "IMF, Reversing Course, Urges Capital Controls". *The Wall Street Journal*. 19 February 2010. http://online.wsj.com/article/SB40001424052748704269004575073610075698010.html.

Davis, K. (1960). "Can Business Afford to Ignore Corporate Social Responsibility?", *California Management Review*, 2: 70-6.

DealBook (2007). "Sovereign Wealth Funds: The New Hedge Fund?" *The New York Times*. 1 August 2007.

Delanty, G. (2005). "What Does it Mean to Be a 'European'?" *Innovation: The European Journal of Social Science Research*, 18(1): 11-22.

Dicken, P. (1986). *Global Shift: Industrial Change in a Turbulent World*. London: Harper & Row, p. 304.

Díez, G. (2011). "A Philosopher's Mission to Save the EU", *Der Spiegel*, 25 November 2011.

Dobbin, F. (2005). "Comparative and Historical Approaches to Economic Sociology", In Smelser, N. J.; Swedberg, R.: *The Handbook of Economic Sociology*. 2nd ed. New York: Princeton University Press.

Domain-B (2002). "Blair calls for global interdependence", 7 January 2002. www.domain-b.com/industry/associations/cii/20020107_blair.html.

Donaldson, T. (1982). *Corporations and Morality*, New Jersey: Prentice-Hall.

Doyle, M. W. (1983). "Kant, Liberal Legacies and Foreign Affairs", *Philosophy and Public Affairs*, I y II (12): 205-35, 323-53.

Dreher, A. (2010): KOF Index of Globalization. http://globalization.kof.ethz.ch/static/pdf/variables_2010.pdf and http://globalization.kof.ethz.ch/static/pdf/definitions_2010.pdf.

Dreher, A.; Gaston, N.; Martens, P. (2008). *Measuring Globalization—Gauging its Consequences*, New York: Springer.

Durkheim, E. (2006 [1897]). *On Suicide*. London: Penguin.

Dwyer A.; T. Xia (2012). *Xmas without China*. Trailer: http://caamfest.com/2013/films/xmas-without-china/.

Edelman (2013). Trust Barometer. www.edelman.com/insights/intellectual-property/trust-2013/trust-across-sectors/trust-in-financial-services/.

El País (2005). "Evolución bursátil de Terra". 15 July 2005. http://economia.elpais.com/economia/2005/07/15/actualidad/1121412773_850215.html.

EU (2011). *Key Figures on European Business with a Special Feature on SME*. Luxembourg: Eurostat Pocket Books. *Vid.* http://ec.europa.eu/enterprise/policies/sme/facts-figures-analysis/sme-observatory/index_en.htm.

EU (2013). *List of Countries, Territories and Currencies*, Publishing Office, http://publications.europa.eu/code/en/en-5000500.htm.

European Commission (2002). *Communication from the Commission Concerning Corporate Social Responsibility*, COM(2002) 347-final, Brussels, 2.7.2002: http://eur-lex.europa.eu/LexUriServ/LexUriServ.do?uri=COM:2002:0347:FIN:en:PDF.

Evans-Pritchard, A. (2011). "IMF Raises Spectre of Civil Wars as Global Inequalities Worsen". *The Telegraph*, 1 February 2011. www.telegraph.co.uk/finance/globalbusiness/8296987/IMF-raises-spectre-of-civil-wars-as-global-inequalities-worsen.html.

Fligstein, N. (1990). *The Transformation of Corporate Control*. Harvard University Press.

Fligstein, N.; Markowitz, L. (1993). "Financial Reorganization of American Corporations in the 1980s". In Wilson, William J. (ed.) *Sociology and the Public Agenda*. Newbury Park, CA: Sage Publications, pp. 185-206.

Florida, R. (2002). *The Rise of the Creative Class: And How it's transforming work, leisure, community and everyday life*. New York: Perseus Book Group.

Fontana, J. (2005). "La construcció històrica de la identitat". In *La construcció de la identitat. Reflexions sobre el passat i sobre el present*. Editorial Base.

Foreign Policy (2007): The Globalization Index, www.foreignpolicy.com/articles/2007/10/11/theglobalizationindex_2007.

Foster J.B. & Magdoff F. (2009). *The Great Financial Crisis: Causes and Consequences*. New York: Monthly Review Press.

Frankl, V. (2000). *Man's Search for Ultimate Meaning*. Perseus Books Group.

Freeland, C. (2011). "The Rise of the New Global Elite". *The Atlantic*, January–February 2011. www.theatlantic.com/magazine/archive/2011/01/the-rise-of-the-new-global-elite/308343/.

Freeman, R. E. (1984). *Strategic Management: A Stakeholder Approach*, Boston: Pitman.

Friedman, M. (1953). *Essays in Positive Economics*. Chicago: The University of Chicago Press.

Friedman, M. (1970). "The Social Responsibility of Business Is To Increase Its Profits". In Hoffman, W. M.; Frederick, R. E.; Schwartz, M. S. (ed.) (2001), *Business Ethics—Readings and Cases in Corporate Morality*, McGraw-Hill, pp. 156-60.

Friedman, T. (1999). *The Lexus and the Olive Tree*, Anchor Books.

Frum, D. (2013). "The Speechwriter: Inside the Bush Administration During the Iraq War", *Newsweek*, 19 March 2013.

Fukuyama, F. (1989). "The end of the history?" *The National Interest*.

Fukuyama, F. (1992). *The End of History and the Last Man*. The Free Press.

Galbraith, J. K. (2004). *The Economics of Innocent Fraud: Truth for Our Time*, Houghton Mifflin.

García Roca, J. (1998). *Exclusión social y contracultura de la solidaridad. Prácticas, discursos, narraciones*. Madrid: Ediciones HOAC.

Gerges F. (2009). "Al-Qaida Today: A Movement at the crossroads", *Open Democracy*. www.opendemocracy.net/article/al-qaida-today-the-fate-of-a-movement.

Ghoshal, S. (2005). "Bad Management Theories Are Destroying Good Management Practices", *Academy of Management Learning & Education*, 4(1): 75-91.

Giddens, A. (1990). *The Consequences of Modernity*, Cambridge: Polity.

Giddens, A. (1991). *Modernity and Self-Identity. Self and Society in the Late Modern Age*, Cambridge: Polity.

Giddens, A. (1994). *Beyond Left and Right—The Future of Radical Politics*. Cambridge: Polity.

Giddens, A. (1999). *Runaway World: How Globalization is Reshaping Our Lives*, London: Profile.

Gill, I.; Raiser, M. (2012). *Golden Growth: Restoring the Lustre of the European Economic Model*. Washington: The World Bank.

Giné, S. (2012). *Asia marca del rumbo*. Barcelona: Dèria Editors.

Giner, S. (1997). *Sociología*. Barcelona: Península.

González, E. (2003). "Cómo se fabricó el 'eje del mal'", *El País*, 9 January 2003.

Goodpaster, K. E.; Matthews, J. B. (1982). "Can a Corporation Have a Conscience?", *Harvard Business Review*, January–February, pp. 132-41.

Grabel, I.; Chang, H.-J. (2010). "Why Capital Controls Are Not All Bad". *Financial Times*. 25 October 2010. www.ft.com/intl/cms/s/0/4d0e3e34-e02f-11df-9482-00144feabdc0.html#axzz2gMQEzT3e.

Greenhouse, S. (1997). "Nike Shoe Plant in Vietnam Is Called Unsafe for Workers", *The New York Times*, 8 November 1997: www.nytimes.com/1997/11/08/business/nike-shoe-plant-in-vietnam-is-called-unsafe-for-workers.html?pagewanted=all&src=pm.

Greenpeace: https://webdrive.service.emory.edu/users/vdhara/www.BhopalPublications/Environmental%20Health/Greenpeace%20Bhopal%20Report.pdf.

Gutiérrez, V.; Muñoz, R. (2011). "Reforma exprés y sin referéndum", *El País*, 23 August 2011. http://politica.elpais.com/politica/2011/08/23/actualidad/1314128715_080054.html.

Habermas, J. (2012). *The Crisis of the European Union. A response*, Polity Press.

Hausman, D. M.; McPherson, M. S. (2006). *Economic Analysis and Moral Philosophy*. Cambridge University Press.

Healy, J.; Grynbaum, M. (2009). "Why Analysts Keep Telling Investors to Buy". *The New York Times*, 8 February 2009.

Held, D.; McGrew, A.; Goldblatt D.; Perraton, J. (1999). *Global Transformations: Politics, Economics, and Culture.* Stanford University Press.

Heredia, S. (2013). "Suiza, en pos del nombre perdido". *La Vanguardia Dinero.* 13 October 2013.

Ho, K. (2009). *Liquidated: An Ethnography of Wall Street.* Duke University Press.

Hofstede, G. (1980). *Culture's Consequences: International Differences in Work-Related Values.* Beverly Hills CA: Sage Publications.

Huntington, S. (1993). "The Clash of Civilizations?" *Foreign Affairs,* vol. 72, 3, Summer 1993, pp. 22-49.

Huntington, S. (1996). *The Clash of Civilizations and the Remaking of World Order.* New York: Simon & Schuster.

Huntington, S. (2004). *Who Are We? The Challenges to America's National Identity.* New York: Simon & Schuster.

IE Business School; Kreab Gavin Anderson (2011). *IV Informe. Panorama de Inversión Española en Latinoamérica.*

IMF (1998). "The Asian Crisis: Causes and Cures". *Finance and Development.* June 1998, 35(2). www.imf.org/external/pubs/ft/fandd/1998/06/imfstaff.htm.

IMF (2000). *IMF World Economic Outlook. October 2000.* Washington.

IMF (2011). "The Right Kind of Global Recovery". Speech by Dominique Strauss-Kahn, 1 February 2011. www.imf.org/external/np/speeches/2011/020111.htm.

IMF (2013). *World Economic Outlook Database,* October 2013.

ISS (2013). Corporate Website: www.issworld.com/aboutiss/Strategy/Pages/Ourvalues.aspx.

Jensen, M. C. (2001). "Value maximization, stakeholder theory, and the corporate objective function", *European Financial Management Review,* 7(3): 297-317.

Jiménez, M. (2010). "US Tried to Block Bid for Panama Job". *El País,* 19 December 2010. http://elpais.com/elpais/2010/12/19/inenglish/1292739643_850210.html.

Jonas, H.; Herr, D. (1984). *The Imperative of Responsibility: In Search of Ethics for the Technological Age,* University of Chicago Press.

Jones, T. M. (1980). "Corporate Social Responsibility Revisited, Redefined", *California Management Review,* 22(2): 59-67.

Judt, T. (2010). "The World We Have Lost", in *Ill Fares the Land,* Chapter 2. New York: Penguin Press.

Judt, T.; Snyder, T. (2012). *Thinking the Twentieth Century.* London: The Penguin Press.

Kanter, J.; Ewing, J. (2013). "A Running Start for a U.S.–Europe Trade Pact". *New York Times.* 13 February 2013. www.nytimes.com/2013/02/14/business/global/obama-pledges-trade-pact-talks-with-eu.html?r=0.

Kay, J. (1993). *Foundations of Corporate Success,* Oxford: Oxford University Press.

Keohane, D. (2013). "Global Financial Assets, There Are Lots". *Financial Times.* 13 February 2013.

Keohane, R. O.; Nye, J. (2002). "Governance in a Globalizing World", In Keohane, R. O. (ed.): *Power and Governance in a Partially Globalized World.* Londres: Routledge.

Keohane, R.O; Nye, J. (2000). "Realism and Complex Interdependence", In Lechner, F.; Boli, J., eds. (2008): *The Globalization Reader,* 3rd ed., Malden, MA: Blackwell Publishing, Chapter 8, pp. 70-8.

Keynes, J. M. ([1933]1972). *Collected Works,* vol. X: *Essays in Biography.*

Keynes, J. M. (1936). *The General Theory of Employment, Interest and Money.* London: Macmillan.

Khurana, R. (2007). *From Higher Aims to Hired Hands: The Social Transformation of American Business Schools and the Unfulfilled Promise of Management as a Profession.* Princeton, NJ: Princeton University Press.

Kristol, I. (2003). "The Neoconservative Persuasion", *The Weekly Standard*, 25 August 2003, 8, p. 47.

Krugman, P. (2013). "Hot Money Blues". *The New York Times*. 24 March 2013. www.nytimes. com/2013/03/25/opinion/krugman-hot-money-blues.html?_r=2.

Kubota, Y.; Obayashi, Y. (2013). "Wrecked Fukushima storage tank leaking highly radioactive water", *Reuters*, 20 August 2013, www.reuters.com/article/2013/08/20/us-japan-fukushima-leak-idUSBRE97J02920130820.

Kumhof, M.; Rancière R. (2010). *Inequality, Leverage and Crises*. International Monetary Fund. WP/10/268. IMF Working Paper. Research Department.

Labunska, I., Stephenson, A., Brigden, K., Stringer, R., Santillo, D. and Johnston, P. A. (1999). *The Bhopal Legacy. Toxic contaminants at the former Union Carbide factory site, Bhopal, India: 15 years after the Bhopal accident.*

Lacalle, D. (2013). *Nosotros los mercados. Qué son, cómo funcionan y por qué resultan imprescindibles*. Barcelona: Deusto.

Le Parisien (2011). "Les Français, champions du monde … du pessimisme!", 3 January 2011, www.leparisien.fr/societe/les-francais-champions-du-monde-du-pessimisme-03-01-2011-1210951.php.

Lechner, F. (2001). The Globalization Website, www.sociology.emory.edu/globalization/debates.html#cultural.

Leonard, M. (2005). *Why Europe Will Run the 21st Century*. London: Fourth Estate.

Leonard, M. (2008). *What Does China Think?* London: The Fourth Estate.

Leonard, M. (2011). "Europa i el desafiament a l'ordre liberal d'Occident", *VIA. Revista del Centre d'Estudis Jordi Pujol* (16): 50-61.

Levitt, S. & Dubner, S. (2005). *Freakonomics: A Rogue Economist Explores the Hidden Side of Everything*. William Morrow/Harper Collins.

Lewis, R. (1996). *When Cultures Collide: Leading Across Cultures*. Nicholas Brealey Publishing.

Liodice, B. (2010). "10 Companies With Social Responsibility at the Core", *Ad Age/CMO Strategy*, 19 April 2010: http://adage.com/article/cmo-strategy/10-companies-social-responsibility-core/143323/.

Lipovetsky, G. (2007). *La felicidad paradójica. Ensayo sobre la sociedad del hiperconsumo*. Barcelona: Anagrama.

Luttwak, E. (1999). *Turbo-Capitalism: Winners and Losers in the Global Economy*. New York: HarperCollins.

Lutz, A. (2012). "These 10 Corporations Control Almost Everything You Buy", *Business Insider*, 25 April 2012, www.businessinsider.com/these-10-corporations-control-almost-everything-you-buy-2012-4.

Lutz, A. (2013). "Wal-Mart Asks Workers To Donate Food To Its Needy Employees", *Business Insider*, 8 November 2013: www.businessinsider.com/walmart-asks-customers-to-donate-food-2013-11#ixzz2lf4QQ7zg.

Mackenzie, D. (2004). "The Big, Bad Wolf and the Rational Market: Portfolio Insurance, the 1987 Crash and the Performativity of Economics", *Economy and Society*, 33 (3): 303-34.

Mackintosh, J. (2011). "Top 10 hedge funds make $28bn". *Financial Times*. 1 March 2011. www.ft.com/intl/cms/s/0/24193cbe-4433-11e0-931d-00144feab49a.html?siteedition=intl.

Mahajan, S. (2006). *Globalization and Social Change*, New Delhi: Lotus Press.

Martínez Inglés, A. (1989). *España indefensa*. Ediciones B.

Marx, K. (1968). *Sociología y filosofía social*. Selección e introducción de T.B. Bottomore y M. Rubel. Barcelona: Ediciones Península.

McClellan, S. (2009). "Decoding Wall Street's Well-Kept Secrets". *Financial Times*. 23 June 2009.

McCormick, J. (2010). "Europe in the World: Towards Perpetual Peace". In *Europeanism*. New York: Oxford University Press, pp. 191-214.

McKinsey (2013). *Urban World: The shifting global business landscape*, October 2013: www. mckinsey.com/~/media/McKinsey/dotcom/Insights/Urbanization/Urban%20world%20 The%20shifting%20global%20business%20landscape/MGI%20Urban%20world%203_ Full%20report_Oct%202013.ashx.

Medialdea, B.; Álvarez, N. (2009). *Liberalización financiera internacional, inversores institucionales y gobierno corporativo de la empresa*. WP07/08. http://eprints.ucm.es/9031/1/WP07-08.pdf.

Merton, R. K. (1995). "The Thomas Theorem and the Matthew Effect". *Social Forces*, 74(2): 379-424.

Mihm, S. (2009). "Why Capitalism Fails. The man who saw the meltdown coming had another troubling insight: it will happen again". *The Boston Globe*. 13 September 2009.

Minder, R. (2011). "Top Spanish Banker Faces Inquiry on Tax Charges", *The New York Times*, 17 June 2011: www.nytimes.com/2011/06/17/business/global/17santander.html.

Mintzberg, H.; Simons, R.; Basu K. (2002). "Beyond Selfishness", *MIT Sloan Management Review*, 44 (1): 66-74.

Moïsi, D. (2009). *The Geopolitics of Emotion: How cultures of fear, humiliation, and hope are reshaping the world*. New York: Doubleday.

Murado. M-A. (2013). *La invención del pasado*. Barcelona: Debate.

Murillo, D. (2007). "Rescatar la ética económica de Adam Smith". In Alcoberro, R. (co-ord.), *Ética, economía y empresa*. Barcelona: Gedisa, pp. 29-44.

Murillo, D. (2011). *Understanding China through a cultural rather than economic perspective*, ESADEgeo Position Paper 21.

Murillo, D.; Sung, Y. (2013). *Understanding Korean Capitalism: Chaebols and their Corporate Governance*. ESADEgeo Position Paper 33, www.esadegeo.com/download/ PR_PositionPapers/43/ficPDF_ENG/201309Chaebols_Murillo_Sung_EN.pdf.

Murths, T. P.; Lenway, S. A. (1998). "Country Capabilities and the Strategic State. How National Political Institutions Affect MNC Strategies", *Strategic Management Journal*, 15(5): 113-19.

Naím, M. (2000). "Fads and Fashion in Economic Reforms: Washington consensus or Washington confusion?" *Third World Quarterly*, 21 June 2000, 3, 505-28.

Naím, M. (2013). *The End of Power: From Boardrooms to Battlefields and Churches to States. Why Being in Charge Isn't What It Used to Be*. Basic Books.

Nussbaum, M. (2010). *Not for Profit. Why democracy needs the humanities*. Princeton: Princeton University Press.

Nye, J. (2004). *Soft Power: The Means to Success in World Politics*. New York: Public Affairs.

Nye, J. (2010). "The Future of American Power. Dominance and Decline in Perspective", *Foreign Affairs*, November 2010.

O'Rourke, K.; Williamson, J. (2004). "Once more: When did globalisation begin?" *European Review of Economic History*, 8, 109-17.

OECD (1998). *Harmful Tax Competition. An Emerging Global Issue*. Paris: Organization for Economic Cooperation and Development.

OECD (2008a). *Growing Unequal? Income Distribution in OECD Countries*. París: OECD Publishing: www.oecd.org/els/soc/41527936.pdf.

OECD (2008b): *Economic Outlook*, www.oecd.org/eco/outlook/38628438.pdf.

OECD (2011). *Divided We Stand: Why Inequality Keeps Rising*. Paris: OECD Publishing: www. oecd.org/els/soc/dividedwestandwhyinequalitykeepsrising.htm.

Palau, J. (2011). "Las agencias de rating. Viven de bancos y empresas". *La Vanguardia*. 14 July 2011.

Palley, T.(2007). "Financialization: What It Is and Why It Matters". *Working Paper* n. 525. The Levy Economics Institute and Economics for Democratic and Open Societies. Washington, DC. December 2007. www.levyinstitute.org/pubs/wp_525.pdf.

Pascual, M. (2006). *¿En qué mundo vivimos? Conversaciones con M. Castells*. Madrid: Alianza Editorial.

Perle, R. (2003). "Thank God for the Death of the UN", *The Guardian*, 21 March 2003.

Pew Research Center (2011). "Twenty Years Later Confidence in Democracy and Capitalism Wanes in Former Soviet Union", 5 December 2011, www.pewglobal.org/2011/12/05/confidence-in-democracy-and-capitalism-wanes-in-former-soviet-union/.

Porter, M. E. (1980). *Competitive Strategy*, New York: The Free Press.

Porter, M.; Kramer, M. (2011). "Creating Shared Value", *Harvard Business Review*, January–February 2011, 89: 1-11.

Preston, L. E.; Post, J. E. (1981). "Private Management and Public Policy", *California Management Review*, 23(3): 56-63.

RAND National Defense Research Institute (1989). "Long-Term Economic and Military Trends 1950–2010", The RAND Corporation, Santa Mónica, April 1989.

Rathbone, J.; Thomson, A. (2011). "Pemex and Sacyr Team Up Over Repsol". *Financial Times*. 30 August 2011: www.ft.com/intl/cms/s/0/95f9fa12-d290-11e0-a409-00144feab49a.html#axzz2fuy84Ly2.

Reality News (2013). *Papel mojado. La crisis de la prensa y lo fracaso de los periódicos en España*. Barcelona: Debate.

Reich, R. (1991). *The Work of Nations: Preparing Ourselves for 21st Century Capitalism*. New York: Vintage Books.

Ritzer, G. (1993). *The McDonaldization of Society*. Thousand Oaks, CA: Pine Forges Press.

Robertson, R. (1991). "The Globalization Paradigm: Thinking Globally", In *Religion and Social Order*, Greenwich: JAI Press, 207-24.

Robertson, R. (1992). *Globalization: Social Theory and Global Culture*, London: Sage.

Robin, M. (2010). *The World According to Monsanto*, New York: The New Press.

Robinson, A. (2013). *Un reportero en la montaña mágica. Cómo la élite económica de Davos hundió al mundo*. Barcelona: Ariel.

Rocher, G. (1983). *Introducción a la sociología general*. Barcelona: Herder.

Roddick, A. (2011). "Questioning the Ethics of Corporate Social Responsibility", *Big Picture Videos*: http://on.aol.como/video/questioning-the-ethics-of-corporate-social-responsibility-516923273.

Rodrik, D. (2011). *The Globalization Paradox. Democracy and the Future of World Economy*. New York: W. W. Norton & Co.

Roubini, N. (2011). "Is Capitalism Doomed?" *Project Syndicate*, September 2011.

Sandel, M. (2012). *What Money Can't Buy: The moral limits of markets*. New York: Farrar, Straus and Giroux.

Santander.(2013). Investor relations website: www.santander.com/csgs/Satellite?pagename=CFWCSancomQP01%2FPage%2FCFQP01_PageResultados_PT23&cidSel=1278684289572&appID=santander.wc.CFWCSancomQP01&canal=CSCORP&empr=CFWCSancomQP01&leng=en_GB&cid=1278677300268.

Santiso, J. (2011). "Fondos soberanos latinos". *El País*. 3 July 2011.

Saul, J. R. (2009). *The Collapse of Globalism*. London: Atlantic Books.

Save the Children (2007). "A Generation On: Baby milk marketing still putting children's lives at risk": www.savethechildren.org.uk/resources/online-library/a-generation-on-baby-milk-marketing-still-putting-childrens-lives-at-risk.

Scherer, A. G.; Palazzo, G. (2011). "The New Political Role of Business in a Globalized World: A review of a new perspective on CSR and its implications for the firm, governance, and democracy", *Journal of Management Studies*, 48(4): 899-931.

Scholtes, P. (1997). *The Leader's Handbook: Making Things Happen, Getting Things Done*. McGraw-Hill.

Schuman, M. (2009). *The Miracle: The Epic Story of Asia's Quest for Wealth*. New York: Harper-Collins Publishers.

Sen, A. (2006). *Identity and Violence: The Illusion of Destiny*. New York: Norton & Co.

Shamir, S. (2009). "Extent of Madoff Fraud Now Estimated at Far Below $50b". *Haaretz*. Associated Press. 6 March 2009. www.haaretz.com/news/extent-of-madoff-fraud-now-estimated-at-far-below-50b-1.271672.

Shiller, R. (2000). *Irrational Exuberance*. Princeton University Press.

Shiller, R. (2012). *Finance and the Good Society*. Princeton University.

Shiller, R. (2013). "Is Economics a Science?", *The Guardian*, 6 November 2013: www.theguardian.com/business/economics-blog/2013/nov/06/is-economics-a-science-robert-shiller.

Simmons, K. (2013). "World Worried About Inequality". *Special to CNN*. 28 May 2013. http://globalpublicsquare.blogs.cnn.com/2013/05/28/world-worried-about-inequality/.

Skidelsky, R. (2009). *Keynes: The Return of the Master*. New York: Public Affairs.

Sklair, L. (2002). "Sociology of the Global System", In Lechner, F.; Boli, J., eds. (2008): *The Globalization Reader*, 3rd ed., Malden, MA: Blackwell Publishing, Chapter 7, pp. 62-9.

Solana, J. (2012). "Whose Sovereignty?" *Project Syndicate*, 12 March 2012. www.project-syndicate.org/commentary/whose-sovereignty-.

Steger, M. (2010). *Globalization: A Very Short Introduction*. Oxford.

Steiner G. (2004). *La idea de Europa*. Madrid: Siruela.

Stevens, P. (2012). *The "Shale Gas Revolution": Developments and Changes*. Chatham House. www.chathamhouse.org/sites/default/files/public/Research/Energy,%20Environment%20and%20Development/bp0812_stevens.pdf.

Stiglitz, J. (2002). *Globalization and Its Discontents*, W.W. Norton & Company.

Stiglitz, J. (2010). "The Non-Existent Hand". *London Review of Books*, 32 (8). 22 April 2010, pp. 17-18.

Story, l.; Thomas, l.; Schwartz, N. (2010). "Wall St. Helped to Mask Debt Fueling Europe's Crisis". *The New York Times*. 13 February 2010.

Tax Justice Network (2010). www.taxjustice.net/cms/front_content.php?idcat=148.

Taylor, M. (2013). "Madness of Choice", *Capitalism and Society*, 8(2).

Tempest, M. (2005). "Treasury Papers Reveal Cost of Black Wednesday". *The Guardian*. 9 February 2005.

The Economist (2007). *Global Business Barometer*: www.economist.com/media/pdf/20080116CSRResults.pdf.

The Economist (2010a). "The Uses and Abuses of Mathematical Models". 11 February 2010.

The Economist (2010b). "The Redistribution of Hope", 16 December 2010, www.economist.com/node/17732859?fsrc=nwl.

The Economist (2011a). "BlackRock. Goliath. The world's largest asset manager has done well out of the crisis. What now?" *The Economist*. 3 September 2011.

The Economist (2011b). "Milton Friedman Goes on Tour. A survey of attitudes to business turns up some intriguing national differences", 27 January 2011: www.economist.com/node/18010553.

The Economist (2012). "The Rise of State Capitalism", 21 January 2012, www.economist.com/node/21543160.

The Economist. (2013a). "The Global Debt Clock". www.economist.com/content/global_debt_clock.

The Economist. (2013b). *Dictionary of economics*: www.economist.com/economics-a-to-z.

Tintoré, E. (2002). "Foro Social Mundial. Las propuestas alternativas". *La Vanguardia*. 31 January 2002.

Todorov, T. (2010). *The Fear of Barbarians: Beyond the clash of civilizations*. University of Chicago Press.

Torres López, J. (2009). *La crisis financiera. Guía para entenderla y explicarla*. Attac.

Triggle, N. (2009). "Swine flu less lethal than feared", *BBC News*, 10 December 2009, http://news.bbc.co.uk/2/hi/health/8406723.stm.

Trivett, V. (2011). "25 US Mega Corporations: Where They Rank If They Were Countries", *Business Insider*, 27 June 2011. www.businessinsider.com/25-corporations-bigger-tan-countries-2011-6?op=1.

Tugores, J. (2010). *El lado oscuro de la economía*. Ed. Gestión 2000.

UN Framework Convention on Climate Change (2013): Kyoto Protocol: http://unfccc.int/kyoto_protocol/items/2830.php.

United Nations (1999). *Global Compact Initiative*: www.unglobalcompact.org.

United Nations (2012). World Population projections, www.un.org/en/development/desa/population/publications/pdf/trends/WPP2012_Wallchart.pdf.

United States Government (2010). "Historical Tables", Office of Management and Budget, www.whitehouse.gov.

US Census Bureau (2014). www.census.gov/popclock/.

US Securities and Exchange Commission and the Commodity Futures Trading Commission (2010). "Findings Regarding the Market Events of May 6, 2010" September 30: www.sec.gov/news/studies/2010/marketevents-report.pdf.

Vargas Llosa, M. (2002). *La verdad de las mentiras*. Madrid: Alfaguara.

Veyne P. (2009). *Foucault. Pensamiento y vida*. Barcelona: Paidós.

Vilanova, M.; Lozano, J. M.; Arenas, D. (2009). "Exploring the Nature of the Relationship Between CSR and Competitiveness", *Journal of Business Ethics*, 87 (supplement 1), pp. 57-69.

Villoria, M. (2009). "Crisis económica, globalización y corrupción", *Revista VIA*, 10, pp. 83-95, Centre d'Estudis Jordi Pujol.

Voltaire ([1759] 2003). *Candide*. New York: Bantam Classics.

Waddock, S. (2008). "Building a New Institutional Infrastructure for Corporate Responsibility", *Academy of Management Perspectives*, August 2008, 22(3): 87-108.

Waddock, S. (2010). "Finding Wisdom Within—The Role of Seeing and Reflective Practice in Developing Moral Imagination, Aesthetic Sensibility, and Systems Understanding", *Journal of Business Ethics Education* (7) 177-96.

Wallerstein, I. (2004). "The Modern World System as a Capitalist World Economy", In Lechner, F.; Boli, J., eds. (2008): *The Globalization Reader*, 3rd ed., Malden, MA: Blackwell Publishing, Chapter 6, pp. 55-61.

Weber, M. (1979). *La ética protestante y el espíritu del capitalismo*. Barcelona: Ediciones Península.

WEF (2013). *Global Risks Report 2013*. www.weforum.org/reports/global-risks-2013-eighth-edition.

Wikipedia (2012). Protests against SOPA and PIPA, http://en.wikipedia.org/wiki/Protests_against_SOPA_and_PIPA#Protests_of_January_18.2C_2012.

Williamson, J. (1990). "What Washington Means by Policy Reform". *Latin American Adjustment: How Much Has Happened?* Washington: Peterson Institute for International Economics.

Wolf, M. (2004). *Why Globalisation Works*. Yale University Press.

Wolf, M. (2012). "Seven Ways to Fix the System's Flaws", *Financial Times*, 22 January 2012, www.ft.com/intl/cms/s/0/c80b0d2c-4377-11e1-8489-00144feab49a.html#axzz2dS2Xx7YS.

World Bank (2013a). *Indicators*, http://data.worldbank.org/indicator.

World Bank (2013b). "What is Governance?" http://go.worldbank.org/G2CHLXX0Q0.

World Bank (2014). *Indicators*, http://data.worldbank.org/indicator/NE.CON.PETC.ZS/countries?display=graph.

World Business Council for Sustainable Development (2000). *Corporate Social Responsibility: Making Good Business Sense*, Geneva: WBCSD.

World Economic Forum (2013). *Global Risk Report.* www3.weforum.org/docs/WEF_#GlobalRisks_#Report_2013.pdf.

Zakaria, F. (1994). "Culture Is Destiny—A Conversation with Lee Kuan Yew", *Foreign Affairs*, March–April, 73, 2.

Zedillo, E. (2011). "Book Review of *The Globalization Paradox* by Dani Rodrik", *Journal of Economic Literature*, 49(4): 41-3.

Zelizer, V. (1979). *Morals and Markets: The Development of Life Insurance in the United States.* Columbia University Press.

About the author

David Murillo, PhD, Lecturer in the Department of Social Sciences, Esade Business School (Barcelona), holds a degree in Humanities and in Business Administration and a PhD in Sociology. In recent years he has been visiting professor at different prestigious universities all over the globe such as the Copenhagen Business School (Denmark), ESAN (Peru) and Sogang University (South Korea). His research embraces the areas of geopolitics, globalization studies and business ethics. His previous book is *Pathways to Systemic Change: Inspiring Stories and a New Set of Variables for Understanding Social Innovation*, written together with Heloise Buckland and published by Greenleaf in 2013. www.esade.edu/professorat/david.murillo